HERE'S LOOKING AT YOU

HERE'S LOOKING AT YOU

THE STORY OF
BRITISH TELEVISION
1908–1939

Bruce Norman

BRITISH BROADCASTING CORPORATION
THE ROYAL TELEVISION SOCIETY

For Becky and Cass

ROYAL TELEVISION SOCIETY

The Television Society was founded in Leeds in 1927 at a meeting of the British Association for the Advancement of Science where John Logie Baird had demonstrated his Noctovisor. Today the Royal Television Society, as it has now become, stands as a unique institution providing a forum where the art and science of television can be discussed by all the major branches of the industry.

PICTURE CREDITS

Cover illustration: *David Scutt*

Published by the
British Broadcasting Corporation
35 Marylebone High Street
London W1M 4AA
and
The Royal Television Society
Tavistock House East
Tavistock Square
London WC1H 9HR

ISBN 0 563 20102 9
First published 1984
© The Royal Television Society 1984

Typeset by August Filmsetting, Haydock, Merseyside
Printed in England
by Hartnolls Ltd, Bodmin, Cornwall

CONTENTS

ACKNOWLEDGEMENTS

The official records tell one story of the birth of television, the people involved tell another. Theirs is not always a very different story but it is certainly more lively, more human and more revealing of what actually happened. Many of the surviving pioneers of television have helped me with research for this book, providing written information, photographs and giving up time to be interviewed. I would like to thank in particular Arthur Askey, Betty Astelle, Douglas Birkinshaw, Jasmine Bligh, John Bliss, Dallas Bower, Alan Bray, Leonard Broadway, Desmond Campbell, Ben Clapp, Elizabeth Cowell, Ned Davis, Gracie Fields, Donald Flamm, Cyril Fletcher, William Fox, L. Marsland Gander, Sidonie Goossens, Bernard Greenhead, Wee Georgie Harris, Dora Jackson, Alan Lawson, Norman Loxdale, Cecil Madden, James McGee, Joan Miller, Victor Mills, Leslie Mitchell, Donald Munro, Ian Orr-Ewing, Jim Percy, Dinah Sheridan, George Watson, Rebecca West, Eric White and Isabel Winthrope. The full transcripts of their interviews are lodged in the library of the Royal Television Society where I hope they will be used by future researchers. I would like to thank Feinman and Krasilovsky, P.C., for giving permission to quote from Pirandello's *The Man with a Flower in His Mouth*.

I would like to thank the BBC Written Archives Centre, Caversham, and acknowledge the help received from the staff of the Royal Television Society, GEC–Marconi Electronics Ltd, Thorn–EMI Ltd and Radio Rentals. I would like to give especial thanks to Mrs J. L. Baird for her interest and permission to quote extensively from Baird's partly published autobiography and, above all, I want to thank T. H. Bridgewater who, in so many ways, is the co-author of this book. He freely gave time, encouragement and information, read the typescript and made suggestions for improvements. The improvements are his, the mistakes that remain are mine.

Bruce Norman
Hatfield
November 1983

THE WHO'S WHO OF EARLY TELEVISION

The Pioneers:

J. L. Baird	(1888–1946): the first man to demonstrate television, Jan. 1926. Demonstrated colour television in 1928.
Karl Braun	German: inventor of cathode-ray oscilloscope (tube), 1897.
P. T. Farnsworth	American: inventor of electronic TV system (the image dissector), 1928.
C. F. Jenkins	American: inventor of mechanical TV system, 1924. Baird rival.
D. Von Mihaly	Hungarian: pioneer of mechanical television, 1924.
Paul Nipkow	German: inventor of the Nipkow disc, 1884.
Boris Rosing	Russian: proposed television system embodying cathode-ray tube as receiver, 1907.
A. A. Campbell Swinton	(1836–1930): the first man to propose the all-electronic method of television, 1908 and 1911.
Jean Weiller	French: inventor of the mirror drum, 1889.
V. K. Zworykin	Russian: pupil of Rosing. Lodged patent in America in 1923 for electronic television system. Published paper on electronic camera, the 'iconoscope', in 1933.

Hastings: (1922–5)

J. J. Denton	Physics lecturer. Gave early advice and help to Baird.
N. Loxdale	Helped Baird construct his original apparatus in 1922–3.
V. Mills	Helped Baird wire and improve his apparatus, 1923.

The Baird Company: (1926–37)

H. Barton Chapple	Engineer: joined Baird in 1928. Editor of *Television*.

8

A. F. Birch	Engineer: joined Baird 1928.
H. Bradly	Producer of Baird's television programmes.
T. H. Bridgewater	Engineer with Baird 1928–32; 1932–5; BBC 30-line Alexandra Palace 1936–.
D. R. Campbell	Engineer with Baird 1929–32; 1932–5; BBC 30-line Alexandra Palace 1936–. Known as the 'father' of television lighting.
B. Clapp	Baird's first engineer, 1926.
W. Day	Baird's co-financier, 1924–6.
D. Flamm	Owner of New York radio station and supporter of Baird in America.
W. C. Fox	Press Association journalist. Baird press officer, 1928–30.
O. G. Hutchinson	Baird's partner and managing director, 1926–31.
Dora Jackson (née Caffrey)	Baird's personal secretary, 1929–.
W. W. Jacomb	Baird's chief engineer, 1928–32. Perfected the 'flying spot'.
A. Lawson	Cameraman, joined Baird 1933. Worked on Intermediate Film.
S. A. Moseley	Journalist and Baird supporter.
Ostrer Brothers	Cinema owners. Took over Baird company 1932.
J. D. Percy	Engineer: joined Baird 1928.
A. G. D. West	Joined Baird as chief engineer 1932.
J. C. Wilson	Engineer: joined Baird 1928. Developed colour.

The Performers:

Miss King	Baird's switchboard operator.
Lulu Stanley	Soubrette.
William Taynton	Office boy: subject of Baird's first television image in 1925.

BBC 30-line:

N. Ashbridge	Assistant Chief Engineer, 1926. Controller engineering, 1929–48.

D. C. Birkinshaw	Television's first chief engineer, 1932. Responsible for setting up Alexandra Palace, the world's first television station, 1935.
P. P. Eckersley	Chief Engineer, 1929–39
J. C. Reith	BBC Managing Director, 1922–7. Director-General, 1927–38.
E. Robb	Sole producer 30-line TV, 1932–5.
L. Sieveking	Producer: *The Man with a Flower in His Mouth*, July 1930.

The Performers (interviewed):

Arthur Askey	Comedian.
Betty Astelle	Singer.
Gracie Fields	Singer.
Sidonie Goossens	Harpist.
Georgie Harris	Comedian.

EMI (1932–8):

C. S. Agate	Responsible for commercial receiver design.
A. D. Blumlein	'All-round genius'; created detailed specification of 405-line system.
L. F. Broadway	Worked on vacuums, cathode-ray tubes for receivers and TV screens. Later Head of Research.
C. O. Browne	In charge of design of cameras and studio equipment and, later, of all EMI equipment for Alexandra Palace and Outside Broadcasts.
J. E. I. Cairns	In charge of manufacture of Emitron cameras.
G. E. Condliffe	Manager of EMI research laboratories.
N. E. Davis (Marconi)	Designed EMI and AP transmitters.
B. Greenhead	Chief liaison engineer between EMI and BBC. 'Saved' the Coronation transmission.
L. Klatzow	Worked on photosensitivity.
H. G. Lubszynski	Developed the Super-Emitron camera.
J. D. McGee	Worked with W. F. Tedham on cathode-ray tubes

and produced first experimental camera tube in Britain in 1932, later developed into Emitron camera.

Isaac Shoenberg — Director of Patent Department and Research Laboratories. Responsible for all major decisions including 405-line television system.

E. L. C. White — With Hardwick and Blumlein, designed all circuits for original EMI equipment at Alexandra Palace.

The Government:

Lord Selsdon — Head of government committee to look into the future of television, 1934.

BBC 1936 – the First Producers:

Mary Adams — Producer: talks.

L. G. Barbrook — 'Film assistant'.

Dallas Bower — Producer: drama, opera, ballet and film: responsible for opening programme Nov. 1936.

Gerald Cock — Director of Television.

Philip Dorté — Head of television Outside Broadcasts.

Cecil Lewis — Producer to 1937: early Outside Broadcasts

Cecil Madden — Programme organiser and producer: responsible for first live show, *Here's Looking at You*, *Picture Page* and light entertainment.

Donald Munro — Productions manager and later ballet producer.

George More O'Ferrall — Producer: *Picture Page* and drama.

Ian Orr-Ewing — Assistant producer: Outside Broadcasts.

Harry Pringle — Stage manager and later light entertainment producer.

Stephen Thomas — Producer: ballet and opera.

The Announcers:

Jasmine Bligh — 'Hostess'.

Elizabeth Cowell — 'Hostess'.

Joan Miller — Switchboard girl, *Picture Page*.

Leslie Mitchell — The 'male announcer'.

The Engineers:

In addition to Campbell, Birkinshaw and Bridgewater from 30-line days there were:

H. W. Baker	Senior transmitter engineer.
John Bliss	Cameraman at the Coronation.
H. F. Bowden	Senior transmitter engineer.
Alan Bray	OB engineer.
T. C. MacNamara	Senior engineer planning and installation.
Roland Price	Cameraman at the Coronation.
Harry Tonge	Cameraman at the Coronation.

The Services

Mary Allen	Head of Wardrobe and Make-up.
Malcolm Baker-Smith	Assistant head of Design.
Peter Bax	Stage manager and head of Design.
Tom Edwards	Chief carpenter.
Leonard Schuster	Executive and financial administrator.
William Streeton	Artists' contracts.
Isabel Winthrope	Joined wardrobe and make-up 1937.

The Critics:

L. Marsland Gander	TV critic of the *Daily Telegraph*.
Grace Wyndham-Goldie	TV critic of *The Listener*.

(Note: this list is not fully comprehensive, but refers only to those people mentioned in the text.)

1

'HERE'S LOOKING AT YOU'
August 1936

BBC Television opened officially on 2 November 1936. It began, by chance, nine weeks before on 26 August with a 78 rpm record of Duke Ellington and a visual announcement which simply stated 'BBC Demonstration to RadiOlympia by the Baird System'. In the 9.40 Home Service News, on the evening before transmission, Sir Noel Ashbridge addressed the listening public:

> We at the BBC are going to do everything in our power to ensure that television broadcasting in this country shall be second to none . . . this is an adventure on which the BBC and the public are entering together, and for this reason we should be frank. Television progress is no further advanced anywhere in the world than it is in this country. You can, with a television set, hear people talk and watch their movements. You can see film. Everyone, scientist and layman, must accept this as remarkable. Only time can show where it will lead.

Neither Ashbridge, the BBC Chief Engineer, nor Gerald Cock, recently appointed the first Director of Television, had expected this sudden dash into production. Nor had the programme planner, Cecil Madden:

> In August, Gerald Cock assembled the whole staff in the Council Chamber at Broadcasting House and said 'I know nothing about television – none of you do, but you've got about four months to think, find out, see what the cameras can do. I suggest you all pile yourselves into cars and go out to see your offices at the Alexandra Palace.' It took about an hour to get there and I found my office on the third floor. There wasn't a stick of furniture in the room, just a telephone in the corner ringing merrily. With some trepidation I crossed the room, picked it up and there was Gerald Cock. 'Ah Cecil,' he said, 'I'm glad I caught you. Wash out everything I said earlier. The Radio Show at Olympia has been a great failure. They can't sell stands. They think television can save them and I've agreed. Don't muck about. You're the senior man. Get hold of your staff and ring me back about five o'clock and tell me what you're going to do. This means programmes in about nine days' time.'

When, in 1935, the Selsdon Committee had advised the government that a regular high-definition television service was both possible and desirable, the BBC was given the job of starting it. Television technology was still being developed. Fewer than a dozen people in the whole country had any experience of television production. There was no equipment, no studio and no money. The government, of course, didn't increase the licence fee but expected it to be funded out of the radio licence. The BBC were given eighteen months to get ready.

The first consideration was to find a high point on which to site the television transmitter and a building close by that could house the studios. The only location remotely suitable was at Wood Green in North London where the east wing of the ageing Victorian entertainments complex, Alexandra Palace, was converted under the general guidance of D. C. Birkinshaw, the corporation's first Engineer in Charge of Television. By August 1936 when the BBC management agreed to provide programmes for RadiOlympia, the studios and equipment were far from complete. Birkinshaw:

> And to be asked to do something three months earlier than the expected date when you're already under the heaviest pressure you can conceive is really rather much.

The Selsdon Committee had insisted that the BBC test two systems of television – the Baird and the Marconi–EMI. The requirement was to waste time, talent and money and provided, said the *Birmingham Mail,* 'yet one more example for foreigners to marvel at our native genius for compromise.'

There were two main studios. One operated the Marconi–EMI electronic television system; the other the Intermediate Film system of Baird. In addition, Bairds had a small announcer's studio using the mechanical 'spotlight' method. These three were for 'live' presentations. Both Baird and Marconi-EMI also had telecine machines for showing film.

Transmissions for RadiOlympia were to begin on Wednesday 26 August and alternate between Baird and EMI. On the toss of a sovereign, Baird was to go first. The broadcast was to consist of fifty minutes of film transmission from telecine, ten minutes of Gaumont British newsreel and forty minutes of 'live' programming from the studio under the direction of Cecil Madden. Madden and his co-producer George More O'Ferrall opted for a variety show: something 'light, bright and fast moving'. Ronnie Hill was commissioned to write a new song and it was Hill who came up with the name *Here's Looking at You.* Madden:

> This caught my imagination and I thought, instead of calling our show *Variety,* let us call it *Here's Looking at You.* This was an extremely good move from the point of view of the press because they saw the whole thing was going to be done with imagination and excitement and they backed us all the way.

On 18 August, Bill Streeton, television's booker, confirmed that all the artists had accepted their contracts: the Three Admirals, 'Masters of Modern Harmony' from the Cochran revue *Anything Goes;* Miss Lutie and her Wonder Horse 'Pogo' which had just completed a year at the London Pavilion; Carol Chilton and Maceo Thomas 'Tapping in Rhythm'; and the singer from Lew Stone's band, Miss Helen McKay. The entire budget for artists was £300. As there was no method of television recording, the show was to be done 'live' twice a day for ten days. Miss McKay received £42. The Admirals shared three guineas a show.

Rehearsals began on 20 August and Gerald Cock issued a private and confidential memo about stand-by arrangements in case of a technical breakdown:

If there is a breakdown lasting (as far as can be anticipated) about one minute, go straight on with the programme as if nothing had occurred. If likely to be longer than a minute, abandon the particular item being broadcast and continue with the next . . . There will be a breakdown microphone ready on both the EMI balcony and the Baird balcony by which Mr Lewis will broadcast informally an apologetic announcement and will continue to do so for as long as the breakdown lasts.

With considerably more confidence than Cock, Marconi–EMI issued details of their electronic system – 'The System of Today and Tomorrow', and added a special note about the quality of reception to be expected from their television sets at RadiOlympia. The picture was to remain 'absolutely steady'. It was to have 'correct tone values without further manipulation'. There was to be 'no flicker'. Bairds, too, described their television system. They avoided mentioning their flickery picture and concentrated on their two methods of 'live' or, in one case, 'almost live' studio transmission:

In the Spotlight Studio, which takes close-ups and three-quarter length shots, a steady beam of light from an arc lamp . . . traces a line . . . over every part of the subject twenty-five times a second making no less than two hundred and forty traces each time. At this incredible speed the point of light ceases to be noticed by the subject and the illumination seems to be nothing more than normal room lighting and causes not the slightest discomfort.

This method of 240-line transmission was a development of the mechanical system that Baird had been working on for ten years. It was intended for announcements only; full-scale studio productions were to be covered by the Intermediate Film technique:

. . . a wonderful new machine which films the studio scene, develops the film practically instantaneously, and sends it out as a television picture thirty seconds after it is taken! In fact before the announcer can walk from the studio into the open air, his picture is speeding through the ether to the television 'lookers-in'.

This was the 'almost live' transmission. Furthermore:

The whole installation, with typical British thoroughness, is built as solidly as the electronic installation of a battleship and is a masterpiece of technical efficiency and engineering ability.

The reference to 'typical British thoroughness' was to remind patriotic viewers that Baird was the local boy and that he claimed the EMI product was not really British at all but American in disguise. The reference to an 'electronic installation' covered up the fact that Bairds, unlike EMI, actually lacked an electronic system altogether.

On 24 August the BBC, steering a neutral path between the rival claims of the two companies, issued its own technical description of the 'premises, aerials and transmitters' at Alexandra Palace and whetted viewers' appetites with a foretaste of the live transmissions:

Dress and make-up will play a part towards the success of RadiOlympia's first televised variety show. Helen McKay will be dressed in white and the Three Admirals will wear white sailor suits. Carol Chilton at the piano and Maceo Thomas the tap dancer will be seen in white, with black shoes which should help emphasise the quick footwork in this act. The Television Orchestra, conducted by Hyam Greenbaum, will wear grey flannels and white shirts.

Transmissions were to take place in both the morning and the afternoon.

Just before midday on 26 August, Leslie Mitchell waited in the dark of the Baird Spotlight Studio. The only one of three announcers not too ill to appear, he was overcome by 'sheer, absolute terror. It was paralysing.' The countdown to the first transmission began. The technicians, having checked and rechecked their equipment, checked again. Madden, waiting to direct the live show, checked his watch. Ambler, the studio manager, adjusted his earphones and waited to cue Mitchell by a well-aimed dig in the ribs. At 11.44 a.m. a still, tense calm fell over the entire building as all eyes watched the hand on the clock as the seconds drained away. At 11.45 precisely, came the smooth sweet sounds of Duke Ellington's 'Solitude' and, onto the television screen, the unsteady announcement of the start of the demonstration to RadiOlympia using the Baird system. This visual tuning signal was primarily for dealers who needed to tune in their sets and lasted for about fifteen minutes. It was backed by further Ellington records and selections from Eric Coates' 'London Again' suite.

At twelve o'clock the doors of Olympia were thrown open to the public. Six thousand people began to crowd in and jostle in the television viewing booths 'like rabbits in a super rabbit hutch' or perch 'like chickens on the tiered seats in front of television sets in the main foyer.' Mitchell, still in the dark of the Spotlight Studio, said his announcement over and over to himself in order not to forget the words:

> You weren't allowed to read from a script: not that you could see it in the dark anyway.

On cue, he introduced the film programme from telecine: 'Some short excerpts from outstanding films of the year.' It was the first airing for Paul Rotha's documentary on books called *Cover to Cover*. It featured Somerset Maugham, Julian Huxley, T. S. Eliot and Rebecca West but was scarcely the blockbuster that might have been expected. The movie moguls, anticipating television as a major threat, were not eager to lend and the shortage of full-length feature material was to remain a major BBC problem for years to come.

The film lasted twenty minutes and was followed by the live entertainment but, because Baird's Intermediate Film system in the large studio was not yet ready, the show was switched to the tiny Spotlight Studio and seriously modified. Madden's proposed spectacular was reduced to three singing spots by Miss McKay. In a long white dress with floral corsage and accompanied by Henry Bronkhurst, she peered into the spotlight and, at 12.22, began to sing:

> Here's Looking at You/From out of the Blue/
> Don't make a fuss/But settle down and look at us:

Which was difficult as viewers were only permitted to stay in front of the television sets for two minutes before being asked to move on.

This wonderful age goes to show/That all the world's a stage,/
First you heard, now you see,/As you wonder what the next thing/
On the list will be,/What hullabaloo!/We're just peeping through/
To say 'how do'/Here's Looking at You.

'Just peeping through' was a more accurate description of the occasion than was intended as the totally unsuitable studio only allowed Miss McKay to appear head and shoulders and the sound of the piano, concealed behind curtains, was muffled and almost inaudible. But the transmission was a success. It went, said *The Times*, 'without a hitch'. This was not so in the afternoon and the afternoon's experience was to be a more accurate indication of what was to be expected during television transmission in the ensuing months.

Mitchell, waiting to repeat his morning announcement, was, at 4.30, delayed by a visual breakdown which stretched into what seemed like an eternity of seven minutes. The second breakdown came when, three and a half minutes into her song, Miss McKay disappeared from the screen and took the sound with her. Mr Lewis, on the Baird balcony, gave informal apologies in sound only – apologies that he repeated every minute for the nine and a half minutes that the breakdown lasted. But, by 5.15, the engineers had the show back on air and, apart from two short interruptions just before the closing announcement at 6.02, the transmission continued uninterrupted with a mixture of live songs from Miss McKay and short film clips of Jessie Matthews, Laurence Olivier, Jack Buchanan and Gertie Lawrence. The *Morning Post* (27 Aug. 1936):

> Reception was excellent (and although) Mr Gerald Cock had warned us that the programme had been hurriedly arranged and that we were not to expect too much . . . he need not have worried . . . we could appreciate the moonlight on the diaphanous dress of Miss Matthews . . . and feel no undue eyestrain.

The Times (27 Aug. 1936):

> (There was) a tendency to flicker and a curious and uneasy shifting of parts of the image . . . on the whole it would seem that entertainments prepared beforehand and filmed for the occasion are at present more suitable than those in 'direct vision'.

Thumbs up for Baird telecine: thumbs down for Baird Spotlight.

On 27 August it was the turn of Marconi–EMI and the potential of Madden's variety show could be seen for the first time. Whereas Baird transmitted at 240 lines and twenty-five frames per second (flicker), Marconi–EMI transmitted at 405 lines and fifty frames per second (no flicker). Whereas Baird planned to use for live coverage either the mechanical spotlight system or the cumbersome static, single camera Intermediate Film technique, Marconi–EMI had an electronic system with three fully operational studio cameras, two of which were already mobile. It meant that with Baird, performers had to direct the action to the camera, but with Marconi–EMI the cameras could follow the action and performances could be more natural and pictures more numerous and varied. With the flexibility of the electronic system, the producer's imagination could be given much greater rein. Madden:

I didn't really know how to present this first show . . . so I turned to the stage as an idea. I divided the big Studio A (the EMI studio) into three stages separated by curtains, one behind the other, and started the show on the front stage with all the cameras, lights, lined up. When the act was over, we opened the next lot of curtains and everything moved down onto the next stage, the lights, cameras, the lot. Then, when that was over on stage two, we moved onto stage three for the climax with the orchestra. As a result, looking down on it from the control room above, with all the cameras, lights, people, everybody going down the stage together, it did look comically like a procession and it was known affectionately as the Madden Processional Technique. And was never used again.

The afternoon live transmission began, as on the previous day, at 4.30. At 4.29, as the film demonstration was coming to an end from Marconi–EMI telecine, Madden, from the control room, phoned down to the stage manager on the studio floor below. The stage manager called to the performers to 'Stand by: one minute to go.' At $4.29\frac{1}{2}$, according to the surviving script, the stage manager blew his whistle, signalled OK to the control room, nodded to the orchestra to roll the cymbals, and through the front curtain, at 4.30 precisely, came Leslie Mitchell: 'There was all this space about you and you could actually see what you were doing.' He's in full-length figure shot:

> *L.M.* Hello RadiOlympia!

Madden instructs the camera to track into close-up. As the curtains open behind him, Mitchell waits for the camera to come to rest and continues:

> *L.M.* Ladies and Gentlemen – *Here's Looking at You*. We now come to another part of this experimental demonstration – direct television from the studios by the Marconi–EMI system, which means that you are watching a programme that is actually going on now. For the next half-hour you are going to see a variety programme – *Here's Looking at You*.

As Mitchell exits left, the camera picks up the Three Admirals who sing the title song unaccompanied. For the first two performances of the show, Mitchell has to make all the announcements alone. He returns to the stage:

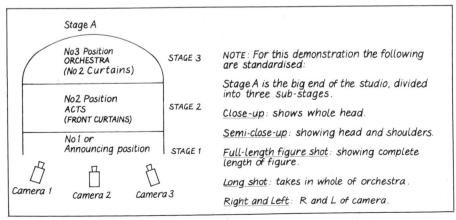

Floor plan and instructions issued to staff and performers involved in *Here's Looking at You* given in the Marconi–EMI studio.

L.M. Now I would like you to meet my colleagues, but by a stroke of very bad luck both Jasmine Bligh and Elizabeth Cowell are too ill to appear. Now. Who's next? The Television Orchestra. Good. Where's the conductor? Come on Greenbaum. This is where you make your bow.

Hyam Greenbaum, 'Bumps' to his friends, was suggested by Sir Adrian Boult as the one musician in London who could cope with any kind of music that television could throw at him. He joins Mitchell in front of the camera:

H.G. Good evening. I'd feel safer with my orchestra.
L.M. Tell me – what are you going to play?
H.G. First 'Rise and Shine'. Then a number by Ronnie Hill called 'Here's Looking at You'.
L.M. I seem to have heard that before somewhere! The title's appropriate anyway. Are you ready?
H.G. Give me a moment.

Greenbaum leaves the stage.

L.M. Well, here's looking at the Television Orchestra.

Mitchell gestures towards the second set of curtains which open to reveal the orchestra. The camera tracks in, pans round the semicircle of musicians, and comes to rest in semi-close-up on Greenbaum. The band strikes up and *The Times* reported (1 Sept. 1936):

Sir Thomas Beecham says he believes that television can do much to improve the musical taste of the nation.

The show continued, uninterrupted by breakdowns, with songs from Helen McKay, more from the Admirals and a comedy routine from Miss Lutie and Pogo the Horse. Bernard Greenhead, EMI Engineer:

The producer of that insert was O'Ferrall. I remember him coming and putting his head round the control-room door and saying, 'I've got a funny horse.' When it was produced, it was two men in a skin, I laughed so much my sides were aching. It was just honest-to-goodness slapstick.

L.M. We now come to the last turn in our programme *Here's Looking at You*. Two international entertainers, new to this country – Carol Chilton and Maceo Thomas who are going to present their song and dance act which they call 'Tapping in Rhythm'. So, ladies and gentlemen, in closing, here's looking at Chilton and Thomas!

Chilton and Thomas were a South American novelty dance act. Chilton, the girl, played the piano while Thomas, the man, tapped up a staircase of thin metal columns on which Chilton had placed even thinner plates. It was an act that combined dancing with gymnastics, high-wire with juggling. He climbed to 8 feet above the studio floor and then, in one spectacular leap, took off and landed, still tapping, on the ground. Madden:

The Emitron cameras could not cut from one to the other instantaneously as they do today. They could only 'fade' – one camera's image slowly disappearing as the next camera's image appeared. And the speed of the 'fade' was a minimum eight seconds. So, in rehearsal, I had to calculate back into the action of the performer to work out when to tell the camera to 'turn over' and hope that the 'fade' would be completed before a performance climax was reached. But with Maceo Thomas' big leap, I had problems. I had to be close on his feet all the time so, when he took off from his column, I couldn't get the action in the close-up camera. I had to mix to another to show the jump and the landing. The difficulty was to make sure the mix was complete before he took off. And sometimes it was and sometimes it wasn't, and when it wasn't all you saw were two confused images superimposed on one another – not the spectacular leap and landing at all.

There were also other serious operational problems. John Bliss, cameraman:

It simply hadn't occurred to the scientists at EMI that we might need a viewfinder.

The only way a cameraman could see what his camera was televising was, with his back to the action, to press his eye to a tiny spyhole, one eighth of an inch in diameter. Here he could see a faint optical image on the actual camera mosaic, upside down and back to front.

It was very frustrating because we had no real idea whether we were in the right position or not and whether we were offering the producer the picture he wanted. He could give us some idea over our headphones when he saw our picture on his monitor but as he had only one of them and not one for each camera and there were usually three cameras on the floor, he couldn't keep track of all of us all at the same time. So, I contrived a little viewfinder of my own out of a piece of bent wire which I tied to the side of the camera with string. Fantastically crude but it served its purpose until EMI designed a proper one for us.

The cameras, too, for all their much-vaunted freedom of movement, actually, in the early stages, moved very little. One sat firmly on a tripod, another was on castors, and the only one that was really mobile was the camera placed on a dolly, a Vinten truck that trundled the camera about and enabled it to track into position. Mobility was doubled after RadiOlympia when Bliss made another dolly out of the chassis of an old Austin Seven. Madden:

So we gave about twelve performances and, of course, all the time, we hoped we got it better. Every time we hoped the thing would move faster and it generally did.

The Times (28 Aug. 1936):

The music hall show was appropriately entitled 'Here's Looking at You' and came over with perfect synchronization of sound and vision and with complete continuity of movement.

The Observer (30 Aug. 1936):

'From Cover to Cover', giving the history of writing and printing and the making of a book, is a good piece of work. That kind of thing will always be welcome. The film criticism, with its excerpts of coming films, is fascinating even in the way it is now being done with bits and pieces hurriedly assembled. The Gaumont British News is also intriguing.

Daily Herald:

> There is a complete absence of flicker from Marconi–EMI . . . it is now clear that (the majority of manufacturers) are convinced that television will in future become a force to be seriously reckoned with.

Morning Post (29 Aug. 1936):

> The number of people attending RadiOlympia on Saturday rose to 28,000 – a new record – and television reception, expected to be within a radius of 25 miles of Alexandra Palace was reported from Bournemouth (96 miles) and Nottingham (102 miles).

Elizabeth Cowell returned from her sick-bed and made her announcing debut on Monday 31 August in the Baird Spotlight Studio. She spoke to the *Daily Sketch*:

> It really was a bit terrifying . . . I went into a pitch-black room. I could see nothing at all at first. I felt hands guiding me towards a platform. About ten feet from a blue light I stood against a white screen. I looked straight into the blue light and began to introduce Miss McKay . . . My sensations were most curious, I felt I was talking to myself in the dark . . . and I made one mistake. In turning to say 'Here is Miss McKay' I looked to the right and Miss McKay came in on the left. But these are the kind of faults, I suppose, I am bound to make at the beginning.

On the following day she joined Leslie Mitchell in the EMI studio to give some variety to the announcing pattern:

> *E.C.* Well, Leslie?
> *L.M.* Now, Elizabeth, tell me, are you going to announce or am I?
> *E.C.* I think it would be a good idea for you to.
> *L.M.* Oh no, that's not fair. But I tell you what. We'll split it up between us.
> *E.C.* Fine.

Despite the archness of the scripted interchange, there was already the start of an informality unknown amongst radio announcers: already the concern with personalities with whom the audience at home could identify.

> *L.M.* I'll do the first half and you do the second half. How about that?
> *E.C.* All right.
> *L.M.* Now, who's next?

In the days that followed, more ideas were tried and tested. The Baird Studio B remained out of commission but, in the Spotlight Studio, both Cowell and Mitchell began live interviewing. Mitchell, on 4 September, spoke to the bandleader Jack Hylton. On the same day, a nervous Elizabeth Cowell talked to the film make-up artist Rita Grant. These five-minute interviews were billed as 'dialogues' and were scripted in order to sustain the interview and 'to prevent anyone from saying something they shouldn't.'

Cowell: Miss Grant is the girl who was up here at Alexandra Palace last Sunday week for the Press Demonstration and I am going to tell you some of her experiences.

Grant: I enjoyed it tremendously and felt very much at home.

Cowell: How long were you here?

Grant: For about four hours rehearsing in the morning and for two and a half hours for the demonstration in the afternoon.

Cowell: Quite a long time.

Grant: But I wasn't tired – I was so excited about it all.

Cowell: What sort of make-up did you use?

Grant: The same as I'm wearing now – blue lips, blue eyes and a white face. It looks all right in here, but when we get outside it looks very funny. I think Bairds find this make-up best for this system.

The blue lips and white face make-up was only used in the Spotlight Studio. Elsewhere in the Baird Studio B and in the EMI studio normal film make-up was used.

Cowell: Have you had any experience of this before?

Grant: I did it years ago in Baird's television in Long Acre and it was quite different from what it is now. I think this is much easier.

Cowell: Well, Miss Grant, do you mind if I ask you a personal question? How do you keep your hair in those beautiful curls?

Grant: Well, everybody asks me that and I don't think I'm going to tell them.

Cowell: I understand that when the press gentlemen were here last Sunday week they didn't believe they were actually seeing you televise. They thought it was a fake.

Grant: That is quite true.

Cowell: How funny.

Television interviewing was a technique that still had to be learned.

Towards the end of RadiOlympia, the BBC experimented with its first Outside Broadcast. OBs were expected to prove one of the great advantages of television over film: to see things 'live', like national ceremonies and sports as they actually happened. But they were only possible on the Marconi–EMI system. Whereas Baird's camera was firmly bolted to the studio floor, EMI's cameras, given sufficient length of cable, could be carried outside the building to take pictures in daylight. In a memo dated 31 August, Mr Cecil Lewis, who was to produce the two-minute item, explained the routine:

The Emitron camera will be required to be set up opposite the main entrance to the offices at the head of the steps on the left side looking from the doorway. Mr Leonard Henry will emerge from the doorway and move towards the camera in s.c.u. (short close up). After he has spoken, Mr Leonard Henry will turn and get into the car, which will move off, followed by the camera. The car will take its usual route from upper to lower terrace, the camera following it and picking it up as it comes along the lower terrace. At the foot of the steps opposite the main entrance, the car will pull up for a moment for Mr Henry to shout a word of farewell, and then drive on again along the lower terrace in a westerly direction, followed by the camera. As the car is lost the shot will be faded.

Microphones will be required to pick up speech on the width of the roadway between the main entrance and the head of the steps opposite and if this microphone is not capable of taking speech at the foot of the steps as Mr Henry passes below, the second mike should be available there. If the boom is available for speech on the upper terrace, its position should be near the right-hand urn looking from the doorway, as it can then be kept out of shot.

On 4 September the experimental item had its first rehearsal and was sufficiently successful for Cecil Lewis to give Leslie Mitchell a closing announcement. It was duly broadcast at the end of transmission the next day:

Well, now that you have seen these two exterior shots mixed back and forth, I think you will be impressed with the possibilities of outside television broadcasts.

But lookers-in at RadiOlympia were, for the most part, not so sure. The trees, they agreed, looked like trees, but not real ones. The daylight made them look artificial. And, from viewing points in Abbey Road (EMI), the Haymarket (Bairds), Broadcasting House and RadiOlympia itself, public acclaim for television as a whole was far from universal. Television screens were extremely small: the picture quality was comparatively poor and the Baird picture flickered. Seated too far away from the television screens and being constantly urged to 'move on', the viewer only had time to see snippets of the variety show. They were quite pleased with some of the acts but felt the lady announcer was both too nervous and too grand. What they took for extempore interviews, though, they quite enjoyed. Films were dismissed as being not television at all but 'the pictures' and interest was only kindled when the movie shot was a close-up. Long shots, breathtaking on the big screen, became little more than a confused fog when reduced to the small.

For the itinerant viewer, television at RadiOlympia was a novelty: but, brought up on a newspaper diet that promised so much from television, it was a disappointment, not a success. For the engineers and production teams a great deal was learnt – there is no better way of learning how to broadcast than broadcasting, but much learning was still left to be done and after the euphoria and excitement of the exhibition was over, L. Marsland Gander, recently appointed the television critic of the *Daily Telegraph*, was able to recollect in tranquillity. Unlike the viewers, he had seen all the transmissions and seen them under reasonable conditions. He wrote on 10 September:

As to the programmes, while anything serves for demonstration, it is obvious that animated lantern lectures, footling interviews and unexciting variety turns will not be good enough for the regular service. Novelty appeal will soon pass. What then?

It was a pertinent question and one which the next few months of broadcasting would answer. But, for the viewer, there would still remain the question of cost. Of the seven different sets on display at RadiOlympia, the cheapest was ninety-five guineas and rose to 150 – the cost of a car – and was way beyond the average purse still in the grips of the Great Depression.

2

THE SCOTTISH INVENTOR
1923–6

The Times: 27 June 1923. Personal Column.

> Seeing by wireless. Inventor of apparatus wishes to hear from someone who will assist, not financially, in making working model. Write Box S 686. *The Times*. E.C.4.

The advertisement was placed by John Logie Baird. Baird was born in 1888, in Helensburgh, near Glasgow. An awareness of scientific achievement was something he grew up with. Percy Pilcher, the aviation pioneer and Glasgow University lecturer, flew his embryonic aeroplane only a few miles from Helensburgh when Baird was ten. A local man, Henry Bell, was responsible for launching the first successful steamship in Europe. His namesake, Alexander Graham Bell, had left Scotland for North America in 1870 and, in 1876, twelve years before Baird was born, had patented the telephone, marketed it and become both a respected scientist and an affluent businessman. Consciously or not, it was Alexander Graham Bell's career that John Logie Baird was to attempt to emulate.

Baird was a precocious experimenter. At the age of fourteen he had constructed a simple telephone, installed domestic electric light and tried to make one of the component parts of television, a selenium cell. By eighteen he had become a student at the Royal Technical College, Glasgow – now the University of Strathclyde.

> The first year I was there I learned a good deal that was very useful and interesting: the remaining years were, I think, almost entirely a waste of time. But what I learned in the first year remained with me all my life and has been of great value.
>
> *(Television Baird*, p. 24)

His detailed study of mechanical engineering set him on an intellectual and practical path from which he was not to deviate.

It was whilst he was at the Technical College that he met the confident and socially superior son of the Moderator of the United Free Church of Scotland, John Reith. Their first encounter came when the short-sighted Baird accidentally interrupted a Reithian conversation with the maths professor:

> As I did so, the heaviest and most overpowering of the students turned round and boomed at me: 'Ha! What's the matter with you? Are you deaf or blind?' I

simpered something inaudible and he turned his back on me.
                                                        (*Television Baird*, p. 14)

The relationship between the two men was not to be very different when, twenty years later, they met again and John Reith was Director-General of the BBC and John Baird the supplicant pleading for access to the air waves.

Baird, partly through illness and partly through boredom, was twenty-six when he graduated from the Royal College in 1914. 'Unfit for Army service', he spent the war years as an assistant mains engineer with the Clyde Valley Electrical Company from which he tried to make a dramatic exit by using the company's facilities to make artificial diamonds. His method was to surround a rod of carbon with a block of concrete and to explode the carbon and turn it into diamonds by passing through it much of the electricity destined for the Glasgow shipyards. The attempt failed, fused the mains and antagonised the management but when, shortly afterwards, Baird left his thirty-shillings-a-week job, he did it voluntarily in order to capitalise on his recently started private venture, the Baird Undersock Company. He was thirty-one and embarked, at last, on his career as inventor-entrepreneur.

The Baird undersock which aimed at keeping the feet warm and dry in winter, cool and unsweaty in summer, was an ordinary undersock that Baird sprinkled with borax. He acted as his own commercial traveller and charged ninepence a pair.

I began to get a little money together and spent some on publicity. I sent a squad of women round the town with sandwich boards . . . They were news, and photographs of them appeared in some of the illustrated papers with the caption 'First Sandwich Women in Glasgow: new occupation for ladies.' The words 'Baird Undersock' appeared prominently on the placards. Some of the newspapers published this without comment, but in two cases I had to pay a small fee to have the name reproduced in the paper. It was first class publicity.
                                                        (*Television Baird*, p. 31)

The lasting value of the undersock enterprise was not the sock but Baird's marketing experience. He learnt to create a demand through advertising. It was a technique he was later to use extensively in his attempt to create a demand for television.

Baird sold the undersock business in 1920 for £1600 and sailed for Trinidad where he invested some of his capital in a factory to make jam and chutney. By the end of 1921 he had exchanged the world of Caribbean chutney for the world of London soap and 'Baird's Speedy Cleaner'. By the autumn of 1922 he had sold the business at a profit and retired to a friend's house in Hastings. He was now thirty-four and it was in Hastings that he began concentrated work on what was to prove the most successful of his enterprises – television.

From the mid-nineteenth century men had been contemplating and later researching the proposition of 'seeing by wireless', and most of Baird's early experiments were based on the ideas of the German inventor Paul Nipkow. In 1884, Nipkow had patented a method of scanning an image by a large disc in which were cut eighteen small holes arranged in a spiral so that the image could be scanned line by line. The disc could be used for both the transmission and the reception of an image by a system that involved the use of the only available photo-element – selenium. Nipkow, even if he had tried, failed to put his idea into practice but, by 1900, the idea of 'distant electric vision' had moved off the pages of the academic journals and into the daily newspapers. As Marconi transformed wireless from discovery to commercial proposition so the notion of 'television' developed from dream to possibility to probability. It was Baird's great achievement to be the first man to produce a television picture.

Baird, with the aid of technical books from the local library, 'laboured alone and unaided in his struggles to achieve television' (Ronald Tiltman, 1933), though not as alone and unaided as had frequently been suggested. In October 1922 Norman Loxdale was a boy of thirteen having problems making a one-valve wireless set:

> It just wouldn't work and somebody suggested 'Well, there's a chap in the Queen's Arcade that supposedly is well up in wireless.' . . . so I wandered down there one day with this box and loudspeakers, knocked on the door and there was this rather tall gentleman there. 'What can I do for you son?' I told him I couldn't get my set to work and he said he would help me. He examined it and he said 'It'll never work like that. You need a grid leak.' I hadn't got one so he said 'We'll soon alter that. There's a bit of string over there. Cut a bit of that off. Now put it in your mouth and chew it.' I looked at him. I thought he was having me on. He then told me how to make a grid leak.

Baird, already the master of makeshift, asked Loxdale to help him construct his apparatus. Loxdale:

> First off he got me to make bits and pieces like brackets and discs. I made three altogether, two of them out of wood from tea-chests got from the Maypole grocers in Castle Hill Road, and one out of card. One of them had twelve small holes and another with larger holes he fitted with bicycle lamp lenses he got from Wheelers in the Arcade . . . Baird was a very clever man. He knew exactly what he wanted and he knew what he'd got to do but he hadn't got the slightest idea how to do it.

Among the other men who helped Baird were the local Post Office engineer, the Hastings Tramways chief engineer, electrical, radio and marine engineers, wood turners, coffin makers, writers, a local physicist, J. J. Denton, who later became a member of Baird's staff, and, perhaps most important of all, V. R. Mills. Mills' association with Baird was first publicly noticed in May 1976 when Mills wrote a letter to the magazine *Electronics and Power*.

> Dear Sir,
>   I have read with much interest and some amusement, the recent correspondence on Baird and television, especially as I am able to add to G. R. M. Garratt's statement 'Baird no more invented television than I did' . . . (as) together in 1923 (Baird and I) did succeed in transmitting an image which was moving and recognisable.

Vic Mills was fascinated by wireless transmission and had just opened a radio business of his own. One night, at home, he was called to the front door. Mills:

I went to the door and there was a man in a dirty old fawn raincoat. It was foggy and wet so I think it was the end of February 1923. I asked him what he wanted and he said 'I'm trying to invent television' – he used the word 'television' because I asked him what it meant and he said 'seeing by wireless' – and he went on 'I believe you know something about radio and if you know something about radio you should know something about resonance. I've got a signal but it's very very weak and I have a lot of noise.' I arranged to go down to the Arcade and see what he'd got and hear his signal. What I saw was this scanning disc – a monstrosity made out of a wooden tea chest lid – with $\frac{3}{8}$ inch holes, perhaps a dozen of them, on a disc about 18 inches going round at about four revs a second.

The basis of all television, mechanical or electronic, is the 'scanning' of an image by a beam of light in a series of sequential lines moving from top to bottom and from left to right. Each section of the image, as the light passes over it, produces signals which are converted into electrical impulses, strong or weak according to the light or dark of that section. Suitably amplified, the impulses are transmitted along wires or through the air by radio waves to be reconverted into light signals in the same order and in the same strength as they were originally given off. That these constantly appearing and disappearing strips of light pattern appear to the human eye as a complete and moving picture depends on the retention of vision. The scanning is so fast that the human retina cannot react swiftly enough to notice how the picture is being constantly built up.

Baird, in his earliest experiments, could only transmit about a yard. There was no wireless transmission and the same revolving disc acted as transmitter and receiver. Baird himself described the equipment:

It was a circle of cardboard into which two spirals of holes had been cut with the sharp end of a pair of scissors. A darning needle formed the spindle, and by

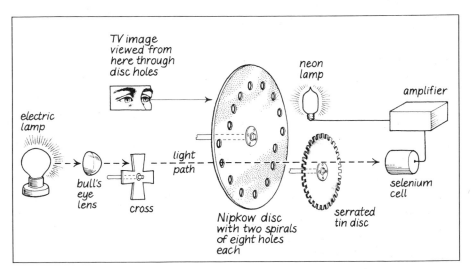

Diagrammatic representation of Baird's first experimental apparatus as described in his memoirs.

means of bobbins this could be revolved. On one side a powerful electric lamp shone through the bull's-eye lens onto a little cardboard cross and cast a shadow. On one side of this revolving disc another tin disc with serrated edges revolved at great speed in the path of the light. The selenium cell, connected by an amplifier, was on the other side of the cardboard disc. The neon lamp glowed when the cell was illuminated and went out when it was in shadow, so that when the apparatus revolved, it was possible to see on one side of the disc the shadow of the cross on the faraway side, a distance of two feet.

(*Television Baird*, p. 42)

However, when Mills first met him, Baird had produced no picture at all. Selenium, like the human retina, 'lags'. It is slow in converting light into electricity and, in attempting to overcome the problem by concentrating the light onto the selenium cell through the serrated-edged disc, Baird had failed to get a clearer signal and only added to the 'noise'. Mills:

It was like a rushing wind. 99.9% 'noise'. Only after a lot of concentration could I hear any signal. I said that with this gear it was impossible to filter out that amount of noise and said the only hope we had of getting a signal was to make a smaller selenium cell. Then we'd get much less noise but that would mean we would have to scan the object in a different manner . . . At that time Baird was scanning the cell and not scanning the picture so I told him to make a small cell and I would come back in a few days' time.

Mills' suggestion was to reduce the noise in order to get a clearer signal by getting Baird's light signal from the scanning disc onto the smallest possible area of the cell by reducing the actual size of the cell itself and by introducing another lens to focus the light from the scanning disc onto the entire cell area. He also suggested that Baird should improve the valves driving the neon lamp and place the cross between the scanning disc and cell so that no longer would the cell be scanned but the cross itself.

Mills:

Next time I went down there, I revamped his optics and the neon circuits and fixed up this new selenium cell I'd told him to make. And while I was adjusting the neon circuit, I put my fingers in front of the selenium cells. Just flicked them and suddenly Baird shouted out: 'It's here! It's here!' My fingers. Baird was looking at the receiving side of the apparatus and when I went to where he was he came to where I was and I think he waved his fingers about. I saw those on the disc.

It was Baird's first 'picture', the silhouette or shadow of Mills' fingers made up of lines corresponding to the number of holes in the disc. The silhouette of the Maltese Cross followed and was seen by Loxdale 'distorted by the curvature of the disc. It was very flickery.' It was late February or early March 1923, the first time anyone had achieved an instantaneous moving picture anywhere in the world. Mills lent Baird his best amplifier and returned to his radio business.

Baird continued to improve his equipment and began to give demonstrations to the press. A report in the *Kinematograph Weekly* prompted a

London cinema owner, Will Day, to give Baird £200 and, on 26 July 1923, Baird and Day together applied for a patent on 'A System of Transmitting Views, Portraits and Scenes by Telegraphy or Wireless Telegraphy'. The patent gives few details – patents rarely do as inventors don't wish to give secrets to rivals – but it describes the circuit much as Mills had rearranged it, though it omits the serrated-edged disc as the improved selenium cell would render it obsolete.

One month before the patent was submitted, Baird had placed his advert in *The Times* for help in 'making working model'. It was seen by the owner of Odhams Press, W. J. Odhams himself. He asked two of his friends, F. H. Robinson, a science writer, and Captain West, Chief Engineer of the BBC, to investigate. They reported back and Odhams told Baird:

> If you could put a machine next door, seat someone in front of it and then on the screen in this room show his face – not a shadow but a face – then I'm certain you would get all the money you want. I am anxious to help but . . . can see no future for a device which only sends shadows.
>
> (*Television Baird*, p. 45)

In January 1924, Baird, thrown out of his room in the Queen's Arcade for causing explosions, prepared to give another demonstration. Mills was summoned to Baird's bedroom at 21 Linton Road to help him wire his apparatus. Baird could still not do this adequately himself and a publicity photograph taken about this time shows Baird presiding over his unwired equipment. But the demonstration was a success and further demonstrations followed. In April, an article appeared in *Radio Times* and, again, in *Kinematograph Weekly*, written by Robinson. He entitled it 'The Radio Kinema' and states, categorically:

> television . . . far from being 'the dream of the future' is an established fact. Not so long ago I visited one John Logie Baird at his laboratory in Hastings and saw a demonstration which proved that he has proceeded so far along the road to radio vision as to make it almost a commercial proposition.

He describes the system. Despite its omission from the 1923 patent, the serrated-edged disc is still present and the selenium cell is still causing trouble, so the system is not yet as practically advanced as the patent might have implied. Nor, perhaps, is the method of transmission. After being amplified, the electric impulses no longer go by wire to a neon bulb but

> . . . are passed into the ordinary microphone circuit of a wire or wireless transmitter and radiated in the usual manner.

However, as Baird was unlikely to have had a wireless transmitter at this date, Robinson's description most probably refers to Baird's theory rather than his practice. But Robinson is clear about Baird's method of reception. The receiver is now quite separate from the transmitter. On this receiving disc

> . . . in place of the holes which are cut in the transmitting disc there are a number of quick acting lamps arranged in positions corresponding to the holes in the

transmitting disc. All of these lamps are wired up to a commutator to which the impulses are fed. The lamps then light up in sympathy with the light flashes passed by the transmitting disc and reproduce the original image . . . It is necessary, of course, to synchronise the transmitting and receiving discs . . .

Robinson does not reveal how or how successfully this was done. But

. . . I myself saw a cross, the letter H and the fingers of my own hand reproduced by this apparatus across the width of the laboratory. The images were quite sharp and clear although perhaps a little unsteady. This, however, was mostly due to mechanical defects in the apparatus and not to any fault in the system . . . Moving images may be transmitted by this means and distance is no object, merely depending on the power of the wireless transmitter and the sensitivity of the receiver employed. Undoubtedly wonderful possibilities are opened up by this invention, its very simplicity and reliability placing it well to the front of many of the variously complicated methods evolved to do the same work. Now that the main principle has been communicated and proved it is not too much to expect that in the course of time we shall be able to see on the screen the winner of the Derby actually racing home watched by hundreds of thousands of worshippers at Epsom.

(*Kinematograph Weekly*, 3 April 1924)

Robinson was right. Television would be at the Derby in seven years' time. He was also right to dismiss most of the other 'complicated methods evolved to do the same work', methods which, like Baird's, relied on the use of mechanical scanners: the work of Von Mihaly in Hungary and Jenkins in the United States. But he was wrong, if he knew of them, to dismiss the suggestions of Rosing in Russia (1907) and Campbell Swinton in Britain (1908 and 1911), who suggested an electronic method of 'seeing by wireless' through the use of the cathode-ray tube. Robinson concluded:

The inventor is confident that no technical difficulties stand in the way of the transmission of moving images by wireless.

(*Kinematograph Weekly*, 3 April 1924)

Baird, if he was to raise money for further work, had to be confident. Vic Mills was not so sure:

After that demonstration in 1924 I had very long talks with Mr Baird. I used to sit on his bed in Linton Road and we talked over the various possibilities of television but I was absolutely certain from the onset that we were going the wrong way. We could not make mechanical vision give a really acceptable picture. It was obvious, if you want to catch a motorbike you have to have another motorbike. And the same with television. If you want to build up a picture you've got to build it up with something that's going to move almost as fast as the light itself. And that's what we do with cathode-ray tubes. I said you can't play about with those spinning discs and think you're going to get television. I told him to go ahead with the cathode-ray tube. I'd read about it in a book printed in 1919 and it made me want to take the long jump and avoid all this mechanical business. But if I knew only a little about the cathode-ray tubes, Baird, apparently, knew nothing. He was simply not interested. He could comprehend the mechanical system but the idea of doing it all electronically appeared to be out of the question.

Mills made another suggestion:

> I said, 'What you should do is to go to some of the big companies, radio companies, who are now sitting pretty with broadcasting nicely ahead of them – everyone will need a broadcast receiver. Why not see them and get them to develop your ideas?'

But Baird had a pathological suspicion of big manufacturing companies, fearing – rightly as it turned out – that the small man would be swallowed up by the huge combine and so, instead, he planned a company of his own. In May 1924, the patent he'd applied for the year before was granted. It was the impetus he needed and in August he left Hastings for 22 Frith Street, Soho, an address found for him by his co-patentee, Will Day. Mills refused to go with him:

> I couldn't justify going into a business which looked right from the outset was bound to be a financial washout. So I didn't. But, looking back, I think Baird was very jealous of the initiative in trying to produce television . . . what of that first apparatus was Baird's and how much of it was my invention? Well, I'll tell you. It was neither Baird's nor mine. Most of that apparatus was just common or garden apparatus that had been known for years. The selenium cell had been known at that time for about sixty years; the Nipkow disc since 1884. So that wasn't his. The arc light we were using wasn't his. But who thought of the light chopper I don't know but it was a useful adjunct though if we'd had a decent amplifer we could have avoided using it. But I can't see what all the fuss was about. Baird put his apparatus together but he didn't produce the first picture alone.

Before he finally moved to London, Baird attempted to prepare the ground and raise wider interest. He tramped the length of Fleet Street before he arrived at the offices of the Press Association. It was here that he met Bill Fox:

> It was a day when I was on office duty and the chief sent for me and said: 'Oh, Fox. There's a fellow down in the waiting room on the first floor, says he's done something with electricity. I don't know what it is. Go down and see what he's got to say but make sure he hasn't got any knives on him. Listen to him but don't promise him anything. And, whatever you do, get rid of him.'
> I didn't want to see any more of these inventor fellows. I was fed up with them. Everyone coming to say he could do something with radio. It was all the rage you see. Well, I went down and found a man of about my own age with a shock of yellow hair, untidy, old sports jacket, baggy grey flannels and forgotten shoes. I was struck because he said few words as if he was unwilling to let any word go. Very parsimonious with his words. He was difficult to talk to but I got the impression that here was an experimenter like myself.
> I took him to Lyons, Ludgate Circus and told him that if he could send a signal from Hastings, by radio, to my home in Golders Green, I'd believe him. He said he thought he could as he was in touch with several wireless amateurs and so we arranged a day and time and the signal and, a few days later, I sat beside my radio set late at night. And then, right on time, came the signal, a very

rhythmic sound based on the rotation of the scanning disc, at about 30 beats a second, just as he had described it – so I kept my word and believed him.

Ever after that he was always on the phone; always wanting to give demonstrations so I could write about them. And he told me that the day we met he'd visited every newspaper in Fleet Street and been thrown out as a lunatic. But he did get a perfect pest.

With only occasional help from J. J. Denton, the physics lecturer, and with the practical assistance of two outside engineers Baird, in his Frith Street laboratory, largely rebuilt the Hastings transmitter. His aim was to transmit a true image as distinct from a silhouette. The transmission of silhouettes, despite the poor performance of the selenium cell, was comparatively easy with low light levels as the light now shone directly onto the cell. But, if Baird was to transmit a face with all its gradations of light and shade, the maximum illumination would be essential, especially as the light would not be conveyed directly to the cell but be reflected from the image. In other words, with silhouettes, light is placed behind the object (a cut-out cross), with actual images, light is placed in front of the object (the human face). Baird wrote, in January 1925, that reflected light would be as much as one thousand times less intense than direct light. To boost the levels of reflected light needed to reach the cell, and to overcome the lag of the selenium, Baird had to go to extremes.

> One disc was eight feet in diameter and had fitted round it spirals of bigger and bigger lenses, until I was using lenses eight inches in diameter. Light, light, more light! But soon I reached the limit. My enormous wheel almost filled the laboratory and as they had to revolve at an absolute minimum of a hundred and fifty revolutions a minute, they were distinctly dangerous. The discs were made in sizes up to five feet in thick cardboard. Beyond that size I used three-ply. On more than one occasion, lenses broke loose, striking the walls or the roof like bombshells. The apparatus would get out of balance and jump from one side of the lab to the other until it stopped or tore itself to pieces. I had some exciting moments.
>
> (*Television Baird*, p. 50)

Apart from the money he had initially received from Will Day, Baird had only his savings to draw on. Day, increasingly concerned that he'd backed a loser, wouldn't advance any more. Baird, belatedly taking Mills' advice, made a tentative approach to the Marconi company but was rebuffed. Salvation came from the most unlikely source. Gordon Selfridge Junior, looking as much for a gimmick to attract people to his store as to help Baird, offered him £25 a week to give three demonstrations a day in the electrical department. Practically the whole of Baird's equipment was transported to Oxford Street and set up by Baird himself at the end of March 1925. Selfridges explained to the public: 'Television is to light what telephony is to sound – it means the *instantaneous* transmission of a picture.' They admitted that the picture was 'flickering and defective' but argued that Edison's experiments with the phonograph were equally hesitant and that Baird's 'present experimental apparatus can be similarly perfected and refined.' They concluded that television 'should rank with the greatest inventions of the century.'

What the casual shopper actually saw was described by Dr Russell, FRS, past principal of the Institution of Electrical Engineers, and published in *Nature* on 4 April 1925:

> . . . the production in the receiver of a recognisable, if rather blurred, image of simple forms such as letters printed in white on a black card . . .

So, no longer shadowgraphs, silhouettes but, for the first time in public, an actual image by reflected light.

> . . . Mr Baird has overcome many practical difficulties, but we are afraid there are many more to be surmounted before the ideal television is accomplished.

In this version of his apparatus, Baird has returned to an improved version of the system he'd worked on with Mills. Russell described the method in some detail:

> In the receiving section of Mr Baird's television apparatus the signals sent out from the transmitter are detected and amplified by very powerful valves, until they are strong enough to light up a neon tube when a signal is received i.e. when a bright part of the object is being dealt with by the transmitting apparatus. A disc, with lenses or holes corresponding to the lenses of the transmitting disc, is rotated synchronously with the transmitting disc, causing spots of light produced by the neon tube to appear on a screen in positions corresponding to the part of the object being dealt with. With these means, a sufficiently recognisable image of the subject is produced.
>
> (*Nature*, 4 April 1925)

The transmission was not wireless but, again,

> He has also been able to substantiate the claim that there was nothing to stand in the way of wireless transmission.

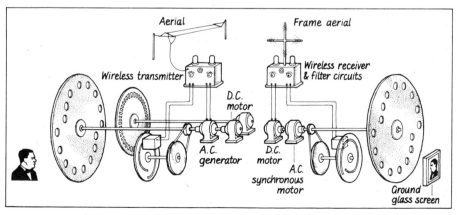

Baird's apparatus as described by Russell in April 1925, drawn and published by Baird in *Experimental Wireless and Wireless Engineer* (December 1926). This apparatus corresponds to the photos of Baird's apparatus at Frith St (see page 75) where, although the transmitter and receiver are on the same shaft, the transmitter is exactly as shown in Russell's diagram.

At about the same time that Russell had seen Baird's apparatus, or even slightly before, the editor of a more popular science journal, *Discovery*, had visited Baird in Frith Street. His description of Baird's equipment is more forthright than Dr Russell's:

> His machinery is astonishingly crude and the apparatus in general is built out of derelict odds and ends. The optical system is composed of lenses out of bicycle lamps. The framework is an unimpressive erection of old sugar boxes and the electrical wiring a nightmare cobweb of improvisations. The outstanding miracle is that he has been able to produce any result at all with the indifferent material at his disposal.
>
> (*Discovery*, 6 April 1925)

Results had, indeed, been achieved but, like the equipment, they were indifferent. Like Russell, he saw, with a certain degree of clarity, letters of the alphabet. But he saw more – a hand and a face:

> The hand appeared only as a blurred outline, the human face only as a white oval with dark patches for the eyes and mouth. The mouth, however, can be clearly discerned opening and closing and it is possible to detect a wink.

The wink was not, in fact, human but belonged to Stooky Bill, the head of a ventriloquist's doll which Baird was using as a stand-in – a non-human that would be neither burnt by the amount of artificial light nor bored by the hours of sitting. But despite the newspaper publicity and the interest created by the demonstrations at Selfridges, Baird was increasingly hard up. He reports that he had little money for equipment, less for food and none at all for clothing.

> Things were very black: my cash resources were almost exhausted and day by day, as success seemed as far away as ever, I began to wonder if general opinion were not after all correct and television was in truth a myth.
>
> (Baird Lecture, 1931)

He tried to float a small company. Offers of practical help came from General Electric who donated some electron tubes and Hart Accumulators who gave some batteries, but there were not enough takers for the shares and it was only after an appeal to his Scottish cousins that £500 was subscribed, Television Limited was born and the work in the Frith Street laboratory was in fact resumed.

In his efforts to reproduce the human face, Baird needed to reproduce halftones. The time-lag of the selenium cell seemed to make it impossible. With or without the use of the light chopper; with or without lenses in the transmitting disc, the cell posed an immutable problem. Baird wrote:

> The dummy's head appeared on the screen as a streaky blob. What was happening was this: when the light fell on the cell, the current, instead of jumping instantly to its full value, rose slowly and continued rising as long as the light fell on it. Then, when the light was cut off, the current didn't stop instantly but only stopped increasing and began falling, taking quite an appreciable time to get to zero.
>
> (*Television Baird*, p. 55)

Baird tried to solve the problem by introducing a transformer into the circuit. He wrote: 'The moment the light fell upon the cell there would be a change from no current to current. And although the current would be small, the rate of change would be great.' There should be no slow build-up; no slow run-down. Several weeks of trial and error convinced Baird he was on the right path.

> One day, it was in fact the very first of October, I experienced the one great thrill that research work has brought me. The dummy's head suddenly showed up on the screen not as a mere smudge of black and white but as a real image with details and with gradation of light and shade.

It was the breakthrough that Baird had been working for.

> I was vastly excited, and ran downstairs to obtain a living object. The first person to appear was the office boy, a youth named William Taynton, and he rather reluctantly consented to subject himself to the experiment. I placed him before the transmitter and went into the next room to see what the screen would show. The screen was entirely blank and no effort of tuning would produce any result. Puzzled and very disappointed I went back to the transmitter and there the cause of the failure became evident at once. The boy, scared by the intense white light, had backed away from the transmitter. In the excitement of the moment I gave him half a crown, and this time he kept his head in the right position. Going again into the next room I saw his head on the screen quite clearly. It is curious to consider that the first person in the world to be seen by television should have required a bribe to accept that distinction.
> (Broadcast Lecture on WMCA and WPCH Radio, New York, 18 Oct. 1931)

Baird's degree of excitement must have been enormous to have caused him, penniless Scot, to part on impulse with two shillings and sixpence. Taynton, however, did not share his enthusiasm:

> Mr Baird came running downstairs in a very excited condition, and almost pushed me in front of him into the laboratory and got me to sit in front of his projection lamps. These were enormous electric bulbs and gave out a tremendous amount of heat. Behind the lamps was a whirling disc and behind that again a quantity of wireless apparatus.
> After I had sat down Mr Baird went into the next room and left me in front of the lights. Without realising that I was spoiling the experiment, I moved back a little way to avoid the glare and heat. After about five minutes, Mr Baird returned and the moment he saw me he said: 'Ah! Why do you go back? – that explains it – you must keep exactly where I put you.'
> Knowing what was required, I did not move this time, and held as long as I could. I was just beginning to feel I could not keep still any longer, when I heard a shout from the next room, 'Open your mouth!'
> I did this and was then told to turn sideways and this was followed by Mr Baird's sudden return to the transmitter saying: 'William, I saw you. Would you like to see what television looks like?'
> Mr Baird seemed very excited and took me through into the other room where I looked through a little square opening at the face of a revolving plate. The square seemed to be covered with a reddish light. A minute or two later Mr Baird

went into the other room and on the little screen his face immediately appeared. It was not very clear but by looking closely I could see his mouth open and close and recognise that it was Mr Baird himself.

I must say I did not then realise the marvel I was witnessing but thought that it had a very long way to go before it could compete with the cinematograph.

(Television 2:38, March 1929)

Baird's Frith Street laboratory was on the second storey. Fox:

Baird had the whole floor, clear of any obstructions, and in the middle of that clear space he erected his transmitter and receiver on one long shaft. When working, he always wanted to be free to pass from transmitter to receiver and vice versa but, although he had the whole floor, he never felt he had space enough.

(Letter, April 1983)

The laboratory was approached up a succession of cold, dark, narrow, concrete stairs with only a thin metal handrail for guidance and support. It was here, on the evening of 26 January 1926, that Baird gave his most prestigious demonstration so far. On it rode most of his hopes for the future of television. With him was Bill Fox:

I turned up, groaning all the way because I'd found him a bit of a nuisance with his constant demands for attention. Anyway, when I arrived, he said he wanted me to hold the visitors book and that nobody was to come into the demonstration who didn't sign it. So you can imagine what it was like for me standing at the top of the concrete staircase with the wind whistling round my ankles. Then I began to hear the sound of footsteps coming from the street door up the steps, patiently, in twos and threes until all these eminent scientists were greeted by me and told to sign the book. They were good boys, they all did and I let them in in groups of about five at a time. You couldn't get in any more than that, the room was so small.

The men who toiled up that Soho staircase were some forty members of the Royal Institution and two newspaper reporters. Prior to their arrival and to avoid any chance of industrial espionage, Baird had carefully concealed his apparatus behind a curtain.

He said to me once, 'You know Mr Fox, the great danger is these big firms will get hold of my idea and take it and I shall be left sitting with nothing.'

What the visitors were permitted to see was reported first in the *Daily Chronicle* on 27 January and on 28 January in *The Times*:

First on a receiver in the same room as the transmitter and then on a portable receiver in another room, the recognizable head of a person speaking. The image as transmitted was faint and often blurred but substantiated a claim that through the 'Televisor' as Mr Baird has named his apparatus, it is possible to transmit and reproduce instantly the details of movement and such things as the play of expression on the face.

The paper made no further comment. The immediate reactions of the scientists, though, had been one of deep suspicion. Fox:

I'd say they didn't believe it a bit. They thought it was all a trick or something equally disreputable. I did hear one fellow say Baird was a mere mountebank, merely after what he could get. Other comments were 'nothing much'; 'absolute swindler'; 'doesn't know what he's about', and one fellow came out very definitely and said 'Well, what's the good of it when you've got it. What useful purpose will it serve?' But I do remember one man, Sanger Shepherd, very well known at the time, saying 'He's got it. The only thing now is to find the money to develop it.' Baird was very pleased when I told him.

Baird wrote later:

I was certainly gratified by the interest and enthusiasm. The audience were for the most part men of vision who realised that in these tiny flickering images they were witnessing the birth of a great industry.

(*Television Baird*, p. 59)

Television, for the next six years, was to belong to John Baird.

3

THE YEARS OF SUCCESS
1926–8

In the development of television, there were four crucial stages: the discovery that light can be transformed into an electrical effect (photoelectricity); the discovery of the effect of light on selenium; the invention of a method of scanning an image; and the invention of the cathode-ray tube. These developments were made over a period of sixty years from 1839 to 1897 and the invention of a really practical method of television was over another thirty years after that.

The first man to recognise the natural phenomenon photoelectricity was a Frenchman, Edmund Becquerel, in 1839 but the first proposals for 'Distant Electric Vision' didn't come until after an Englishman, Willoughby Smith, announced the discovery of the photoconductive effect of the metal selenium. In 1866, whilst responsible for laying a transatlantic cable, Willoughby Smith needed a new method of ship-to-shore communication:

> Whilst searching for a suitable material the high resistance of selenium was brought to my notice but at the same time I was informed that it was doubtful whether it would answer my purpose as it was not constant in its resistance . . . it was while these experiments were going on that it was noticed that the deflections varied according to the intensity of light falling on the selenium.
> (Letter to Society of Telegraphic Engineers, 3 March 1876)

The upsurge of interest that followed was the result not so much of Willoughby Smith's discovery as of the invention of the telephone in 1876. If hearing by electricity was now possible so, the argument ran, was seeing. In the decade that followed, there were many suggestions: some experiments. Most of them were related more to picture telegraphy – the reception of printed pictures for newspapers – rather than to television itself, the instantaneous reception of 'live' moving images, but, prominent among the 'television' researchers were, in the United States, Mr Alexander Graham Bell himself, Mr Brown of Philadelphia, Mr Sawyer of New York and Mr Carey of Boston: in France, Monsieur Senlaq and, in England, Professors Ayrton and Perry and Mr Shelford Bidwell. But, of all these scientists, the most important was Paul Nipkow whose proposals were contained in his German patent No. 30105 granted in 1884.

Nipkow's disc was the scanning device on which all subsequent television experimenters had to rely until, in 1897, J. J. Thomson in Britain discovered the electron and Braun in Germany produced the cathode-ray tube. These two

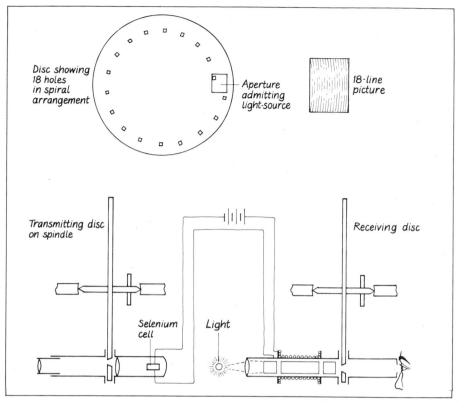

This diagram (redrawn from Nipkow's original patent) shows the scanning disc with its spiral of apertures, and the selenium cell suggested as the light-sensitive element at the transmitter.

developments meant that an electronic system as an alternative to the mechanical was, at least in theory, possible.

Between 1875 and 1925, there were more than fifty serious proposals for 'distant vision' and when Baird began his experiments with a mechanical system in 1923, the methods were well documented. 'The only ominous cloud,' Baird wrote, 'was that in spite of the apparent simplicity of the task, no one had produced television.' The two men closest to success and therefore closest to rivalling Baird were D. Von Mihaly of Hungary and C. F. Jenkins of the United States. *Wireless World and Radio Review* of 19 March 1924 gave a detailed description of Von Mihaly's 'Telehor'. Von Mihaly had abondoned the Nipkow disc but not the principle. Instead of a disc he was using a mirror-drum scanner 'for the purpose of splitting the picture into picture elements and for rearranging the current fluctuations into picture elements of different brightness.' It was a technique that Baird was later to develop himself.

By 1924, Von Mihaly, like Baird, was claiming he could transmit shadow-graphs. By June 1925, Jenkins, only ten weeks after Baird's demonstration at Selfridges, was giving his own demonstrations of the slowly revolving sails of a model windmill. The reporter on the *Washington Sunday Star* claimed, wrongly:

> . . . the first time in history that man has literally seen far-away objects in motion through the uncanny agency of wireless.

As Jenkins continued to demonstrate, reporters continued to overreact:

> Motion pictures by radio are here! I saw them with my own eyes. The present motion pictures are silhouettes . . . but the shadow-like figure moved – it danced.

In the international race for television Baird, who was already experimenting with Stooky Bill, was ahead but, unlike Jenkins, he hadn't the benefit of a permanent staff, regular finance or convenient premises. However, Baird kept ahead. Even before the now famous demonstration to the members of the Royal Institution, the magazine *Electrician* on 15 January 1926 announced 'British Company formed to exploit television invention' and, eight days later, *Popular Wireless* reported that television seemed even now a commercial proposition, that Television Limited was applying to the Postmaster-General for a licence to broadcast and that the demonstration to the Royal Institution members was imminent. The *New York Times* on the same day, 23 January, picked up the stories from London and wrote:

> The international race for the perfection of television . . . has been won by Great Britain.

The catalyst for this flurry of press announcements was Oliver George Hutchinson. For Will Day, television was seen primarily as an extension of the cinema: to bring to the cinema screen pictures of ceremonial or sporting events as they actually happened. Baird was always keen to exploit this potential but he was equally keen on developing television as a form of home entertainment. Day, increasingly disillusioned with Television Limited, sold out to Hutchinson, the same cheery Irishman to whom Baird had finally sold his Speedy Cleaner business in 1922. They were to form a new company, the Baird Television Development Company, with Hutchinson as co-director responsible for the business. He was present at the 26 January demonstration and it was probably Hutchinson who implied that it had been given at the Royal Institution's own headquarters and under the Institution's own auspices rather than in Frith Street – thus giving it an official status that would be of commercial benefit to Television Limited.

This was the first in a long line of half-truths that were told on behalf of the Baird company and which, in the end, did the company more harm than good, though, on this occasion, all Baird received personally was a stiff rebuke from the Institution's secretary. It was also Hutchinson who was most likely responsible for the kite-flying information contained in the concluding paragraphs of the *Times* report:

> It has yet to be seen to what extent further developments will carry Mr. Baird's system towards practical use. He has overcome apparently earlier failures to

construct light sensitive cells which would function at the high speed demanded, and as he is now assured of financial support in his work he will be able to improve and elaborate his apparatus. Application has been made to the Postmaster-General for an experimental broadcasting licence and trials with the system may shortly be made from the building in St. Martin's Lane.

The move to Motograph House at 26 Upper St Martin's Lane was made on 26 February. *Engineer* magazine paid a visit on 18 June and reported:

> . . . when a face of a person in the upper part of the building was made to appear on the screen of the receiving apparatus in the basement. Instructions to move the head, open the mouth etc. were sent from the receiver to the transmitter by telephone and every movement was duly reproduced on the screen. True, the results left a lot to be desired, for they did not in any way compare with those of the modern cinematograph but they served to demonstrate that television has been made possible and that in all probability infinitely better results will be secured in the near future.

The refrain 'in the near future' was to become a familiar one and equally familiar, the secrecy:

> Unfortunately Mr Baird is not at present willing to allow us to publish full technical details of his apparatus, but we hope to do so in due course.

Baird's stage management of these demonstrations was superb – the maximum drama for the maximum effect. On 3 July 1926, *Nature* reported:

> . . . the transmission by television of living human faces, the proper gradation of light and shade and all movements of the head, of the lips and mouth and of a cigarette and its smoke . . .

The cigarette smoke was a stroke of publicity genius which General Electric in America repeated in December but . . .

> . . . just as in the early kinematograph films, there is a constant flicker, but this will doubtless be got rid of in whole or in part in the new Baird 'Televisor' . . .

In other words, 'in the near future'.

> It is natural that Mr Baird and his partner Captain Hutchinson should contemplate a great future for television. They are taking steps in the direction of having a broadcasting system of television for London. Every possessor of a 'televisor' will be in a position to see on his screen the performers in opera and plays as well as hearing them. They expect to make a start in this new system of broadcasting next year. The new discovery will in no way interfere with the ordinary British broadcasting. The Post Office officials, seeing the probable advent of a new British industry, regard the scheme with benevolent neutrality.
>
> Those of us who remember the advent of the telephone in 1876, and remember also how little its importance was then realised, will hesitate to criticise this new invention. There is endless scope for improvement. Mr Baird, who, like Graham Bell, is a Scotsman, has been so extraordinarily and so rapidly successful in the past that we have great hopes that he will soon perfect his invention to the commercial stage. We wish him every success.

The article was signed A.R. the same Dr Russell who had closely followed Baird's progress over the past two years.

Baird, having made up his picture with twelve lines, then sixteen, had progressed to thirty:

> I found this the minimum necessary to transmit the human face. To decide the most suitable shape to take in the face without wasted space I made endless measurements and ultimately decided on a long, narrow picture in the ratio of seven units high to three wide. The number of lines was arrived at by making drawings from photographs divided into strips. I tried experiments with different numbers and came to the conclusion that thirty strips and a picture frequency of twelve and a half per second was the best compromise. The amount of detail was limited by the wireless transmitter which also limited the number of pictures I could send. It was a compromise between flicker and detail: more flicker more detail, but less flicker less detail. My picture finally had a fair amount of flicker and a fair amount of detail, but was surprisingly good considering the small number of lines . . .
>
> *(Television Baird, p. 61)*

Baird, having transmitted just one yard in Hastings; then the width of the laboratory and from one room to another in Frith Street; and, now, from the attic to the basement of Motograph House, was anxious to try transmission over a much longer distance. He informally approached H. L. Kirke, the chief research engineer of the BBC, and several transmissions were arranged whereby a television picture was relayed to the BBC over a telephone line from Baird's laboratory and then broadcast, late at night after radio programmes had ended, from the BBC aerial which was on the roof of Selfridges:

> I received it again by wireless at my laboratory. The picture came through practically unaltered and it is interesting to record that the company actually transmitted television in 1926, although unofficially. I was bound to silence and did not mention the matter at the time. It amused me to hear people say that while I could send television in the laboratory it could not be sent over the British Broadcasting Company.
>
> *(Television Baird, p. 62)*

These first 'illegal' wireless transmissions 'came to an abrupt end', said Baird, when they were ordered to cease by 'someone up above' – the most likely 'someone' being Baird's student contemporary John Reith, Managing Director of the BBC.

Baird, denied the facilities of the BBC, applied to the Post Office for a licence to transmit experimental television himself. It was granted and a 250-watt transmitter was built at Motograph House. The aerial was placed on the roof and a receiving theatre was installed two floors below. Bill Fox was soon to become Baird's press officer:

> Motograph House fortunately possessed two flag poles, reasonably well spaced and a flat lead roof well above the circle of surrounding buildings. This formed the layout of the first wireless station devoted exclusively to the broadcasting of television signals. Mr J. L. Baird was still without a staff of assistants, so when it

came to running up the aerial, Captain O. G. Hutchinson repaired to the roof and for the time being became a simple labourer under Baird's direction. Between them, the aerial was rigged and hoisted. Its appearance created little comment in the neighbourhood for at that time, August 1926, practically every wireless set required as high and efficient an aerial as could be secured and the aerial bore few signs to show it was being used for transmission purposes. If any comments were made at all they came from well-informed amateurs who found fault with it from a reception point of view. Remarks which were quite justified for it was not all that could be desired for reception purposes. Nevertheless, it worked and with it experience was gained which was invaluable when a larger station came to be built.

The call sign of the station was 2TV. Another station, 2TW, was completed on a house eight miles away in Harrow-on-the-Hill.

Almost nightly, pictures are being sent from London to Harrow, generally of the faces of the operators, for testing purposes, and the time is not too far distant when broadcasting of television should become as popular as broadcasting at the present time.

(*Morning Post*, 10 August)

This advance has been made possible through British research and British invention. Mr Baird has proved that the British research worker is the equal, if not the superior, of any foreign rivals.

(*Wireless Trader*, 18 August)

The American press acknowledged the superiority:

Mr Baird has definitely and indisputably given a demonstration of real television. It is the first time in history that this has been done in any part of the world.

(*Radio News*, September 1926)

The *New York Times* had already announced Baird's intention to put television receivers on the market at fifty pounds each as soon as the television station was in operation. And Hutchinson, as part of the publicity build-up, claimed that 500 televisors were already being made.

In November 1926, as the company began to grow, Baird took on his first employee – Ben Clapp. Clapp had his own amateur radio business and was doing some work for an American company – Wannamakers – and experimenting in long-distance radio transmission between the UK and the US. To answer Wannamakers' questions about television, Clapp visited Baird at Motograph House and, unexpectedly, was offered a job:

I just had a small room at the back of the place where we built amplifiers on the lines that he suggested. 'Shall we do this Mr Clapp: shall we do the other: shall we try this Mr Clapp: shall we try the other?' He always called me Mr Clapp. And I'd do it and he would take them into the lab where he had his transmitter/receiving equipment and try them out.

Facilities for research were minimal:

We just had an ordinary wooden bench. There were no mechanical tools, just soldering irons, hand drills, no lathes or anything like that. We just had to do everything ourselves. We had certain people outside who would make things for us but they didn't know what things were for, they merely worked to instructions that were given them.

The holes in the discs were drilled with increasing accuracy to give better picture definition. 'Plastic' lenses replaced glass ones so the discs could be run faster and safer.

Baird was a very charming man and could be pleasant to talk to but he was eccentric. When I knew him better he used to come into the lab, take off his shoes, pull his socks down, turn a piece of sock underneath and put on the old slippers he used to slop about in. He was rather keen on having good food but he had no idea of the value of money at all. He took me to a little place in Leicester Square. We had a coffee each and he gave the chap a ten-bob tip.

Baird's studio was a large room with an aperture in the wall and a huge bank of lamps which illuminated the subject to be televised. Behind the aperture was the familiar transmitting disc now between 4 and 5 feet in diameter and with 4-inch lenses, and all the other equipment including the neon tube, receiving disc and a greatly improved photoelectric cell. The viewer saw the picture through a fixed lens in a wall in the room adjacent. This worked well whilst the discs were on the same shaft but, when the receiver was taken into the basement for 'long distance' transmissions, the problems of synchronising the two discs became crucial. The *Engineer* reported that the problem of synchronisation had been 'successfully overcome' but the rheostat that controlled the speed of the two motors that drove the discs didn't, in fact, work very well. The viewer would see only half a face which would move up and down in the frame until it steadied as the operator adjusted the disc speed. But, as soon as the hand was removed from the control knob, the picture would drift again: 'it would disintegrate and you just saw nothing except a lot of spots and stripes.' This was just one of several technical problems Baird still had to solve but, having 'achieved television', he seemed to lose interest in personally following up development beyond the initial stage. Tony Bridgewater, Baird engineer:

Baird was a serious experimenter but he was always concerned with anything new. Once something had been done, like achieving a passable black and white picture, as far as he was concerned there was nothing more to do. He'd invented that. The fact that it was wobbling and crude didn't seem to be regarded at the time as anything very serious.

Baird left others to try to perfect his 'invention' whilst he concentrated on other related ideas. He was interviewed by the *Morning Post* on 10 August 1926:

Things have moved fairly fast since the inception of Television Ltd., and there seem to be distinct possibilities of a three-colour transmission in the near future since I have already secured definite results in that direction.

Concluding a long article about him, the *Wireless Trader* wrote:

The fertile brain of Jules Verne presented many strange and wonderful inventions . . . in our laboratories there still exists a need for men who can combine the imagination of a Verne with the cold, deliberate work of the men of science.

Baird was the Jules Verne of television and the invention that gained him most publicity was Noctovision. 'Searchlight that can't be Seen: Television Discovery' cried the *Daily Mail* on 16 December 1926:

> Mr. J. L. Baird, inventor of the Baird 'televisor' who gave the first demonstration of television on 27 January this year, is the producer of this invisible ray and describes as follows the experiments leading to its application: 'In my first demonstration of television it was necessary for the person being "transmitted" to sit before an intensely brilliant light. Its intensity was so great, in fact, as almost to blind the sitter. Before, therefore, my "televisor" could be feasible commercially it was essential that this enormously brilliant light should be dispensed with. For six months I have been concentrating on reducing the brilliance of the lighting and it is now possible for my "televisor" to see a person who is sitting some distance away in total darkness. This is accomplished by isolating and then employing rays which are outside the visible spectrum. The human eye cannot see them but the sensitive "electric eye" of my apparatus detects them readily.'

Baird had first tried to get rid of the need for the intense white light by using ultraviolet. Hutchinson had been the human guinea-pig and the rays hurt his eyes. Baird tried infrared, invisible to the human eye but not to the photoelectric cell that he was using, and so Hutchinson, apparently sitting in the dark, appeared on the 'televisor' as clearly as if he'd been televised by 'white' light. Dr Russell, of *Nature*, was given a demonstration on 23 November 1926:

> . . . the assistant's head was shown brilliantly illuminated on a screen and all the motions that he made could be readily followed.

On 30 December, Baird demonstrated to the Royal Institution, almost eleven months to the day that he'd first shown them television. They were impressed: 'It is an amazing development and one with possibilities almost illimitable.'

Many people regarded Noctovision as an even more important discovery than television as it was thought that the infrared rays could penetrate fog sixteen times better than ordinary light. The *Daily Mail*:

> 'It is difficult,' said Captain O. G. Hutchinson, who is associated with Mr. Baird, 'to estimate what may be the importance in war of this invention. It becomes feasible to follow an enemy's movements when he believes himself to be in total darkness. Attacking aeroplanes approaching under cover of night will be disclosed to the defending headquarters by the electric eye of the televisor. They will be followed by searchlights emitting invisible rays and, as these rays will be unseen by them they will continue to approach until, without warning, they are brought down by the guns of the defence.'

The *Mail*, in its editorial on the same day, commented:

> . . . that the possession of such an apparatus would require to be carefully

controlled. It would, for example, never do for nervous maiden ladies to realise that they could no longer rely on being able to go to bed in the dark.

A steady stream of demonstrations and newspaper articles followed. In *The Observer* (16 Jan. 1927) Baird looked forward to the use of infrared rays in fog. Infrared lighthouses would prevent shipwreck; infrared signals would prevent railway crashes. In April 1927 he demonstrated to Admiral Mark Kerr the fog-penetrating potential for the Royal Navy. 'One of the biggest things we've had for a very long time,' said the Admiral. By June the story was picked up in America by the *New York Herald Tribune* and even by small provincial papers like the *Roanoke News*, Virginia, in which Baird states that he's perfected what he calls a 'noctovisor' and plans experiments at sea. In August and September he demonstrated Noctovision at the Leeds meetings of the British Association. The crowds were so great that the police had to control them.

But Noctovision wasn't all. 'On Tuesday 6 September, at the University Reception, Mr Baird will exhibit and explain the Phonovisor . . . which makes use of an interesting television phenomenon and enables vision to be recorded and reproduced in the same way as sound.' Sir Ambrose Fleming had seen a demonstration of the device in July and Baird had explained Phonovision at length to *The Observer* in January:

> (there is) . . . a peculiar phenomenon which occurs in television, namely, the fact that every scene has its corresponding sound when the receiving televisor is replaced by earphones. For example, one face may make a noise like the hum of a bee, another like an aeroplane flying high in the sky; a third will be heard like a circular-saw and a fourth like the purr of a cat, and so on, the sound changing with every movement . . . the sound of the living face can be recorded on the phonograph record and on playing this record again the moving face is reproduced on the televisor screen so that we have here a method of storing living scenes on phonograph records.
>
> (*The Observer*, 16 Jan. 1927)

Amateurs listening to 2TV transmissions were aware of these sounds and puzzled by them. Baird, testing his television amplifiers and listening through headphones to the noise that the vision signals were making, had realised their significance and patented the first ever method of television recording. The video cassette was not to be commercially available until forty-five years later; the video disc not for another fifty-five. *The Times*, in September, was firmly anticipating 'Television by Gramophone' and *Punch* was happily anticipating the consequences:

> I can easily imagine a Sunday evening in 1950 in the suburbs of London (near present-day Guildford). There will be none of the usual indecision as to whether to have a little music – 'my daughter plays so nicely now' – or whether to show the visitor the family photograph album backed by remarks like: 'Yes, that's Harry at Brighton in July, 1920 – or was it August now?' The two alternatives will, by 1950, simply be combined, since the family portraits can be played over to the visitor on the gramophone. In which case the accompanying conversation will go like this:

'Now Mrs Smith, that noise like a rusty hinge with a bereaved saxophone obligato is Uncle James . . . Here's another one of him . . . you can hear the difference at once. That harsh, dry rattling is his beard; he's toned it down several octaves now! Silent beards are so much more becoming, don't you think?'
. . .

Altogether, Baird spent little more than three months on Phonovision – gained publicity and then dropped it. In 1941 he wrote with hindsight:

I was now a celebrity, but instead of using this to get into the right circles, I . . . continued to shuffle round in the lab in a state of dirt and dishevelment, absorbed in my bits and pieces. I paid for my carelessness later on when big business got hold of television and myself. Oh why didn't I cash in while the going was good?

The first indication that big business was getting hold of television came on 27 April 1927, the same day that a new company was founded, the Baird Television Development Company, and at the same time that Baird was demonstrating Noctovision to Admiral Kerr. The news came from America that the Bell Laboratories of the American Telephone and Telegraph Company had transmitted television the two hundred miles from Washington to New York. Herbert Hoover, speaking into a telephone and scanned by a Nipkow disc, was 'both seen and heard in New York' on a receiver linked to Washington by wire.

Baird's world monopoly was broken. It didn't please some of the new shareholders in the Baird Television Development Company but they had their confidence restored when Baird, on 24, 26 and 27 May, demonstrated his own ability to transmit over long distances – and, at 438 miles, double the distance achieved by the Americans. 'Television Marvels: Glasgow Looks in on London' cried the *Glasgow Herald*. 'Young Scottish Inventor's Great Achievement.'

Hutchinson and Clapp had been despatched with a televisor to the Central Station Hotel in Glasgow. Two telephone lines were used to link the hotel with the laboratories at Motograph House – one line for sound and the other for vision, just as the Americans had done, and synchronisation improved by the use of a new arrangement of filter circuits. Baird, in London, was seen in Glasgow by Professor Taylor Jones who reported that Baird's features, barely two inches across, were sufficiently clearly marked for a person to recognise an acquaintance, that Baird had overcome the chief difficulties of television and that 'there are great possibilities for future development.'

The theme 'great future possibilities' is repeated over and over again by newspapers and individuals throughout this period of Baird's progress and, for the most part, they remained just that – future possibilities. However, the demonstration allowed Sir Edward Manville, Chairman of the Baird Television Development Company, to debunk the American achievement as 'a crude form of television' which occupied thousands of engineers to Baird's three and used a system patented by Baird eighteen months before and which Baird had shown was already out of date. Shareholders were reassured that the Baird company's research is 'in our opinion, eminently satisfactory.'

The competition from America spurred Baird to make more and more spectacular and so newsworthy demonstrations of his superiority. The *Daily Mail*, reporting the London–Glasgow demonstration, looked forward to something even bigger:

> Next week, some of Mr. Baird's experts leave England for the United States to arrange for a demonstration of seeing as well as hearing across more than 3000 miles of ocean between London and New York. Transmission will be by wireless not cable.

Baird was convinced it was possible. Ben Clapp:

> He came into my lab one day and said to me: 'Mr Clapp, can you go to America tomorrow?' And I said, 'What for?' And he said: 'Well, we'd like to get a picture across the Atlantic.' The idea was that I would go and rig up a receiving station in America, with an amateur possibly, if I knew one, and transmit the picture from a landline from Motograph House to my house in Coulsdon where I had my transmitter and someone would operate that transmitter and I would try and receive it in New York. That was about April 1927.

The US press were in a state of anticipation. Baird had told the *New York Times* in March that whilst television was not yet perfected, he promised to sell televisors to the public that year and broadcast scenes from a new studio he was building at Purley (Coulsdon), a station which, in fact, was never built.

> 'Television will never supplant the legitimate stage or the motion picture,' says Baird, 'but there is not the slightest doubt of the influence it will have on them both. Special television theatres will spring into being. They will contain a screen but neither orchestra nor film. Each will be linked by wire with a central broadcasting station. There, players will act and tenors and sopranos will sing, and there the finest orchestras in the world will play. Simultaneously at many centres audiences will see the production, hear the players or singers and during the intervals listen to the finest music.' Baird bases this prediction of the televisionary future on the past history of the motion picture. 'Can you not remember those early films with their flickering images, uneven lighting and perpetual illusion of heavy rain?' he asks. 'Could you foresee the magnificent projection that followed soon after? All this was due to nothing more than the mechanical perfection of a simple principle that has never changed. So it will be with television.'

Ben Clapp left for America in September 1927:

> I had to build all the equipment myself and take it into America as experimental radio equipment – I daren't have mentioned the word 'television'. I packed it into a large box – a big receiving disc with thirty holes in it, neon lamp, amplifiers, motor to run the disc – all the things necessary for a televisor. And, of course, a viewing lens to view the picture through. The televisor itself produced a picture of about an inch and a half by an inch which, when viewed through a lens, increased its size according to the type of lens we were using.

Night after night, Baird, with the help of Denton, sent wireless signals from Motograph House to Clapp in Hartsdale, New York:

The first image I saw was just the dummy he used – Stooky Bill – but we did eventually put in people. But you couldn't recognise anyone. It was much too crude with merely a skeleton outline. Though you could see movement.

It took almost six months and a move from Motograph House to Long Acre before Baird was ready to give a demonstration. He made his first attempt on 6 February 1928 – and failed. On 8 February he succeeded. *The Times* reported from New York on 9 February:

> Four men sitting in a darkened cellar in a suburb of New York last night saw the faces of a man and woman in London. The pictures were transmitted by wireless and they were seen as if through frosted glass . . . It was about ten o'clock that Mr Hart (owner of the short-wave wireless station 2CVJ) detected the first sign of the vision sounds coming from London, a loud, irregular humming noise. Instantly, a whirling screen, somewhat bigger than a man's hand, was covered with tiny dancing rectangles of varying brilliance. By degrees they assumed the pattern of a head – a man's head as it was presently seen. Several times the pattern was lost and regained again, but it remained constant long enough for the watchers to see that the subject in London was moving in a human way.

Synchronisation was poor, the signal was weak but the *New York Times*, admitting the imperfections of the picture, dramatically acknowledged the achievement:

> (Baird's) success deserves to rank with Marconi's sending of the letter 'S' across the Atlantic – the first intelligible signal ever transmitted from shore to shore in the development of transoceanic radio telegraphy. As a communication Marconi's 'S' was negligible: as a milestone in the onward sweep of radio, of epochal importance. And so it is with Baird's first successful effort in transatlantic television.

Shares in the Baird Television Development Company boomed and were kept booming when Clapp and Hutchinson, who had joined him in New York for the demonstration, returned to England in the S.S. *Berengaria*. Setting up their televisor in mid-Atlantic, the Baird team invited the ship's chief wireless operator to 'view' his fiancée, Miss Selvy, who was in the Baird studio at Long Acre. 'Lovers Meet by Television'; 'Liner Romance'; 'Seeing from Mid-Atlantic'; Miss Selvy was 'delighted that the experiment was so successful.' And Baird was telling the *Boston Transcript* that 'Americans crossing the Atlantic or the Pacific will be able to see, in colours, baseball, football, cricket and other sports.' In all the excitement there was little comment on the fact that wireless operator Brown had great difficulty in recognising Miss Selvy at all and it was only a letter printed in the *Daily Express* that emphasised the technical reality:

> Seeing across the Atlantic was a spectacular experiment. But . . . three years ago Mr Baird demonstrated the crude televising of faces. He is still televising crude pictures of faces. When he can send (if only from one room to another) moving pictures comparable with the very earliest cinema film, then he will have indicated that he is capable of making real progress with his system. But I fear

that detail and depth of focus are as far from his grasp as ever.
(Norman Edwards, Managing Editor, *Popular Wireless*, 28 Feb. 1928)

The company had left the cramped premises of Motograph House and moved to 133 Long Acre in the last days of 1927. For the first time, during those months of Noctovision and long-distance television, Baird was to have money for staff and equipment. The company, launched with a capital of just £125,000, now had a realistic chance of achieving its aims which, according to the prospectus, were 'to develop commercially the Baird Inventions for Television, Invisible Ray, Speaking Films.' Joining the board of Baird and Hutchinson and Sir Edward Manville, already director of twenty other companies including Birmingham Small Arms and Daimler Hire and vice-president of the CBI, were two other professional businessmen, Sir James Percy and Francis Shortis. Joining the staff, in addition to Clapp and Denton, were A. F. Birch, J. C. Wilson and W. W. Jacomb who was chief engineer from 1928 to 1932.

At Long Acre, with the whole first and second floor and a section of the roof, the company had available an area eight times bigger than in St Martin's Lane and, four months after taking possession and immediately after the *Berengaria* transmission, the demonstration of television 'developments' began again. 'Television Feat: Transmission by Daylight' headlined the *Morning Post* on 2 July 1928, reporting a demonstration that had been given to the eminent scientist Professor J. A. Fleming. A transmitter, housed on the roof, transmitted pictures by daylight to a receiver several floors below. Stooky Bill was used in the first trials and then human beings and, because the daylight was brighter than the artificial light available the pictures were no longer just close-ups of a head but, on occasions, wider shots of the whole body.

These demonstrations, like the ones in the previous year, were carefully orchestrated. The *Morning Post* commented, 'All that is now necessary is for the inventor to succeed in transmitting colours.' And, four days later, Baird did. *Morning Post*, 7 July: 'Big Step Forward: Mr Baird's Triumph':

> The receiver gave an image about half as large again as an average cigarette card, but the detail was perfect. When the sitter opened his mouth his teeth were clearly visible and so were his eyelids and the white of his eyes and other small details about the face. He was a dark-haired, dark-eyed man and appeared in his natural colours against a dark background. He picked up a deep red-coloured cloth and wound it round his head, winked, and put out his tongue. The red of the cloth stood out vividly against the pink of his face while his tongue showed as a lighter pink.

Flowers were sent for from nearby Covent Garden, and strawberries: ' "Like one?" asked the communication telephone, and the strawberries looked as though they could be lifted out of the basket.' The technique, largely developed by Wilson, was to scan the object with a Nipkow disc in which there were three spirals of thirty holes each, one spiral covered with red filters, one with blue and one with green. The receiver, matching the Nipkow disc, presented the red, blue and green images in rapid succession to the eye to form a 30-line colour picture.

Stereoscopic television followed in August and September. It was not a success and even at the time, the staff that Baird was continuing to gather round him had their doubts about the wisdom of so many demonstrations. Bill Fox became full-time publicity manager for Baird between 1928 and 1930:

> Because of Baird's constant demonstrations, people, who should have known better, thought he was a twister. I warned Baird. I said, 'Look, you're doing far too many demonstrations. They won't trust you.' But he couldn't leave it alone.

Jim Percy, son of the company director, joined Baird in June 1928:

> He became a showman . . . Long Acre was wide open – we had pressmen round all day long and any variation on his system he instantly had a press conference and showed it to the people who would publish his results. But he was being driven beyond the capability of his system: being driven down a road faster than he could run. Noctovision was a case in point. It was a dead failure. It was a good idea but he hadn't got the techniques or the equipment available to make it work. Phonovision was another brave effort but you never saw much of a picture when it was played back through an ordinary pick-up.

Tony Bridgewater joined the company in July:

> Baird used publicity a great deal and used it recklessly – though I suppose that it was necessary when it came to going to the public for money.

Desmond Campbell joined in January 1929:

> He hadn't very good commercial judgement. He just thought the great thing was to get it all publicised and then everything else would follow. People would come to want it if it was publicised enough – irrespective of whether it was good or bad.

Bridgewater was put to work making amplifiers for more television sets for more demonstrations:

> An amplifier was about the last thing Baird was interested in. They were a necessary evil for him. He didn't understand them: he just knew he had to have them and if he could find somebody who would make one, that was fine. . . . and certainly in the early days, it was one of Baird's weaknesses that he wasn't careful enough – particularly careful enough in selecting the right personnel with the right knowledge to be useful to his development.

There was one prominent exception – Jacomb. Jim Percy, his assistant:

> Baird would say to him he wanted a certain thing done and Jacomb would say to me 'Here's the circuit diagram, make it by eight o'clock tomorrow morning and have the batteries charged' and he'd go off to dinner in the United Services Club in Pall Mall. If it hadn't been for Jacomb, Baird would never have reached the peak of mechanical excellence in television transmission and reception that he did. Baird produced the ideas but he was not a very practical man and it was Jacomb who could instantly assimilate what was required and translate it into precision hardware. He really was the key to Baird's success – as far as it went.

Baird himself was convinced that his approach to television and his concern for the widest possible publicity were right and justified:

Research was stimulated all over the world. Television *was* a practical possibility. These demonstrations stimulated progress in an incalculable degree . . . I was not interested in shares or money but I felt I was doing something worth doing.

(Television Baird, p. 81)

As a result, in the summer of 1928, the atmosphere at Long Acre was, metaphorically and literally, electrifying. Jim Percy:

It pulsed with a tremendous sense of achievement. Here was something very new that we could work. We weren't quite sure how long it would take or how it would eventually be done but we were certain it was working. The whole team under Jacomb was so inspired by a sense of discipline from the workshop right up to the offices with Baird sitting on top giving the ideas, that it was a sort of magical period of hopes and endeavour.

And the magic, for a while, was to continue.

4

THE RIVALS
1928–30

The long-term aim of the Baird Television Development Company Limited, so far as domestic television was concerned, was the sale of television sets – the company's major source of potential income. To sell sets, Baird needed to be able to broadcast. To be able to broadcast, he needed a licence and the only broadcasting licence, issued by the government through the Postmaster-General, was held by the BBC. The rivalry between the company and the corporation was to be long and bitter.

Baird had stated as early as July 1926 his intention to have 'a broadcasting system of television for London.' Again, nine months later, in the *Daily Chronicle*: 'Our aim is to have research laboratories and a power station on a parallel scale to the BBC.' Baird had either to break the BBC monopoly or join it and, in September, the *Westminster Gazette*, anticipating pictures 12 inches square, reported 'Joint work with BBC likely.' It wasn't likely as far as the fledgling BBC was concerned, not yet five years old and preoccupied with establishing radio, nor as far as many scientists were concerned either. A. L. Rawlings of the Admiralty Research Department wrote in April 1927:

> Television must be classified as one of the problems like the nature and cure of cancer which, after baffling mankind for a generation, still eludes us. At the same time, scientific experts are accumulating useful facts, and television might yet be realised.

In August the following year, 1928, after the great long-distance demonstrations and after the shares in the Baird company had risen from one to thirty shillings, the press, fed by Baird, were once more announcing that television was only weeks away.

The eminent scientist A. A. Campbell Swinton, who had suggested the electronic approach to television as early as 1908, wrote to *The Times* on 20 July:

> In numerous publications, the public are being led to expect, in the near future, that, sitting at home in their armchairs, they will be able to witness moving images approximating in quality to the cinematograph . . . such achievements are beyond the possible capacity of any mechanism with moving parts . . . and the only way it can ever be accomplished is by using the vastly superior agency of electrons.

On 4 August, the Baird Company announced that they were to broadcast their own programmes. Campbell Swinton, in a letter to a friend at the BBC, thought that this was

> . . . one of the most impudent efforts I remember . . . I cannot help wondering how the BBC is going to counter this advertisement which, as it seems to me, can scarcely go unanswered.

And he complained that *The Times* had edited one of his letters. He quoted the offending paragraph, which, given the laws of libel, it's not surprising *The Times* omitted:

> . . . I fear that my view is simply that Baird and Hutchinson are rogues, clever rogues and quite unscrupulous, who are fleecing the ignorant public, and should be shown up. But there is a difficulty in doing so, I fear, because of the papers liking fat advertisements.

The following day, *The Observer* stated categorically that 'Practical Television is Here' and reiterated Baird's plan to broadcast his own programmes. Campbell Swinton, in a final riposte, wrote to *The Times* on 21 August:

> As it seems to me, television, as at present developed, is not ready for general public use at all, and is not likely to be so for quite a long time.

Baird's retort was headlined in the *Evening Standard* on 10 September: 'New Broadcasting Rights Sought: Pioneer Television Firm as Rival to the BBC.' It was a declaration of war.

At Long Acre, a new transmitter was just being completed. A special little house beside the aerial on the roof held the new plant and the new station was capable of handling up to $\frac{1}{4}$ kilowatt and worked on a wavelength of 200 metres. And, at the Radio Exhibition at Olympia, from 22 to 29 September, Baird exhibited three versions of the televisor. The crowds round stands 13 and 14 were, according to the magazine *Television*, 'the biggest of the week' but actual demonstrations of television on exhibition premises were banned. Bridgewater:

> The radio industry didn't want the competition so Baird took an empty shop in Maclise Road, just outside Olympia, and demonstrated there. It wasn't long before it became known that television could be seen by going round the corner and people came in great numbers.

What the public saw was a procession of celebrities like Harry Tate and the actress Peggy O'Neil. R. F. Tiltman, Baird's first biographer, was there:

> I have never seen features televise better . . . and her show gave a vivid impression of the potentialities of Baird's system as an entertainment force.
>
> (R. F. Tiltman, *Baird of Television*)

In the week following, another makeshift studio was built on the fourth floor at Selfridges for the proclaimed benefit of 'the thousands of people turned away at Olympia.' Whilst it was stressed that the broadcasting of vision was, at the moment, limited, 'extended facilities' were soon expected. Do-it-yourself television kits were on direct sale whilst, for the non-mechanical, televisors ranging in price from £20 to £150 could be ordered from the Baird Company. Two of these receivers were on working display and the public, with little immediate reason to buy, were, again, urged to view. Amongst them, doubtless incognito, were members of the BBC. An internal BBC memorandum circulated on 1 October:

> The Baird machine may be said to give a recognisable human head. It is curiously unlike any particular face . . . only very slow movements are possible, anything of even normal speed producing a wild blur. The impression is of a curiously ape-like head, decapitated at the chin, swaying up and down in a streaky stream of yellowy light . . . the effect being more grotesque than impressive.

The memo went on to catalogue the reaction of spectators.

> The faces of those leaving the show showed neither excitement nor interest. Rather like a Fair crowd who had sported 6d to see if the fat lady was really as fat as she was made out to be.

It was a comment completely at variance with the excited comments given to the press by Bairds.

The system that Baird now used to scan the image was the 'flying spot' – an improvement by Jacomb of a technique first proposed and patented by the Frenchmen Rignoux and Fournier in 1908. The subject, instead of being flooded by light or sitting in the complete dark and scanned by infrared, was scanned by a Nipkow disc 14 inches in diameter, made of aluminium and in which the heavy lenses were replaced by thirty small, precision-cut holes arranged in the usual spiral. The disc, placed between the subject and the light source, produced a succession of light spots moving across the surface of the subject being scanned and, as the speed of the disc increased, the spots appeared to become lines which, thanks to the retention of vision of the human eye, built up into the 30-line picture. Apart from the glow from the 'flying spot' itself, the studio was completely dark in order to allow the variations of light intensity reflected by the subject to be picked up by the photoelectric cells placed close to it.

On 9 October, Baird invited officials of the BBC for a demonstration of the new system at Long Acre – probably unaware that they had already had a sneak preview. Eckersley, the BBC Chief Engineer, wrote, three days before, that 'on the eve of a demonstration, I should like to sum up what has been my point of view for a long while.' He expressed that view to members of the BBC management, including the Director-General:

> If it is thought by the Control Board that what they see demonstrated, i.e. what has been done by Baird, justifies in itself a service, then let us go ahead, but I warn everyone that in my opinion, it is the end of their development, not the beginning, and that we shall be forever sending heads and shoulders. Are heads and shoulders a service? Is it worth it for the minority who can afford sets? Has it any artistic value? Is it not in fact simply a stunt?

The actual demonstration merely confirmed Eckersley in his opinion. Further memos circulated inside the BBC, such as this one, dated 10 October:

From the angle of the service, yesterday's demonstration would be merely ludicrous if its financial implications didn't make it sinister. The demonstration considered in terms of service 'might well be considered an insult to the intelligence of those invited to be present . . . The Baird method, therefore, is either an intentional fraud or a hopeless mechanical failure. In either case we have a primary duty to the listening public to do what we can to promulgate the truth and to prevent the excitement of false hopes in the crash of which we are bound to suffer by a remote implication.

The Corporation issued a public statement:

In order that its listeners may not suffer disappointment by anticipating the possibility of seeing as well as hearing its performances, the BBC wishes to make it plain that it has not so far been approached with apparatus of so practical a nature as in the opinion of the Corporation to make television possible on a service basis.

The magazine *Tit-Bits* (11 Oct. 1928) supported the BBC attitude:

For three years in succession the dawn of the era of 'looking-in' has been loudly trumpeted. Television fever has become a sure symptom of the silly season. As long as optimistic claims did no more than provide good daily copy in August, they were no more objectionable than other forms of fiction. During the past six months over £1,000,000 have been provided in Great Britain alone for the promotion of companies concerned in the manufacture of apparatus for the transmission and reception of pictures by wireless broadcasting. . . . It is high time that the facts were realised and the danger of disappointment looked in the face.

The article continued by rebuffing the accusation that BBC engineers were jealously trying to abort a promising invention and argued that it was the duty of the BBC to prevent people from being misled; that the BBC's 'warblings' should have been more emphatic and concluded that 'until some entirely new principle is discovered, general television will not be realised.' But the media-clamour, mostly pro-Baird, continued. 18 October, *Evening Standard*: 'Mr Baird and the BBC: Inexplicable Attitude to Television.' *Evening News*: 'Television with or without the BBC: Company undaunted by the Cold Shoulder.' *Tit-Bits*, on the same day, wrote at length:

There is no secret that the Post Office would have been better pleased if the BBC had not rejected the recent proposal for co-operation. As things stand now, the Baird Television Co., with its considerable political and financial backing, will go 'all out' for a licence to operate a 3kw station of 200 metres, transmitting both speech and vision . . .

Speech, of course, was the sole prerogative of the BBC and the suggestion that Baird should broadcast sound, even if only as an adjunct to vision, was an attempt, essential from Baird's viewpoint, to break the BBC monopoly. *Tit-Bits*:

. . . (our view is) that they will attempt to transmit pictures alone, relying thereafter on the pressure of public opinion to have their licence extended even if it is necessary to modify the powers of the BBC by special legislation.

In December, the magazine *Television*, the journal of the Television Society, heavily pro-Baird and indirectly funded by him, urged its readers to sign a petition demanding the broadcasting of British television now and 'Help the British Empire to maintain the lead she undoubtedly has today in this new triumph of scientific research and inventive genius.'

But the lead was getting shorter. The Bell Laboratories in America, having beaten Baird to long-distance television in April 1927, followed him with daylight television in August 1928 and colour in June 1929. General Electric, having demonstrated halftones – the face of a man smoking – only ten months after Baird in December 1926, had preceded him in September 1928 by producing, in their laboratories at Schenectady, the world's first televised play – a melodrama entitled *The Queen's Messenger* – and, from the steps of the state capital in Albany, demonstrated live action in an outside broadcast. Whilst Baird struggled to find a broadcast outlet in Britain, by the end of 1928 in America, there were eighteen licensed 'visual broadcasting' stations transmitting television to the public. They included Station WGY in Schenectady, which had introduced a half-hour of faces of men 'talking, laughing and smoking' three days a week since May, and C. F. Jenkins, the 'tinkerer' from Washington, who had been broadcasting a 48-line picture of silhouette films since June, three nights a week for an hour. It was this kind of freedom to experiment that led Sydney Moseley, the *Daily Herald* journalist, to accuse the BBC publicly of, by not immediately buying British, 'playing into the hands of the Americans'.

Baird began to fight on two fronts. To counter the American threat abroad, he sent Clapp and Bridgewater to Australia, Percy to South Africa, Fox to Holland and went himself to Germany. Later, he sent Campbell to America. Demonstrations were given, personalities paraded, governments impressed and, for the most part, nothing happened – except in Germany where a Baird transmitter was installed in Berlin and a new company was formed, Fernseh A.G., of which Baird was a fourth part. At home, to prepare for battle with the BBC and be ready for experimental broadcasting in London, Baird had built a new studio at Long Acre. Fox:

> Up to date as it could be. Dark blue curtains lined the wall with a design in orange and gold at the junction with the ceiling and floor. The ceiling was covered with orange coloured material while the floor was covered with felt and grey matting. A few good chairs, a table and a grand piano completed the furnishings.

The studio was a mere 15 feet square and the heavy curtains were to deaden the sound. Later, the walls had to be lined with copper to keep out outside electrical interference. Next to the studio was the control room, 12 by 10 feet. The controls consisted of a Nipkow scanning disc mounted on a metal table and behind the disc a bright lamp of 1000 watts. On the other side of the disc was the lens which focused the 'flying spot' beam through the 12- by 6-inch hole in the wall onto the subject in the studio. Campbell:

> That control room was a very hush-hush place. God knows why when you think

about it. There was nothing new or inventive in it. It was only a 12 volt DC motor turning a disc. I must admit a very special disc that had to be made in Germany, sandwiched between, believe it or not, two fly-wheels of a Douglas motorbike. And to be quite honest there was nothing in that control room that anybody who had the slightest experience of circuitry, should have found difficult. I think after about a week, I would have been quite pleased to take over the whole apparatus without worries.

Bridgewater:

To show the result, the sound and vision signals were carried by wire into a demonstration room next door to a Noah's Ark televisor, a rather large wooden cabinet about $2\frac{1}{2}$ feet wide, 2 feet tall and 18 inches deep which housed the disc and the motor. It was nicknamed the 'Noah's Ark' because of its shape – only about a dozen were made. Under the table on which it stood were housed amplifiers and batteries. Everything was batteries, even the high tension for the amplifiers, which had to be 600 volts, and it was very dangerous. 600 volts direct current can kill and, some years later, a Baird man *was* killed.

Campbell:

The first thing that absolutely shook me was there was no testing apparatus. We hadn't even a voltmeter. We had no idea how strong our signal was. In fact Birch, who had been a naval wireless operator, had to put on his headphones and talk us in: 'Yes, that's right. Now come on, we want some more gain somewhere. Come on, that's too much.' And that was the only method of finding out. I thought it was extremely odd. So the first thing I said was that we must have a modulation meter. And they sort of looked at me blankly. Anyway, I made up a modulation meter.

When Birch left the company, Bridgewater and Campbell took over the running of the studio. They were paid £3.10.0d each and their first job was 'to have a signal available to show people on the Stock Exchange what television had come to.' All part of the plan to pressure the BBC by recruiting influential public opinion.

Baird's Visitors' Book still survives. It reads like a *Who's Who* of the influential – politicians, sportsmen, actors and actresses, businessmen, the press. One of the better-known journalists 'filmed' was Rebecca West:

I was with John Van Druten and I remember asking him what I had looked like and he said, 'Well, you just looked like all women look like.' Baird had shown us stills of the television images of other women he'd filmed and we all looked just the same. We did see that it was a wonder but John and I walked away saying 'Well, he'll never make a fortune out of this but it's going to be a big thing.'

Baird, after being turned down by the BBC in October, continued to lobby the sympathetic Postmaster-General, Sir William Mitchell-Thompson, later Lord Selsdon. A parliamentary committee of investigation, which included Reith, Eckersley and Eckersley's deputy Noel Ashbridge, decided that Baird could have experimental broadcasting facilities via the BBC if yet another demonstration, but this time carefully controlled, proved satisfactory.

There were four stipulations: that Baird was to install a transmitting station at Savoy Hill and broadcast via the BBC station 2LO; the transmission was to be viewed on televisors identical with those offered for sale to the public; four televisors were to be at the General Post Office to be viewed by Post Office experts and another four at Savoy Hill for the experts of the BBC.

The demonstration was fixed for 5 March 1929. Baird wrote:

> It was a nerve-racking ordeal, as we were to stand or fall by the result of one crucial demonstration. If a wire were to slip or a valve to burn out at a critical moment, the demonstration would fail and we should be faced by a devastating fiasco.
>
> (*Television Baird*, p. 85)

The demonstration consisted of a head and shoulders parade of singers and actors – one of them Jack Buchanan. There were no technical hitches, the demonstration seemed a success but Baird, who had been watching at the Post Office with his friend and mentor Sir Ambrose Fleming, was forced to wait over three weeks before the Postmaster-General made his pronouncement in *The Times* of 28 March:

> In the Postmaster-General's opinion, the system represented a noteworthy scientific achievement, but it is not considered that at the present state of development television should be included in the broadcasting programmes within existing hours . . . the Postmaster-General is, however, anxious that facilities should be offered as far as practicable without impairing the broadcasting service, for continued and progressive experiments with the Baird apparatus, and he would assent to a station of the BBC being used for that purpose outside broadcasting hours.

For Baird, it was a breakthrough, if only half of what he asked for. However:

> In granting facilities for these experimental demonstrations in which the public can, if they so desire, take part, neither the Postmaster-General nor the BBC accept any responsibility for the quality of transmission or for the results obtained.

Forced to bow to public, press and political pressure, the BBC haggled with Bairds over costs and times of transmissions, but the first 'demonstration' began, on schedule, on 30 September 1929 at 11.04 a.m. It was introduced by the ubiquitous journalist, Sydney Moseley:

> Ladies and Gentlemen, you are about to witness the first official test of television in this country from the Baird Television Development Company and transmitted from 2LO, the London station of the British Broadcasting Corporation . . .
> I must explain that as the facilities for broadcasting both speech and vision simultaneously are not yet available, we shall transmit first of all speech, and afterwards those of you who have televisors will have an opportunity of seeing the speakers. Listeners not yet in possession of televisors should leave their sets tuned in in the ordinary way.

The reason that sound and vision could not be transmitted together was not the result of BBC parsimony. They had only one transmitter and it could either broadcast sound signals or vision signals but not both at the same time – a situation that was to last for another six months. So, at 11.08, Sir Ambrose Fleming sat for two minutes staring at the spotlight whilst he was televised in silence. At 11.10, as the vision was cut, he spoke. Following the same routine came two further academics, a monologue by Sydney Howard, songs by Miss Lulu Stanley and a few words from Baird himself. Bridgewater:

> And every artist had to sit down as the scanning beam was so low.

Morning transmissions were soon extended to include transmissions late at night on Tuesdays and Fridays. Bridgewater:

> That was a very tiresome business. We'd work all day, kill time in the West End till midnight and then go and do this broadcast – without a penny extra pay. Campbell and I were the two technicians who made it work, but that was a fairly simple job. You switched the disc on, switched the lamp on, switched on the amplifiers and the picture came on. It was all pre-set. The only thing you really had to do was to get the subject focused which you did with a lens in the control room. And you peered through the hole in the wall to see if there were sharp spots, then, as the disc got up speed, sharp stripes on the person's face. You had then to get your subject sitting in the right position because at that time the disc was fixed so you had to place the subject in relation to the beam of light and not move the camera in relation to the subject. If you had a small person we had a typist's chair that had a little bit of adjustment on it. But if that wasn't enough we had a range of telephone directories we just shoved under him until we got the right height.

Control room technician soon became studio front person. Bridgewater:

> Although we had an announcer for the morning, Brigadier Russell, a brother of our company chairman – nice little job for his retirement – he didn't care to come in at midnight, so I did it. And we'd heard that all the BBC announcers wore dinner jackets so I thought the smart thing was to do this on television. So I kept a dinner jacket at the studio and a dicky I bought from a shop in Soho that sold outfits for waiters and one of those bow ties on elastic. And I used to have my dicky shirt dyed blue because the equipment couldn't cope with anything bright. So, I'd get there about ten to twelve. Campbell was usually there before me switching things on and I'd rush into the dressing room, throw off my jacket, throw off my collar and tie, shove on the dicky – I didn't have to change my trousers as only my top was shown and, two minutes later, I emerged as a blue-shirted announcer and would sit in front of the thing and announce Miss So and So who was going to sing or Mr So and So who might play a violin. We always used to try and be like the BBC because that was what we thought we were expected to be. And, while the show was going on, I'd go into the control room and see if Campbell wanted any help and then back into the studio if there was to be another act, push the artist onto the chair, get the height right and carry on.

In the spring of 1930, the BBC moved their 2LO transmitter from the roof of Selfridges to a new site at Brookman's Park, near Potters Bar, to provide two transmitters, one for National broadcasting, the other for Regional. Two transmitters meant, for Baird, the possibility of broadcasting sound and vision simultaneously. Sydney Moseley, who had taken over from Hutchinson the job of Baird's business manager, leaked to the press the proposed date of the first dual transmission. It didn't improve relations with the BBC:

> Dear Moseley,
> . . . I think we had better get together on this as soon as possible to see if there is anything that can be saved from the wreckage and also to get the new arrangements worked out and agreed.

Miss Cicely Courtneidge was asked to appear at the new opening and she submitted her programme to Moseley for approval. He called her song, 'I've Fallen in Love', 'too twaddlish for broadcasting' and Miss Courtneidge replied that if she didn't sing that she would not sing anything – and didn't. So, at eleven o'clock at night on 31 March 1930, dual transmissions began with Annie Croft and, in Miss Courtneidge's place, Miss Gracie Fields:

> I was put in this little room, it seemed as big as the smallest telephone kiosk you see in the street, and they put me in there and they said 'You're going to sing through here.' Well, all I could see was, well, it looked like a brick wall. 'Are you kidding? Are you pulling my leg?' They said 'No. You see. It goes in there and it's going to be seen miles away.' Somebody *is* pulling my leg. Well, all right, I'm used to singing in so many places, and I go in there and get myself locked inside and start to sing.

The *Evening Standard* reported that Miss Fields was seen 'complete with curls and distinctive expression.'

On 14 July 1930, again with the co-operation of the BBC, Bairds presented the first play to be transmitted in England on television – Pirandello's *The Man with a Flower in His Mouth*. The 'flower' was a cancer. It was performed 'in a space which even puppets would not appreciate' by a cast which included Gladys Young, Lionel Millard and Earle Grey; the producer for the BBC was Lance Sieveking and his co-producer was of course Sydney Moseley. Bridgewater:

> This was the first olive branch you might call it, that the BBC offered and was a very good hopeful sign of increasing co-operation. They brought quite a big team with them including Brian Michie and George Innes in effects and they saw our problems of keeping something in the picture and not having a blank screen and having a broken up background and so on. And I must credit them with this that they exploited this very limited crude medium to the utmost. Much more than anybody amongst the Baird people ever thought of doing or conceived possible.

As well as being shown on televisors, the play was presented to the press and guest celebrities like Signor Marconi on a big screen of little light bulbs, especially erected in a tent on the Long Acre roof. To reach the roof, according to Sieveking, the guests were put in a large open-air goods-hoist, without railings, and hauled up by chain and derrick. Down in the studio, Sieveking read the opening dialogue as the flying spot scanned one of C. R. W.

Nevinson's specially painted scenic backgrounds – a card 3 by 1½ feet – very little of which could actually be seen.

> Narrator: An avenue lined with trees. Electric lights gleaming through the foliage. Among the houses to the left a miserable all-night café with tables and chairs on the pavement. In front of the houses on the left a dim lamppost. It is not long after midnight. Faintly, from a distance, there comes the sound of a departing train.
> (Sound effects)
> The man with a flower in his mouth is seated at one of the tables, silently observing the customer who, at a neighbouring table, is sipping a mint frappé through a straw.
> (Music)
> Man A: Ah, so you've missed the train.
> (Singing begins in background)
> Man B: Yes, I got to the station and there it was just pulling out.
> Man A: You might have caught it by running.
> Man B: I suppose I might.

The play was chosen because it had only three characters, plenty of long speeches and little action. As with all performers, the actors had to slide in and out of the fixed studio chair in order to stare into the spotlight from the static camera and deliver their lines – but with the added complication that, as the camera could never accommodate more than one head at a time, actors had to change places after almost every speech. To conceal this changeover, a 'fading board' like a huge table tennis bat was lowered in front of the actor who then hurried out of camera range. But any sudden movement, including the movement of the 'fading board', caused the camera, in Sieveking's words, 'to shudder, blink and become quite hysterical before it could focus again.' The 'fading board' was abandoned and replaced by another device:

> I made a large chequer-board and slid it cautiously on a wooden rail in front of the magic eye. The broken-up surface distracted its attention and when the board was slid away again the camera calmly focused on the new object without indecent flurry.
>
> (Sieveking, *Illustrated*, January 1951)

The device acted like a theatre curtain as well as, with its contrasting black and white squares, preventing the loss of synchronism. But the technique of moving slowly in and out of the spotlight was one that had to be learned. Bridgewater:

> You didn't push your head quickly in or out and you taught the artist to do the same. Sometimes they would forget and if they did, well, the home receiver would lose synchronism – instead of being stationary the picture would be dancing up and down. Of course we didn't necessarily know at the transmitting end whether the person at home was losing synchronism or not. All we could do was try and make sure that we provided the least provocation by moving slowly and carefully.

The actors found the blue and yellow make-up 'strangely unnatural': Earle

Grey found the spotlight 'sinister and hypnotic': the big screen on the roof began to melt with the heat from the light bulbs and the *Manchester Guardian* wrote its first review of television drama:

> For not having a televisor of my own, I had to rely on the apparatus of a multiple store. This could only be seen by one person at a time. As there were over one hundred waiting and our time before the machine limited, I arrived at the screen at the instant of fade out.

The BBC Control Board Meeting on 22 July discussed the transmission and minuted that 'no material technical progress had been made such as would justify our Programme Branch co-operating any further. Our future action would be only that the Engineering branch holds a watching brief,' in other words the minimum co-operation stipulated by the Postmaster-General. For Baird, it was a major setback.

5

PROGRESS TO THE DERBY
1930–2

Baird, with no income from the sale of televisors, his capital running out and a continuing lack of enthusiasm from the BBC, was down but not out. Experimental broadcasting via the BBC transmitter continued, but, for a while, Baird focused his attention on his other concern, big-screen television for the cinema. The big screen that had shown *The Man with a Flower in His Mouth* consisted of 2100 light bulbs in thirty vertical lines of seventy each and activated by a revolving brush. It was a development of the system he had described seven years before in his first patent:

> At the receiving station a brush fitted on the end of an arm, revolving in perfect synchronism with the disc at the transmitting station, passes over a series of contacts. Each contact is connected to a small electric lamp and the lamps are arranged in rows to form a screen. The varying current received passes through each lamp in succession causing each to be illuminated proportionately to the light or shade of the point of the picture it corresponds to so reproducing the image transmitted.
>
> (Baird Patent, 1923)

Invited to watch the big-screen performance on the Long Acre roof was the booking agent for the Coliseum Theatre. As a result, 'Baird British Television' was advertised for a two-week season beginning on 28 July 1930. Personalities were hired to appear in the studio at Long Acre whilst the viewing public at the Coliseum, linked to Long Acre by phone, were urged to ask the person on the screen to make particular gestures. Gesticulating to order were George Lansbury, the Labour politician, Ruby M. Ayres, the romantic novelist, the scout leader Baden-Powell and Oswald Mosley.

As well as showing 'live' television on the big screen, Baird planned to show film on the television big screen as well. For a year he had been experimenting with the transmission of talking film by television, and telecine, the method of showing on 'tele' vision 'cine' film, was to become a major ingredient of television broadcasting. Baird was not, on this occasion, the first to give a practical demonstration. Just as Bell Laboratories had demonstrated big screen in America in 1927, a Boston radio station, WLEX, used film in its occasional telecasts as early as 1928. The idea was simple enough. The running film would be scanned by the flying spot and transmitted as if it was a normal studio image. But problems arose when it was discovered that the two systems of projection, film projection and television projection, were not compatible. A film picture is shown by flashing individual frames on and off the screen: a television picture is built up one spot and one line at a time. Merely point a television camera at a movie picture and it produces flicker, black lines, half a picture or no picture at all. The problem can be solved if the projected film, instead of flashing on and off, can be in continuous motion. Continuous motion projectors were already in existence and Campbell persuaded Baird to buy one from a cinema in Charing Cross Road. Called a Mechau, it was German designed and provided a continuous picture by arresting the flashing images optically by a complicated system of mirrors. Bridgewater:

> Campbell realised this could be easily adapted to our television projector. So he made a small projector that shone its beam into the gate of this film machine where the image appeared and, lo and behold, through the disc on the receiving end, was a continuous image and from that moment on we had the means to show film on television.

The Times reported in August 1929 the first demonstration to the press:

> Experiments made by the Baird Television Development Company have shown that, within limitations, talking films can be transmitted by television and received by means of the ordinary apparatus used for the reception of television images. At a demonstration given in London yesterday a short 'talkie' made by George Robey was seen and heard through the television machine with a substantial measure of success.

The Coliseum performance was the first time the technique was publicly demonstrated on a large screen and the same piece of George Robey film was an integral part of the overall Baird presentation. Robey first appeared in cabaret on the Coliseum stage then, while he hurried to nearby Long Acre, Baird showed the Robey film and, finally, a little out of puff, Robey ended his performance by appearing on television on the Coliseum big screen as he performed in the Long Acre studio.

However, the large-screen experiments never became a priority and, partly as a result of the BBC rebuff, Baird continued his experiments at Long Acre to improve the technology of television for the small screen – and the production. Bridgewater:

> We were looking for some little change from this everlasting head and somebody singing. It got awfully boring at times so we tried a ballet lesson. The dancer was my sister and we put her on a table which had been specially made to the exact height in order that her feet and legs up to the knees could be seen by the spotlight: filling the area of the screen equivalent to the area occupied by a head and shoulders.

On her toes, on a table and in the virtual dark made for a performance that was 'very limited. But anything different was good and it was a good publicity gimmick as well.'

In the late 1920s the studio was reconstructed and brought into permanent use on 1 April 1931, 'a nice new control room, a proper switchboard' and, in addition to a new Nipkow disc projector, Baird, on Wilson's recommendation, introduced a mirror-drum scanner. Invented in 1889 by Jean Lazare Weiller and used by Von Mihaly in Germany and General Electric in America, it produced a 30-line picture from thirty mirrors tilted at slightly different angles in order to scan the image as the drum revolved. Campbell:

> Baird said to me one day that we ought to do twenty-five pictures a second instead of twelve and a half and asked me if I'd like to try. I said, 'No, I don't think it's safe.' 'Oh, yes. It's quite safe.' 'No,' I said, 'I don't think it is. When these bits of glass strip start going round fast they're going to fly off. I don't want to touch it.' So he got someone else and the result was they nearly got cut in half.

Clapp:

> We blew up the whole big mirror drum. All the glass mirrors fell off because of the speed it was running and Mr Baird said, 'I think we'd better go home now Mr Clapp. I think we'd better go home.'

The Nipkow disc was not immediately abandoned but was slowly phased out as experiments with the drum revealed its superiority. The beam could be tilted slightly to give greater scope for movement in the studio; greater optical efficiency meant more light on distant views and this, coupled with the greater size of the reconstructed studio itself, which allowed performers to retreat some distance from the camera whilst still within range of the scanning beam, meant that the television picture could, very briefly, show a person full-length.

In charge of Baird's programmes, and arguably the world's first television producer, was Sydney Moseley's brother-in-law, Harold Bradly. In July 1931, a reporter from the *New York Herald Tribune* was invited to watch Bradly in action:

> In watching Bradly take auditions we noticed him telling a dancer that she must step only within a certain space within the beam of light. He practised with her and in response to her queries as to whether she might kick, he advised her to go home and practise within a 3-foot square.

It showed the improvement made by the drum and the larger studio. In the smaller, older studio, kicking would not have been possible. Further improvements to the picture definition were made by experiments with the photocells. Campbell:

> There were originally four fixed just above the hole where the spotlight came through. Now, in projected spotlight television, the photocells really represent the studio lights so in the new studio I took the cells off the wall and put them on two little movable stands connected to the control room by leads 18 feet long. Later the two groups of cells were increased to four and if I put them at the back of the subject it produced a nice back lighting effect. If I put them to one side, it would light that side of the face and not the other. In effect I was developing them into lighting in the sense that lighting is used in a film studio.

The photoelectric cell, being red and infrared sensitive, produced some startling if unexpected results. Campbell:

> Bradly thought we'd televise Lulu Stanley, our permanent soubrette. She was a

very dark Welsh girl and was in a red bathing dress. Well, we never rehearsed anything so she did her little dance and she might just as well not have had her bathing dress on. She looked absolutely nude. And a great pal of ours at Savoy Hill rang us in the middle and said: 'For Heaven's sake take her off, we can't get on with our work in the control room.' And that, incidentally, was the first time the engineers at Savoy Hill would condescend to look at television.

The red sensitivity of the cells also caused a new set of problems for costume and make-up. Bridgewater:

> The gas in the neon lamp gave a pink discharge colour and made some colours even redder than they really were. People had pink faces and bright red lips which the cells, because of the red sensitivity, saw as white. So we overcame that by using a dark make-up, blue or black, anything to get away from red.

Productions in the studio became a little more adventurous, a little more serious. Percy:

> Bradly used to hire local artists cheaply for their stint in front of the box. Cyril Smith, for example, world-famous accompanist, would tinkle away behind the curtain, unseen, for thirty shillings a night. Peanuts. He hired singers, ventriloquists, cartoonists, comics who appeared head and shoulders and attempted to amuse. Bradly had a hard time trying to find people who could maybe entertain for eight minutes and who could keep any sort of audience in front of a small red picture, prancing up and down.

Artists who performed at Long Acre included Rupert Harvey, with his cartoons and songs, Percy Edwards with his bird impressions, Jan Bussell and his puppets and Betty Astelle, then appearing with Bobby Howes at the Savile Theatre in *For the Love of Mike*:

> They said you've got to have something with tremendous definition so that we can see which is you and which is what you're wearing. Which was a good start as I had a black satin dress with huge white sleeves and black dots on. But the studio seemed very small: it was always a very stuffy place to work in; the light was tremendously flickery and all it seemed they wanted me to do was to stand there and make funny gestures.

The Baird Company issued a list of programme times and artists and these appeared in the daily press. Reception was over an unexpectedly wide area – the Channel Islands, Dublin and even further. Campbell:

> Bridgie was going out to lunch once, down to the local Express Dairy, when a man stopped him and said he'd seen him in North Africa. Bridgie got a little bit indignant – he'd never been to North Africa: but it turned out that this fellow had made up a disc and made a receiver and recognised Bridgie's face in Morocco.

But distance, achieved by medium-wave transmission, was at the expense of definition. Percy:

> You could tell a man from a woman: you could tell a blonde from a brunette and you could tell, if you jumped it up and down a bit, a £1 note from a ten-shilling

note. But the definition was very crude, even on the monitor sets we had in the same building, but after it went through the air, and through somebody's radio set and onto a home-made televisor, then it must have been difficult to make out what was going on or if you even had a picture at all.

In preparation for the start of dual sound and vision transmissions in 1930, the Baird Company had commissioned from Plessey's one thousand televisors. In a letter to the Television Society in April 1929, Hutchinson had put the figure at 'about 4000'. They were nicknamed 'Tin Box' sets and were marketed for twenty-five guineas. For the first time, Bairds had the chance to make some money. But sales were slow and the tiny television audience was mostly made up of amateur enthusiasts who bought Baird television do-it-yourself kits for sixteen guineas and 'who were so delighted with the results that they'd watch all night whatever you showed them.' In an attempt to boost the sale of televisors, a set was installed, courtesy of Bairds, in 10 Downing Street. Ramsay MacDonald wrote his thanks: 'You have put something into my room which will never let me forget how strange is the world – and how unknown.' And Sydney Moseley, in October, announced that Baird television was soon to be seen in Yorkshire. The BBC reminded him that this was not to be the case; that they, and they only, would determine how much longer experimental transmissions would continue and pointed out, ominously, that 'there has been very little indication of public interest.' As Bairds prepared to mark down their sets to eighteen guineas, Baird, desperate to boost sales, announced that after six years of promises he was going to broadcast the Derby.

Baird had already demonstrated daylight television in 1928 on the rooftop at Long Acre. The following year he had continued his experiments on the pavement just outside the front door and now, in 1931, began to experiment with a mobile van parked in the street. In the rear of the van was the transmitter – a mirror drum similar to the one he had been trying in the studio. It was ideal for daylight television as its thirty mirrors provided a 30-line picture with much less light than was necessary for a disc. The picture was conveyed by cable from the van to a receiver in the Long Acre offices. The press were summoned on 8 May. *Daily Mail*:

> . . . the panorama of the street was there – small boys looking at the transmitting machine in the road, a white-coated seller of chocolates and so on.

According to Jim Percy, it was seeing horses going up and down Long Acre on their way to Covent Garden market that convinced Baird that the time for televising the Derby had, at last, arrived.

> If I was working late, Baird would say, 'Would you like your supper, Mr Percy?' Lyons Tea Shop. Free meal. Sure. But there was always a catch in it and on this occasion before the Derby, I was in the caravan parked outside 133 Long Acre and doing some work on it when, about seven o'clock, he came and took me across to a restaurant in St Martin's Lane. We had a good supper and he then brought out a black lead pencil and said, 'Now, I'd like you to make up this bit of equipment by eight o'clock tomorrow morning because I want to have a

variation in the lens system.' And I said, 'I haven't got any paper to take down your notes, sir.' And he said, 'Och, it doesn't matter,' and he looked at the white, spotlessly clean tablecloth, drew a circuit on it – a lens arrangement – and swept it off the table and gave it to me and said, 'There you are.' And the waiter came along and Baird told him to put the cloth on the bill. And I had to take this damned tablecloth with these dimensions and everything laid out on it and make up a lens arrangement and modify the circuit.

In order to broadcast the Derby, Baird needed to transmit during the hours reserved for radio. The BBC were approached for a special dispensation. It was given on condition that only the London national wavelength was used for half an hour between 2.45 and 3.15; that speech, which would not be broadcast, would be conveyed to Long Acre on a telephone line separate from any rented by the Corporation and that Baird's signals should in no way interfere with the BBC radio commentary. The television broadcast was scheduled for 3 June. Percy was put in charge of the caravan:

It was the forerunner of the enormous wheeled vehicles and aerials and terrific machinery that are now taken round every sportsground in the country. But ours was just a wooden caravan that was towed by an ancient De Soto, the company car and the most powerful thing we had. And I parked the van alongside the winning post at Epsom. We had a petrol generator which didn't work very well; a land line to Long Acre which the Post Office were very late in laying and we just sat there watching all the horses, practising and trying to get a picture to Long Acre with this very primitive mirror drum.

Bridgewater was with the receivers in Long Acre:

As the scanner was fixed in one position near the winning post, looking across the track to the other side, anything that came within its purview was seen. And what it saw in the middle of the track was little more than the width of two horses. Before the race the horses could be seen milling round and movement made an enormous difference to a crude television picture. Movement, even if it was the subtle and slow movement of somebody's face, always made such a difference to the recognition and interest. If the horses stopped you'd only just know it was a horse but moving made all the difference. The picture came to life. But when the race came on all that Campbell and I could do was to put on the sound commentary and wait for the finish. And when the finish came you just saw these figures flashing by. And, if it weren't for the commentary, you wouldn't have known which horses they were.

Baird acknowledged that the reception wasn't perfect, 'but the horses could be seen and it created quite a sensation.' The *Daily Herald*:

The result astonished us all. We had found the stepping-stone to a new era in which mechanical eyes will see for us great events as they happen and convey them to us in our homes . . . we could see the horses passing in file: we heard them named by the announcers as they passed. We could almost recognise their jockeys.

Although the BBC's interest in Baird was now reduced, officially, to just an engineer's 'watching brief', the BBC management were split in their attitude to television. In simple terms, John Reith, Director-General, was anti whilst Noel Ashbridge, who had replaced Eckersley as Chief Engineer, was cautious but pro. On 5 September 1930, he wrote to Reith:

> During the last two years Television has got very little nearer to a commercial standard of clarity etc. In spite of this, however, it is highly probable that television will approach such a standard by some means or other during the next ten years. For this reason we ought to remain in close touch with Baird and any other individual or firm seriously engaged in research on this subject . . . This does not mean that we should allow ourselves to be forced into transmitting a regular service prematurely, but the BBC must retain control as far as service to the public is concerned.

Following the successful transmission of the Derby, it was probably Ashbridge who was responsible for the BBC offering the Baird Company the occasional opportunity to televise BBC programmes from Studio Ten beneath the arches of Waterloo Bridge. However, after a meeting between the BBC and Baird on 17 August 1931, two days before the first transmission, it was stressed inside the BBC that:

> It is no part of the function of the BBC to concern itself directly with the development of commercial inventions or to allow itself to be used by outside concerns as an instrument of research, unless the invention appears likely to become applicable to the service after a reasonable period of research.

Having given an inch, the Corporation was concerned that Baird should not take a mile. The broadcasts continued on a once-weekly basis. Throughout September internal BBC memoranda were using terms like 'keep the pace as slow as is compatible with the maintenance of decent relations'; 'guerilla warfare'; 'careful not to concede too much for peace' and referred to Baird's, in fact more Moseley's, 'crafty old policy'. But, on 12 October 1931, Ashbridge paid his first visit to the new studio at Long Acre. He reported:

> The first picture I saw was easily the best television I have seen so far and might be compared, I think, with a cinematograph close-up of, say, fifteen to twenty years ago. Were it possible for the ordinary public to buy an apparatus of this kind and run it without difficulty or undue expense, I think we should just have reached real programme value . . . I feel that someone must develop television for broadcasting and if Bairds do it adequately, so much the better. If not, sooner or later the BBC will be forced to do it and at great cost to the listening public.

Three days later, on 15 October, Bairds transmitted their first programme from a new BBC location, Studio Seven at Savoy Hill – a performance of Jack Payne's band with BBC sound and Baird vision. It was notable for the way that the Baird team were able to use the mirror-drum scanner. Having placed the machine on wheels, it could now pan, ever so slightly, to left and to right and meant that the transmitted picture was no longer restricted to the conductor's head and shoulders but could move off to a musician as well. Bridgewater:

> So we were beginning to find better use of what rather limited equipment we had. We were able to use it a bit more imaginatively, more intelligently.

As the BBC appeared almost ready to switch on to television, America had already done so. Small stations vied with the big in an experimental free-for-all that offered cartoons, boxing, football, fashion shows, talks, films, Tom Mix and Jean Harlow in a wide variety of transmissions produced by a bewildering variety of mechanical techniques. It was into this television jungle that Baird himself arrived in the autumn of 1931 in a final attempt to get the company 'on air' in the United States. But he came as the representative of his company – no longer its controller.

Baird Television Limited, after four years of outgoings and very few receipts, had been forced into voluntary liquidation in the spring of 1931. It had been saved only by the 'devious financial wizardry' of Sydney Moseley who had raised the money to buy the company back from the receiver, paid off the shareholders and then sold the company to the Ostrer brothers, controllers of Gaumont-British Pictures. For Baird, it meant that his constant fear of being 'swallowed by one of those big companies' had been realised. It also meant that whilst in America he would not have the wholehearted support of his new bosses who were more interested in what television could do for the British movies than what it could do for American home entertainment. Alan Lawson joined Bairds in November 1933:

> I was led to believe that the reason the Ostrers bought into Bairds was because they didn't really want television to succeed. It would be a threat to the cinema. I think that, by buying it, they thought they'd be able to control it.

Baird had kept an office in New York since 1930. Campbell:

> Most of my work was demonstrating, running the film and also arranging for some young woman to come and sit in for us as we had in London. We approached a theatrical agency and boiled our girls down to three. I was certain which one we should have – she was about sixteen at the time and very pretty but I was outvoted. Her name was Ginger Rogers.

In order to get airborne in the United States, Baird needed a radio station as sponsor and, on 18 October 1931, Donald Flamm, owner of radio station WMCA New York, spoke to his listeners:

> It is my pleasure to introduce to you tonight a man whose inventive genius has brought about a new art. As the advent of the motion picture revolutionised public entertainment, so will television bring about an entirely new era in home entertainment. . . . Within a few moments I shall introduce you to John Logie Baird, the Father of Television – a man who, like so many other great inventors, was confronted with difficulties which a lesser spirit would have deemed insurmountable. However, with indomitable courage, this man met his problems, fought and conquered them. . . . He has placed television in Great Britain upon a plane where it is accepted fact. Television there is no longer a cause for great excitement, as it is here – it arouses no more comment than does a Transatlantic broadcast in America. . . . It remains only for certain legal formalities to be met – for a television wave to be assigned us by the Federal Radio Commission – before WMCA starts to broadcast its television programmes. Then the American public will be given the benefit of the millions

of dollars worth of experimental work which the Baird company has done in Britain.

In the talk that followed, Baird detailed his work to date and anticipated the usual bright future – 'the problem of television is solved' – whilst mentioning, in passing and in contrast to the attitude of America, 'the lack of interest and, in some cases obstructionist attitude of the broadcasting authorities in Europe.' But it was not only Europeans who could be obstructionist. Flamm's application for an experimental television broadcast licence, on behalf of the Knickerbocker Broadcasting Company, was met with a strong objection from the Radio Corporation of America. This objection would have to be investigated by the Federal Radio Commission before any decision on the licence could be made, and would take several months. Baird returned to England and on the very day that he successfully demonstrated short-wave transmission at Selfridges, he heard that Flamm's application had been rejected. Foreigners were not to be allowed the freedom of the American air waves. An appeal to President Hoover proved useless. The office at 145 W 45th Street was closed. Baird was out of America. The Ostrers, the owners of Bairds, were probably quite pleased – the American venture was a great loss maker – but for Baird it was a loss of face, as well as finance, another blow that left him with an antipathy towards Americans and the RCA in particular. This resentment was to surface later.

With defeat staring him in the face again, he turned to the event that had revived his flagging fortunes before. He announced his second attempt to televise the Derby – bigger and better than before. It also gave him the opportunity to combine his interest in small-screen television with both his own and his bosses' interest in the big screen as it was proposed to transmit the picture simultaneously to the BBC and to the Metropole cinema in Victoria.

Campbell and Bridgewater were again at Long Acre to receive the pictures by telephone line from Epsom and pass them on to the BBC; Clapp and Baird himself were on stage at the Metropole and Jim Percy was again in charge on the course at Epsom where the caravan now contained three mirror drums instead of the previous year's one. The centre drum was to provide the picture for domestic television whilst the three drums combined were to provide a 'zone' picture for the cinema. 'Zoning' was a system whereby a scene was scanned in three separate sections which, when transmitted side by side, made up one large picture. It was a technique used in the legitimate cinema by Abel Gance in *Napoleon* and had been first demonstrated by Baird as a system suitable for television eighteen months before in January 1931, when Herbert Strudwick, the Surrey and England cricketer, was 'zoned' for the benefit of the press. *The Times* reported that Strudwick's movements 'could be clearly seen'. HMV, soon, as EMI, to be Baird's chief television rival, extended the system to five zones only to abandon the whole technique as impractical for television. In the light of subsequent events it was ironic that *Today's Cinema* was so convinced that 'Baird has at last hit on the very method which will bring television into the cinema.' On 2 June 1932, the *Daily Herald* reported:

With five thousand people in the cinema, fifteen miles from Epsom, I watched the finish of the Derby. It was the most thrilling demonstration of the possibilities of television yet witnessed. It made history. . . . As we sat in the darkened cinema distance was annihilated. We were the first people in the world to see such a spectacle on the cinema screen. 'Marvellous! Marvellous!' shouted men and women around me. . . . Mr J. L. Baird, the inventor who made the marvel possible, stepped onto the stage and received a bigger cheer than the Derby winner 'April the Fifth'. He was too thrilled to say a word.

Ben Clapp:

Baird was standing beside me on stage and he suddenly said: 'Mr Clapp, I'm finished.' And there was a chair beside him and I pushed it under him and I think he'd have gone on the floor if I hadn't done so he was so exhausted.

Baird's collapse on stage at the Metropole was the result of years of increasing physical and mental tension brought on by hard work, high excitement and bitter disappointment. Lost in America, Baird was soon to lose again in Germany where the Nazis were to force Fernseh to get rid of their Baird interests whilst, at home, he was reduced to the status of an employee. It was ironic that it was the old enemy, the BBC, that came to the rescue.

Thanks to the enlightened policy of Noel Ashbridge, the Corporation had already made plans for their own 30-line transmissions and had new Baird equipment installed, along with Bridgewater and Campbell, in Studio BB in the basement of Broadcasting House. After the Derby broadcast in June, the Long Acre studio was closed and, in August, the BBC began a regular service of television. It was the best shop window that Baird could have hoped for.

1a *Here's Looking at You*: Miss
Elizabeth Cowell in the announcing
position. Note the curtained-off stage,
the basic overhead lighting, the
microphone suspended from a boom
and the Emitron cameras on the
unwieldy 'iron man'

1b The final line-up. From left to right:
the Three Admirals, Carol Chilton,
Leslie Mitchell, Elizabeth Cowell,
Maceo Thomas, Helen McKay and
Miss Lutie with Pogo the Horse. The
Television Orchestra in the rear

1c The Three Admirals. Stand lights and 'iron man' on left, camera on mobile
'dolly' on right. Headphone kept studio technicians in contact with the director in
the control room

2a Baird in Frith St *c*. March 1925. (Composite photograph) In this early version of his apparatus, the transmitting disc is on the left with the serrated-edged disc or chopper in front of it and a lamp illuminating the hand. On the right is the receiving disc. The image of the hand is viewed down the cardboard tunnel

2b Baird in Frith St holding two Stooky Bills. The subject, directly illuminated by the bank of bulbs, is seen by the disc through the hole above the doll's head

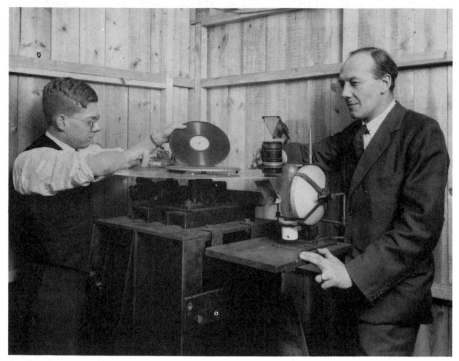

3a Phonovision: a recording about to begin. J.D. Percy places the wax record on the combined turntable and scanning disc, and W.C. Fox adjusts the projection lens

3b Television in mid-Atlantic on S.S. *Berengaria*, February 1928. Captain Hutchinson (right) watches Ben Clapp adjust the televisor. The picture is viewed on the rectangular screen on the left.

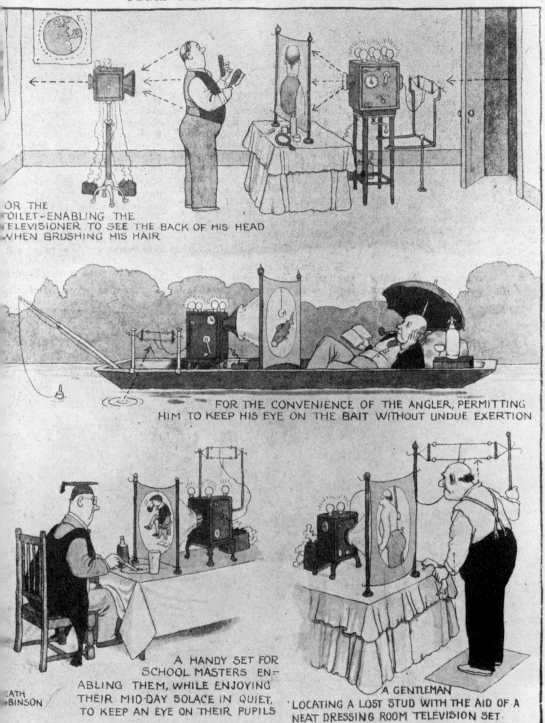

OR THE TOILET—ENABLING THE TELEVISIONER TO SEE THE BACK OF HIS HEAD WHEN BRUSHING HIS HAIR

FOR THE CONVENIENCE OF THE ANGLER, PERMITTING HIM TO KEEP HIS EYE ON THE BAIT WITHOUT UNDUE EXERTION

A HANDY SET FOR SCHOOL MASTERS ENABLING THEM, WHILE ENJOYING THEIR MID-DAY SOLACE IN QUIET, TO KEEP AN EYE ON THEIR PUPILS

A GENTLEMAN LOCATING A LOST STUD WITH THE AID OF A NEAT DRESSING ROOM TELEVISION SET.

Drawn by W. HEATH ROBINSON

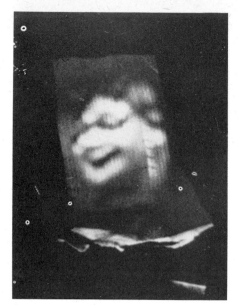
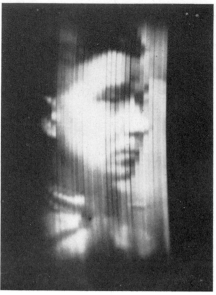

4a Thirty-line images photographed directly from the televisor. The picture of
A.F. Birch, 1929 (right), shows a great improvement in definition compared with
that of Stooky Bill, 1926

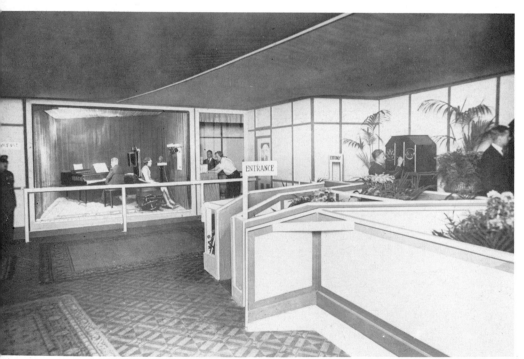

4b Demonstration of Baird television at Selfridges, September 1928. The studio
(left) with pianist and performer seated in front of a microphone and bank of photocells, and the adjacent control room were exact replicas of the set-up at Long Acre.
The public viewed the picture on the 'Noah's Ark' televisor on the right

4c/d *(Above left) The Man with a Flower in his Mouth,* July 1930. Earle Grey (centre) in the title role, Lionel Millard in the hat and Gladys Young. The producer (top left) is Lance Sieveking and the chequered 'fading board' is operated by George Innes. *(Above right) The MFM* showing C.R.W. Nevinson's specially painted scenery

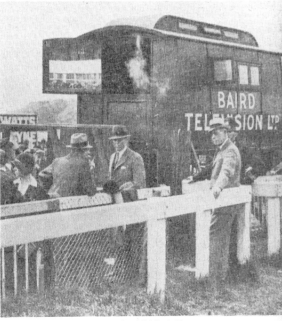

5a/b *(Above right)* Baird's Outside Broadcast van at the Derby, July 1931 *(Above left)* The commentator on the roof of Baird's van at the Derby in June 1932. The sound was not allowed to be broadcast on BBC radio but was relayed direct to the Metropole cinema

6a The control room at Portland Place. Rotating caption stand (foreground) with Bridgewater (left) seated at the sound controls, Bliss (centre) on vision control and Campbell (right) on the 'camera' which looked through the glass window into the studio

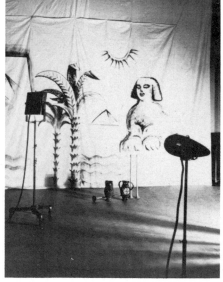

6b/c *(Above left)* The control room as seen from the studio. *(Above right)* Control-room view of the studio dressed for the ballet *Cléopâtre*, March 1934. Photocells on stand (left), torpedo–shaped microphone (right)

6d The Corps de Ballet in *La Danse des Egyptiennes*. The actual performance was, apart from the light from the 'flying spot', given in the dark

6e The first television broadcast from Studio BB in Broadcasting House, 22 August 1932. Louie Freear, Fred Douglas, Betty Astelle, Betty Boulton

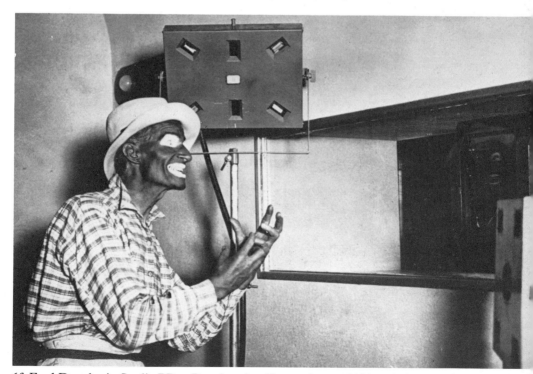

6f Fred Douglas in Studio BB at Broadcasting House, August 1936, as he appeared in the opening programme. Photocells (above and right), 'flying spot' came behind control-room glass (centre)

6

30 LINES
1932–5

The BBC inaugurated their experimental 30-line service on 22 August 1932. Baird made a rare appearance:

> I wish to thank the BBC for inviting me tonight and express the hope that this new series of television transmissions will lead to development of broadcasting, increasing its utility and adding to the enjoyment of the great listening public.

Betty Astelle was one of the performers:

> The next day in the *Daily Express* there was a huge thing about this invention that had gone to the BBC and how it had been seen on various screens. They mentioned all the important people and then finished up saying: 'And then there was Betty Astelle, a baby-faced blonde who could be clearly seen making movements.' So much for my singing and dancing.

Baird claimed that the transmission was the best he had ever seen and Douglas Birkinshaw, appointed Engineer in Charge, BBC Television, reported:

> Everything went off without a hitch of any sort either technically or in the programme – a result I had hardly dared hope for in view of the appalling lack of time for preparation – excepting that we got a howl back for a moment owing to the loudspeaker being fully faded up and also the picture was momentarily obliterated as one photoelectric cell group-plug was pulled out of its socket during the shifting of the cells about in the studio.

The 30-line experiment had three aims: to give Baird the opportunity for further research, to give the BBC experience of television technology and to see if a good producer could make television good entertainment for the public.

The producer appointed by the BBC was Eustace Robb, an ex-Army officer who had had showbusiness experience with Brunswick records and who was a man with 'drive and initiative and determination not to be beaten'. But Robb's production was limited by his technology. Birkinshaw:

> We couldn't provide Robb with anything new or very adventurous. The limits were built into the equipment from the start. He could arrange the limit of movement of the artist – he or she could move a certain amount to one side, a certain amount forwards and backwards but it was mostly movement on the spot – and he could run through the songs and acts and see that they were right. But, you see, when you've only got the equivalent of one camera, four lights and a microphone and nothing else to worry about like telecine, recording, satellites and all the rest of it, it really does simplify what is required of you.

Nevertheless, Robb was able to show how much better productions could be compared with those that were done at Long Acre. The BBC itself acknowledged the fact when, only four months after 30-line transmissions had begun, they published a summary of 'Chief Broadcast Events in 1932':

> From 22 August, television programmes have been broadcast on Mondays, Tuesdays, Wednesdays and Fridays of each week from 11.00 to 11.30 p.m., sound being transmitted on 398.9 metres and vision on 261.3 metres.
>
> The programmes, which have been remarkable for the variety of talent that has been seen and heard, included Mr and Mrs Mollison, an exhibition of art treasures opened by Lord Lee of Fareham, a display of exclusive fashions by a leading London Modist, ju-jitsu and fencing, ventriloquists, Carl Brisson, Erik Bertner, a performing seal, a selection of Christmas toys, a music-hall programme reminiscent of the nineties and Delysia.
>
> The year culminated in a Boxing Day pantomime, Dick Whittington, the first television pantomime ever put on the air, complete with cat, property rats, subtitles showing changes of scenes, drawings of mosques and minarets and the Mansion House London.

In retrospect, the performance that had the longest lasting impact on the BBC was probably that given by the seal (actually a sea-lion). It was appearing at the Victoria Palace theatre and, because no taxi would take the fare, was collected by television's chief engineer Douglas Birkinshaw in his Panhard open tourer:

> I just concentrated on the driving and she was such a good passenger she sat in the back, laid her head on the back of my driving seat, her whiskers tickled the back of my neck, she was perfectly well behaved and we arrived at Broadcasting House without any trouble.

The trouble came later when the BBC issued a Circulating Memorandum: 'For Your Information: Performing animals will, in future, only be admitted to the BBC by the goods entrance.' That memo has never been rescinded. Bridgewater:

> Eustace Robb opened our eyes to what could be done. He did the most incredible things. Take the ballet for example. No longer was the ballerina stuck on top of a table and restricted to one area, one square foot. Robb soon picked up the idea which we showed him that if you kept the movement going then you could sacrifice detail and the picture was still interesting. He adopted all sorts of clever techniques. First of all the dancer would come into close-up so that you established what she looked like and who she was and he'd make her just look pretty and just give a few little movements and then, very gradually, she'd trip backwards and you wound the focus on the camera and followed her and began to see more and more of her. And then, when she got far enough back against the backcloth, she could actually go into her dance routine. And you could even get two or three figures doing this. Of course, they had to be very carefully kept close together and there was a lot of technique involved to make it really practical. But it *did* work.

Among the first dancers to subject themselves to these conditions, which included, for technical reasons, a black and white check floor, black and white costumes, a white backdrop and performance in semi-darkness, was the world-famous ballerina Adeline Genée. On 15 March 1933, partnered by Anton Dolin, she danced her farewell performance – *The Love Song*. Watching the performance in the studio, *Television* reported:

> The man operating the projector had to focus throughout as in a film and anticipating so much movement in a wide arc was tricky work. Eliminating shadows was an anxiety but the effect in the end was superb.

Watching the performance on the screen was Arnold Haskell, distinguished ballet critic:

> A black-out, and another blaze of light, gradually dimming down until a small speck takes shape. That is Adeline Genée, first like a passport photo that has been left overnight in the rain, then, as the details of her costume can be distinguished, like some old faded family portrait. As she dances, the image takes on some meaning, perhaps because we know and love what it represents. We think that we can see the fine carriage, the grace and precision of movement.
>
> (Arnold Haskell, *Balletomania*, 1954)

Genée herself limited her comments to noting that the area available for performance was too small and her black and white frock made her feel like a member of the Ku Klux Klan.

So that, on occasions, more than two people could appear in shot together, the BBC carpenter's shop constructed scenery and ramps. Bridgewater:

> We had the Balalaika Orchestra and, in order to get six players into close-up, still playing the balalaika, Robb had some steps built. About 6 foot wide and the top step about 6 foot high. These were mounted on wheels and two studio attendants underneath these steps, with the whole orchestra on top, pushed the thing forward towards the camera and, as it came, you could pick one or other of them playing. That was the kind of imagination that Eustace had.

The equipment at Broadcasting House had the advantage over Long Acre of being new, if not newly designed. The operational layout was better planned. The studio was larger than at Long Acre and, next to it and on the same level, was the control room separated only by a glass window. A proper control desk was provided for the first time and here the three engineers responsible, Birkinshaw, Bridgewater and Campbell, the 'BBC' of the BBC, controlled sound, lighting and vision. Sound consisted of a large, torpedo-shaped microphone and whilst the equipment was first class, reproduction wasn't. The pianist was placed behind a curtain, partly so that he could have light to read his music and partly to ensure the sound volume of the piano balanced with the voice of the performer. The result was a sound that was distinctly muffled.

The 'lighting' consisted of four banks of photoelectric cells on wheels. The power of each bank was controlled by a separate knob on the control desk and, as each bank could be balanced against another, it now became possible to get particular lighting effects – a strong front light and a weak back light or vice versa depending on the action in the studio. Campbell:

. . . I could light one side of the face and not the other or produce a nice backlighting effect. Give a little jiggle of the knob and the thing could be reversed.

The spotlight projector no longer beamed into the studio through a small hole in the wall but through the glass that partitioned the control room from the studio. It was no longer fixed but could be 'waved about so that it followed the artist'. Bridgewater:

It was on rails. There was an iron tubular-steel framework with two cross-bars front and back and the projector itself was on wheels which ran along these two cross-bars so that you could pull the whole thing sideways, one way or the other, and therefore, by doing that, you adjust to the subject rather than pushing the subject all the time into your field of view. It could focus from extreme close-ups to as far as the back of the studio – 25 or 30 feet. And you could see whether it was in focus or not by just peering into the studio because you could see the scanning strips and you could focus quickly. And the final point of flexibility was that you could tilt the scan up or down so that if somebody wasn't just the right height, you could adjust to them – not the other way round.

Birkinshaw:

I must say that all this swinging horizontally, vertically and moving backwards and forwards called for a certain skill on the part of the operator – all three movements often having to be made simultaneously.

There was also, for the first time, a picture monitor. It was small, the picture was ill-defined and it flickered like the light from the 'camera', but it showed the action in the studio and could be seen by all three engineers at once.

There was soon an afternoon broadcast and, in April 1933, Robb produced the first television revue entitled *Looking In* with Anona Winn. By July, he had introduced a zoo programme. And, for most performers at Broadcasting House, television was becoming less a lark and more a serious business. Betty Astelle:

It meant you had to have a big repertoire of songs and dances. You couldn't keep on doing the same things; even though it was a small audience you had to change your material and, because it was in this flickery light, you couldn't have any words written up on a board, you just had to jolly well learn them. So you had to be very clever at making them up if you forgot. You could rehearse movement. It was just like coming into a dark room and you'd know that the projector could go from A to B sideways and so you'd know that beyond a certain line you'd be out of vision and within that line you were in vision. What you were actually doing was creating a television technique. If you were doing, say, two choruses and a dance you would come up to the projector for the singing and go back and do the dancing in long shot, then back to the projector for singing again. Unlike Long Acre, you didn't have to swim so hard, wave your arms about – you could be a little more natural.

For the Baird company, the establishment of 30-line transmissions was excellent. At last they were being recognised by the monopoly broadcasting organisation but not everyone in that organisation was happy with the mewling and puking infant in the basement. There was trouble with the Henry Hall Dance Band. Studio BB was their rehearsal room. Bridgewater:

> The theory was that Henry Hall would just clear out, take his musicians away when he'd finished and we'd set up our photo cells and scenery. But the times didn't fit and the apparatus we wanted to leave lying around in the studio got in the way of the band and there was general friction.

As early as 25 August 1932, three days after opening, Birkinshaw was pointing out that the technical side of the operation was being looked after by only three men and that all of them had to be present at every audition, rehearsal and performance on every day. But help was not forthcoming. Nor was it offered six months later when Birkinshaw complained that ventilation in the control room had not been installed and nor had the promised larger window between control room and studio. The memo ended:

> The object of this memorandum is to ask whether it is not possible for television to be allowed to progress a little faster – for we can indeed make it progress a little faster – and if not, it would be a little more encouraging if a word of explanation here and there could be given to me as to why these things cannot be done and when we may expect to get out of the groove in which we appear to be sticking.

There were two reasons for the BBC's unwillingness to progress any faster. The first was the extent to which strides were being made elsewhere to develop a better system of television – an electronic system – and the BBC's involvement in these developments could not be revealed to the engineers in the basement. And the second was that, electronic or mechanical, the attitude of the BBC mandarins to any form of television was still, to say the least, equivocal. Birkinshaw:

> Broadcasting House was all chromium plated and very precious and, of course, the whole thing was regarded as a more or less sacred edifice with the pontiff, in the shape of Sir John Reith, at the top. And into this edifice came a group of young people who conducted strange rites in the basement, who required all sorts of things to come into the BBC like scenery, performing dogs, seals. It was rather like having such things going on in the boardroom of the Bank of England. It was just not considered de rigueur. And there was a barely concealed spirit of overall resentment that this nonsense should be going on at all. I think BH rather wished we would go away. And I think, too, that Sir John Reith would have preferred to see sound broadcasting further advanced before anything like television happened.

In 1934, the BH studio reverted to radio and television was shifted up the road to 16 Portland Place. Birkinshaw:

> And we benefited greatly because we could reconstruct the interior on the lines of our accrued experience.

The new studio was a converted first-floor drawing room – 28 feet wide instead of the previous 18, and the new control room was bigger too – 22 by 14 feet with a large window into the studio; but operational improvements were slight and where they were possible at all were more improvements of technique than technology. Campbell, with more space and larger and more sensitive photocells, was able to refine his 'lighting' to a point where he could create or eliminate a shadow on a performer's nose. It was, too, the innovative Campbell who made a caption scanner – a circular drum with a dozen flat facets into which could be slipped a postcard-size caption. Bridgewater:

> It seems a commonplace nowadays to have a caption but it was entirely new for us, the idea of having something that said 'Goodnight' or the name of the next artist. It was a very nice little tool much used by the producer.

The caption card was scanned by a separate Nipkow disc and the picture could be mixed with the picture output from the studio

> . . . in any desired proportion. If necessary, the two outputs can be super-imposed: thus, if a doorway were drawn on a card and an artist were standing in a suitable position in the studio and the two outputs were mixed, the artist could be shown standing in the doorway. Lookers-in to the London National Television transmission will have noticed the many and varied ways in which the producer enhances his presentation by a liberal combination of this projector with the studio.
>
> (Birkinshaw, *World Radio*, March 1934)

Another way that the producer was able to enhance his presentation was to use, as an alternative to the plain white background, a painted backcloth. Robb:

> At one time we never attempted to use scenery at all, but now some form of backcloth is employed for practically every long shot.
>
> (Robb, 'Preparing the Programmes', *Popular Wireless*, May 1934)

As the producer and the engineers became more familiar with their technology so the scope and imagination of the programmes, as well as the number of programmes, increased. Robb:

> Entertainment value *does* exist in the present television programmes, in spite of all that is said about their merely holding scientific interest . . . we are able to infuse considerable variety and attraction into the programmes. And topicality is always uppermost in our minds. . . . Television is building up a technique absolutely its own. While we like to put over stage items as near to their theatre performances as possible, all programmes are developed specially for television.
>
> (*Popular Wireless*, May 1934)

In his private notebook, he recorded a typical day:

> Ten o'clock Rehearsal, Finish at 1.30. Russian ballet. Programme in which will appear Mesdames Danilova, Riabouchinska, Toumanova, Kirsova, Baranova and M. M. Massine, Woizikowsky, Algeranoff, Shabelevsky. Seated on the floor with Massine. Working out suitable presentation of ballet for television purposes. Portions of Alhambra orchestra used. Strange spectacle of Ephraim Kurtz, the conductor, seated on a box on piano; there is no room for him elsewhere but he enters into the spirit. Inspection of dresses with the designer

Monsieur Lourie, who makes a sketch for the alteration of each dress. Mrs Harris arrives with needle and thread to carry out alterations: she must receive her instructions in detail. Stitches hard all day – black epaulettes – black apron – black braid to cover white which will go invisible. Miss Peacock rushes out between office hours for gloves and bonnet. Engineers have choreography explained to them so that they may know what to expect. They have to follow quick movements and focus the artists all the time. Last-moment retouching of scenery.

Robb came back to the studio at five o'clock:

Preparation of studio for the night's show. Scenery must be put into position and props in place. Go through programme routine with Mr Campbell and explain to the various engineers their different duties. Mr Bridgewater will have to watch the microphone moves in the studio and keep a watchful eye that the artists do not come too close to the Televisor or edge too near the black curtains which separate the orchestra – this would create a bad picture. Mr Savage must be told the order of the captions and title cards to be used in the caption machine, and Campbell will want to know how and when he is to fade out at the end of scenes, and if in certain cases, the artists will make their own exits.

Announcement has to be dictated in a suitable form to suit each type of programme. The announcer must be advised on any special points to be stressed in the announcement. On a special night such as the appearance of the Russian Ballet, flowers to be bought for presentation to complete atmosphere of the theatre.

Leave at seven o'clock.

Return at ten o'clock. Make up the artists. Last-minute inspection of faces. Laughter at comic faces and altered costumes . . . .

Phone bell rings in the Television Control Room from Broadcasting House Main Control Room to tell us to start. Everyone on the tips of their toes – off we go.

Astelle:

Eustace Robb was enormously enthusiastic about television. He was a great believer in it and was very good fun. If anything went wrong, it was just funny, there was no hassle about it. We just all roared with laughter; so, presumably, did the viewers.

L. Marsland Gander, television critic of the *Daily Telegraph:*

But the fact that the BBC appointed Eustace Robb, a retired army officer, shows that they were not taking the thing very seriously.

Georgie Harris was a music-hall artist who'd played for Mack Sennet in *Keystone Cops* and who starred in other early movies with Janet Gaynor and Harry Langdon. He was interviewed by Robb in 1934:

He said to me that they were experimenting with the Baird process and had I anything to suggest. I said there were one or two little things and that I would even be happy to write them. He said he'd like to use Sarah Allgood – a very well-known Irish actress who was playing in *Juno and the Paycock* at the old

Vaudeville Theatre. And that gave me an idea. I could write a little thing and she could be the cook and I could be the page-boy in the same hotel which would give me an opportunity to tell her what I'd seen and heard around the hotel.

A kind of early *Crossroads*.

It also would give me the opportunity of doing some impersonations of what I'd seen through a keyhole or through a door. He thought that was a good idea and asked me to see what I could concoct. I submitted something and they accepted it for which I got the princely sum of three guineas.

A threefold improvement on the one-guinea fee at Long Acre.

I presented myself at Portland Place and the first thing I had to be taught was make-up. Now, having been in the theatre all those years, the make-up they presented to me at that time was absolutely grotesque. A pure white face, like a clown, and black on the sides of my nose; silver on the top of my eyelashes and lids.

The reason for the grotesque make-up was to counter the continuing oversensitivity of the system to red.

Anyway, I got used to that type of make-up and we used to rehearse in the morning. We just pantomimed in the area in which we were going to work to familiarise ourselves with, say, a little doorway – for the page-boy and cook routine we just had a door with 'kitchen' painted on it. That was the scenery. And I'd suggest to Sarah that it might be a good idea if I make as if I'm looking through a keyhole and you can pass at the back of me and I'll come this way and we can change positions. It was interesting because we would work in complete darkness except for this light flickering in your face. It was just for all the world as though you were acting in front of the motion picture projection machine that you used to see when you were in the movies in the old days. And it just gave you enough light to see where you were going. Not that you were going to crash into anyone or out of the scene because you were confined almost to the spot.

Unless you were an acrobat. Arthur Askey met a girl coming out of the studio with her head covered in blood. Her partner had swung her round in the darkness and banged her head onto the studio wall. Harris:

You only had a few inches to work in but as I'm not very big myself I was able to adapt to a small space. Once I'd got used to the fact that you couldn't – to use an old theatrical expression – cover stage, well then I stayed in one spot only waiting for an exit. But, once the camera started, you did your dialogue to the camera and that was that. You moved your head rather more than you did your body and you acted primarily with your face and head. It was almost as if you were on a swivel. You had to be darned careful that you stayed with that camera.

Programmes were regularly reviewed in *Television*:

I always welcome an orchestral combination in the studio as a relief from the monotony of the piano. Of the lighter fare I most enjoyed the programme of Helen Raymond and tiny Georgie Harris whose face appeared at the bottom of the picture. The effect was produced by focusing the comedian in the semi-distant position, with only his face in the beam. Later when the announcer declared that a telegram from Bombay complained that he could not be seen, he was raised on a chair and we got a full figure picture. His abrupt exit is explained by his falling backwards from the chair into the arms of a studio attendant who was there to catch him.

Bridgewater:

> We had a couple of enterprising studio attendants called Lee and Bentley who got rather a kick out of catching performers – particularly lady gymnasts. Thrown out of the picture into the dark, these scantily dressed gymnastic women might be glad of a helping hand. So Lee and Bentley used to stand there and, the story goes, make the most of their catches.

Harris:

> As we got going we started to develop a little more. For example, they built me a little igloo set and I came on as an eskimo and sang a number with my head through the igloo door and these items were built up until they became little productions on their own. The first shows we did were from 11 to 11.30 at night and, if you had a television set, you would be able to pick them up but, failing this, the BBC asked people to tune in to sound and a lot of people were listening to these first TV shows by sound only. And a lot of people said 'I heard you last night' instead of saying they'd seen me. It became quite a novelty and people tried to find someone with a television set so they could all look in.

It was such a novelty that the London *Evening News* on 5 November 1934 made a story out of the fact that Georgie Harris was to shave himself on television wearing pyjamas:

> Apparently the BBC had no objections to pyjamas for I learned today that Mr Harris will do an act called 'I Never Slept a Wink Last Night' prancing round the television studio in pyjamas and trying to shave himself by the light of a flickering television scanner.

The greater novelty, though, was that Harris had to get special permission to wear pyjamas: 'they somehow felt it was deshabille – running the thin line of censorship.' As programmes became more complex, routines had to be carefully planned in advance and detailed instructions given to the engineers. *Skyline* was produced on 3 June 1935, the script survives:

> . . . when the first girl has done her exit, Billy Milton steps back into the picture and sings last few bars of the song.
> Milton re-enters after exit of girl – fade on Milton's exit.
>
> Announcement – 'Let's now take a peep at the kitchen in one of New York's greater hotels. What nationalities shall we find there?'
>
> Fade to caption: Astor Hotel.
>
> Chorus of Paddy – screen with door in it placed just behind the back line. At the end of the tune discover Sarah Allgood in close-up position singing: into lines. Entrance of Georgie Harris through the door – she turns and calls, after which

try and show him approaching her. Dialogue between the two as close as possible, panning slightly if necessary.

Lens in – Georgie Harris – big close-up for song.

Birkinshaw:

> The programmes would be regarded as beneath contempt by a modern programme compiler but we were prepared to put on anything which could produce something of interest in a very small space.

The *Daily Telegraph* said about *Skyline* that 'captions and fade-outs preserve the sense of artistic unity and there are some realistic touches with moving silhouette scenery.' Eustace Robb was beginning to take television out of the realm of mere scientific curiosity. But, in a programme transmitted in April 1935, despite the first television appearance of Margaret Bannerman, 'the famous West End star', of impressionist Hermione Gingold, 'effective as a giraffe-necked woman in a costume copied from a Bertram Mills Circus poster', and singer Ted Andrews (father of Julie), the ostrich feathers of Mathea Merryfield's fan dance showed up the continuing limitations of the emerging medium:

> For better definition, black plumes were placed in the yellow ostrich feathers carried by Mathea Merryfield. Even so, some of the beauty of her dance was lost as her figure flitted before the inevitable whiteness of the backcloth.
>
> (*Television*, April 1935)

The picture received direct on the small 7 by 3 inch monitor in the control room was always better than the picture received at home and the reason for this was because the picture, on its journey from studio to viewer, was degraded three times. The telephone lines that carried the Broadcasting House signals to the Brookman's Park transmitter were poor and, despite the efforts of Harry Rantzen (father of Esther), who doctored the lines, the improvement was only slight. Aerial transmission from Brookman's Park was by medium wave only. Ultrashort-wave transmission to improve picture quality was still under research. And the domestic black and white mirror drum receivers, marketed by Bush for Bairds and improving rapidly, were still fairly basic and only as good as the pictures they received. L. Marsland Gander:

> The 30-line sets were hopeless really because they produced a narrow, vertical picture.

Eustace Robb:

> Actually, it is a most admirable size and was not arrived at by accident, as so many think. It was worked out most carefully both from practical and technical considerations. For films the existing shape would have to be modified. Take dancing for instance. One has got to have what are technically known as 'lifts' and without a fairly tall scanned area there would be difficulties right away. And without picture depth any form of effective scenery would be quite out of the question.
>
> (*Popular Wireless*, 5 May 1934)

The domestic receiver also 'hunted'. Bridgewater:

> It would go up and then a bit further up and a bit further down and finally it would go up and not come down again and all you'd see were whirling stripes and spots and you'd have to grab the knob.

L. Marsland Gander:

> It was a question of synchronisation. The thing reminded me of one of those fruit machines where, if you got the combination right, you could see something.

Bridgewater:

> The various things that would upset a picture you'd never think of now. I mean, for example, just putting a hat on or off. Even pushing your hands up too quickly, that could lose you synchronism and, as well, you might hit the photoelectric cells. We had to be awfully careful.

L. Marsland Gander:

> The question was always, in those days, 'has it got entertainment value?' and, I'm bound to say that it hadn't. In spite of the superhuman efforts of Eustace Robb you could only see tiny little midgets in a sort of haze and I wouldn't agree with the engineers that you could recognise faces. You could recognise that it was a human being but I couldn't recognise Arthur Askey or Gracie Fields.

Newspaper interest in television remained high but the viewing audience remained extremely small. Birkinshaw:

> A small keen enthusiastic audience of dedicated experimenters: the sort of thing you'd expect with the birth of a new science.

The *Sunday Dispatch*, in September 1933, estimated a total sale of 3000 sets, including the do-it-yourself kits. Baird thought the number was about 5000. The BBC were not sure:

> The BBC is anxious to know the number of people who are actually seeing this television programme. Will those who are looking in send a post-card marked Z to Broadcasting House immediately. This information is of considerable importance.

The figures, if they were ever discovered, were not published. There was no future for 30-line television.

7

THE ALTERNATIVE SYSTEM

A. A. Campbell Swinton's denouncement of Baird in 1928 was based on knowledge and experience. Born in 1863, Campbell Swinton had played a part in many of the scientific developments that took place around the turn of the century – the telephone, the gramophone, electric light, X-rays, photography and, in 1896, he marked a turning point in the development of wireless when he introduced the young Marconi to the British Post Office. In 1908 he also marked a turning point in the concept of television when he wrote a letter to the editor of the scientific journal *Nature* (18 June):

> (television) can probably be solved by the employment of two beams of cathode rays (one at the transmitting and one at the receiving station) synchronously deflected by the varying fields of two electromagnets placed at right angles to one another and energised by two alternating electric currents of widely different frequencies, so that the moving extremities of the two beams are caused to sweep synchronously over the whole of the required surfaces within the one-tenth of a second necessary to take advantage of visual persistence.
>
> Indeed, as far as the receiving apparatus is concerned, the moving cathode beam has only to be arranged to impinge on a sufficiently sensitive fluorescent screen, and given suitable variations in its intensity, to obtain the desired result.
>
> The real difficulties lie in devising an efficient transmitter which, under the influence of light and shade shall sufficiently vary the transmitted electric current so as to produce the necessary alterations in the intensity of the cathode beam of the receiver, and further in making this transmitter sufficiently rapid in its action to respond to the 160,000 variations per second that are necessary as a minimum.
>
> Possibly no photoelectric phenomenon at present known will provide what is required in this respect, but should something suitable be discovered, distant electric vision will, I think, come within the region of possibility.

This was the first time that anyone, anywhere in the world, had proposed to solve the entire problem of distant electric vision, electronically.

Electronic television works on the same principle as the mechanical system but much more quickly and effectively.

Whereas in the mechanical system the image is scanned by the Nipkow disc and the strength of light given off converted into a series of electric impulses by the photocells, in an electronic system the function of the scanning disc is replaced by a moving beam of electrons (cathode rays). The essential parts are enclosed in a glass envelope, often referred to as a 'pick-up' tube. Although the basic principle has not changed, the detailed design of the tubes has been modified over the years: for example, the size of the tube has been reduced to a point where some are scarcely larger than a fountain pen. By contrast, the tube first developed in this country on the basis of Campbell Swinton's original concept was 18 inches long and about 9 inches in diameter at one end, and its mode of operation, in simplified terms, was as follows.

Within the 'pick-up' tube is the screen (a) which consists on one side of a 'mosaic' comprising thousands of minute 'droplets' of photosensitive substance deposited on a thin wafer of insulating material and, on the other side, a plain metal surface known as the signal plate. The image from the scene is focused by the camera lens (b) onto the mosaic and electrifies or charges each droplet in proportion to the intensity of the light falling on it. A narrow electron beam emerging from the 'gun' (c) is directed at high velocity towards the mosaic, sweeping across it with a combined horizontal and vertical scanning motion and discharging each droplet in turn. The action of these successive discharges results in proportionate electrical impulses on the signal plate and these then form the 'television signal' which is amplified and transmitted.

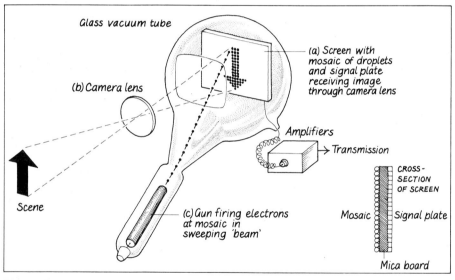

The Emitron TV Camera.

At the receiving end these electrical impulses are reconverted into light by a cathode-ray tube. At the base of the tube an electron gun, controlled by the television signal, shoots a stream of electrons at a fluorescent glass screen. As the stream hits the screen, it glows as a tiny dot of light. The stream crosses the screen with a scanning pattern identical to that in the camera, horizontally from left to right and top to bottom, leaving behind it a trail of dots – each one, as in a newspaper picture, lighter or darker than the rest. Although there is actually never more than one dot on the screen at a time, the viewer sees these dots as a complete picture, just as with a mechanically derived picture, because of the persistence of vision. In modern systems the completed picture is 'painted' twenty-five times a second.

The discoveries in physics that were eventually to lead to high-definition television began in 1887 when Heinrich Hertz discovered radio waves. J. J. Thomson's discovery of the electron and Braun's invention of the cathode-ray tube followed in 1897. In 1906, Diekmann and Glage patented the first proposal for using a cathode-ray tube for producing patterns and the first patent for using a cathode-ray tube for television was filed, in Russia, on 13 December 1907, by Boris Rosing. The patent was not published in England until July 1908, one month after Campbell Swinton's proposals in *Nature*.

Rosing and Swinton were two minds grappling quite independently with the same problem. The difference between them is that Rosing suggested the use of cathode rays for reception only whilst Swinton suggested them for both reception *and* transmission, in other words, for the whole system. Campbell Swinton firmly believed that the cathode ray would solve the three main problems of television – the speed limitation of the mechanical system that prevented good picture definition; the synchronisation of transmitter and receiver; and the time-lag of photoelectric conductors like selenium – but he also knew that technology was not yet far enough advanced to prove him right.

In November 1911, in his Presidential Address to the Röntgen Society, he elaborated his ideas with a diagram which, in the words of J. D. McGee, the man who led the development of the electronic camera for EMI, 'would still pass muster as an outline diagram for a modern electronic system.' But, as Campbell Swinton explained:

> I do not for a moment suppose that it would be got to work without a deal of experiment and probably much modification. . . . It is, indeed, only an effort of my imagination.

Some effort: some imagination!

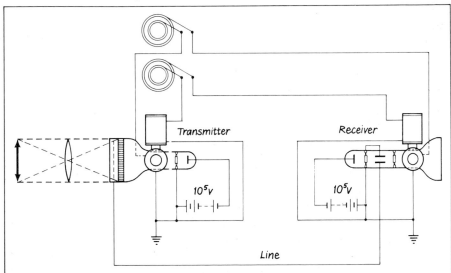

Campbell Swinton's Scheme, 1911. In his Presidential Address to the Röntgen Society, Campbell Swinton outlined the basic system upon which high-definition television was later developed. Note the use of cathode-ray tubes both as transmitter and receiver.

Campbell Swinton continued to expand and elaborate his system as technology, especially in radio, advanced. An elaboration of his 1911 proposals was published in 1924 in *Wireless World* and, whilst the press prepared to go wild over Baird's mechanical system, Campbell Swinton, almost alone, stuck doggedly to his electronic ideas. These were again emphasised in 1928 when he ended a paper by commenting on the exhibitions of mechanical television by Baird, Bell Laboratories and GEC:

> As experimental shows, they were no doubt magnificent but . . . surely it would be better policy if those who could afford the time and money would abandon mechanical devices and expend their labours on what appears likely to prove the ultimately more promising methods in which the only moving parts are imponderable electrons?

Apart from experiments made in 1903–4 when 'no reliable results could be obtained' Campbell Swinton's theories had to remain unsupported by any practical demonstration. Rosing, on the other hand, with more restricted ideas, was able to confirm them by experimentation. Boris Rosing was Assistant Professor of Physics at the Imperial Institute of Technology in St Petersburg. His pupil and assistant between 1910 and 1912 was Vladimir Zworykin:

> Rosing had a cathode-ray tube receiver, a kinescope as it is called, and the double mirror drum wheel for transmitting . . . during my time we constructed the cathode-ray tube (and achieved) stationary geometrical figures, very fuzzy, like a triangle and some kind of distorted circle and so on but with very, very intense light.
>
> (Interview with Dr Zworykin by Mr G. R. M. Garratt, Deputy Keeper,
> Communications Section, Science Museum, May 1965)

Rosing, despite attempts to overcome the problem, never achieved moving figures because of the slow reacting selenium cell he was using.

But perhaps his most important contribution to television was the effect he had on Zworykin:

> He started me to dream about television so when I succeeded to reach the United States which was in 1919, I started to look for a place where I could work in television.

Zworykin began his work in the US with Westinghouse, and in 1921, he had followed Rosing's example and made a cathode-ray tube, a 'kinescope', for receiving a television picture. Westinghouse were not impressed by television, they were more concerned at the time with washing machines, and it was not until 1923 that

> I had got part of the system working – the kinescope, I had all this in patents . . . and in addition I did evolve the first idea of the iconoscope.

The 'iconoscope' was Zworykin's name for his cathode-ray transmitter, in other words, his television 'camera'. With all early television cameras, whether mechanical or electronic, one of the main problems was the colossal amount of light needed in order to get a reasonable picture. Baird was to have the problem; Zworykin's mentor had already experienced it:

> One of the biggest troubles Rosing had and the same with everybody else – they tried to transmit the picture point by point. It meant the amount of electrons which can be made from the point corresponding to the time when the light is on a particular point is very small. That principle will remain true when you use the Nipkow disc or any kind of scanning. My principal contribution to television was storing of the image before it was scanned.

Zworykin lodged his patent for the 'iconoscope' in 1923 but it was several years before he was given the opportunity to develop it fully and the opportunity came largely as a result of the publicity that Baird and Jenkins were getting in the USA in 1927:

> I went to New York to meet David Sarnoff of RCA and Sarnoff said 'They tell me you have started a new method of making the television?' I said: 'Yes, it should not have any mechanical parts and all this foolish thing.'

Sarnoff was highly sceptical but, at the end of 1927, Zworykin was set up in his own experimental laboratory at RCA, began transmission testing by the end of 1928, using film, and, by 1929, had two groups of engineers, one group working on the transmitter and the other on the receiver. 'Things,' said Zworykin, 'began to boil.' But they did so in the utmost secrecy and, whilst patents were constantly registered, Zworykin did not publish his paper on the iconoscope until 1933. However, RCA's awareness of the television potential that they possessed was probably a major contributing factor in their decision to object to the Baird system having a broadcast outlet in America. They needed to prevent the possibility of mechanical television establishing itself in New York before they could market their electronic one.

In England, the commercial interest in television, largely generated by Baird, was, by 1930, no longer exclusive to him. A number of companies were preparing to enter the market for mechanical television sets and, in addition, Marconi were developing transmitting equipment. In 1932 they announced that 'television has a future outside as well as inside the amusement field . . . an apparatus has been developed for the commercial transmission of news.' The apparatus consisted of a moving tape on which a special typewriter printed words at a speed of 60 or 120 a minute. The image of the moving type was scanned by mirror drum, transmitted by wireless and reproduced on a visual display receiver. The *News Chronicle* gave it the Baird treatment: 'New Television Marvel – Words typed on screen in England seen in Australia. Marconi Secret Out.' Further experiments were conducted across the Atlantic with the co-operation of RCA but, whilst the device itself failed to provide an alternative to Morse code, the experiments were important because they increased the Marconi Company's experience of short-wave, high-frequency transmission – an experience that was to prove invaluable for two other companies who were to become involved with Marconi in Britain's development of electronic television – Columbia and HMV.

In 1930 the Columbia Graphaphone Company under Sir Louis Sterling was HMV's biggest rival and a large part of their latest success was due to Isaac Shoenberg, a Russian émigré who had worked for the Russian Marconi Company and who had been chief engineer of the Russian Wireless and Telegraph Company in St Petersburg at exactly the same time that Zworykin was helping Boris Rosing with his television experiments. To help circumvent the large royalties demanded by an American company on their patents for sound recording equipment, Shoenberg, 'an engineer-scientist with a dash of the visionary', had recruited a young engineer from Imperial College, London, called Alan Blumlein. Blumlein, an electronics genius, invented a gramophone recording system completely free of American patents and, in the process, laid the foundation for the stereophonic system which is used today.

HMV had an almost equally strong research department and their work on new methods of sound recording and their passing interest in films led naturally to an interest in the transmission of pictures and an interest in television. C. O. Browne and W. F. Tedham began to work on developing an effective cathode-ray picture receiver. Test transmissions were provided by a mechanical system, a 30-lens mirror drum scanning movie film and projecting the image onto a bank of five photocells to give a 150-line picture (5 by 30-line). This was the zoning system shown to the Physical Society in 1931, but five channels were too cumbersome and HMV began to look into the possibility of a single channel. A start was also made on electronic television.

In December 1930 Koller, in the United States, had published his discovery of a photocathode that made possible a stable vacuum photocell that could be formed as a fine-structured mosaic. This, ten months after Campbell Swinton's death, was the breakthrough that was to make electronic television a reality. Tedham immediately developed the photocell whilst, at the same time, beginning to develop a high-vacuum cathode-ray tube to replace the inefficient gas-focusing system that Rosing and Zworykin had used in 1910.

Tedham's television experiments coincided with the start of the Great Depression. The sale of records and gramophones began to fall. Columbia and HMV were forced to merge and form a new company – EMI, Electric and Musical Industries. Their research teams merged too and, under Shoenberg, formed one of the greatest teams of scientific brains ever assembled in Britain. Their brief was, literally, to engineer company salvation by developing a commercially viable electronic television receiver to offset the effect of falling sales of radio players. It was at this point, 1 January 1932, that the EMI research team was joined by J. D. McGee:

> I quickly found that Tedham was very familiar with the literature of the whole field but especially with Campbell Swinton's proposals. He was completely convinced, and he soon convinced me, that they pointed the correct way to achieve really effective television. The high vacuum cathode-ray tubes were already giving very promising television pictures using C. O. Browne's mechanically generated signals and the photocathode and vacuum techniques were already well established.

Whilst concerning itself with cathode-ray receivers, EMI did a great deal of work on mechanical transmission. It needed the mechanical signals in order to test the new receivers and also to test the transmission of movie films. But:

> Both Tedham and I were impatient to tackle the next logical step, the (electronic) signal-generating tube, and tried to persuade our management to allow us to include this in our programme. In vain we argued that no television service could hope to be successful unless, besides picture signals from film, it had signal generating cameras which were effective not only in illuminated studios but also out-of-doors in conditions of poor illumination. As we could see that no organisation in the UK was doing this we argued that it was essential for EMI to take up the technical challenge.

The challenge was not accepted – except by Tedham and McGee, in secret. During the spring and summer of 1932, they discussed methods of constructing a tube for transmission based on Campbell Swinton's suggestions. Should the target in the tube be single or double sided? If single, how could a photosensitive mosaic be made? Methods were evolved, patents applied for – some granted, others rejected, to the surprise and annoyance of the inventors, on the grounds that RCA in America had got there first. McGee:

> This, and many similar instances, is very strong circumstantial evidence that the state of technical thinking in the RCA and EMI laboratories, at the time, was not very different.

Of even greater concern was the problem of how such a tube could work but,

> in spite of these uncertainties, Tedham and I could not resist temptation to disobey orders and give it a trial and see what happened, especially as we had available most of the required components and techniques. So in the autumn of 1932 we constructed an experimental tube. . . . We borrowed a signal amplifier from C. O. Browne and drove the scanning coils on the neck of this tube in parallel with those on a display tube from the same scan generator. We projected a simple draught-board picture onto the mosaic and after some minor adjustments a picture appeared on the receiver. It appeared to us as if by magic.
>
> I am afraid we were very unprepared for this surprising success and, looking back, we were extraordinarily naive about the whole thing. We did not even take photographs of the apparatus and the transmitted picture. Rather like Edison and his colleagues, when they got their first incandescent lamp to work, we looked on fascinated until, to our chagrin, the picture began to fade.

What survives is the tube itself, displayed in the Science Museum, London. But why didn't the experimenters continue? McGee:

> Echo answers why! We were young, inexperienced and we had done this contrary to the instructions of the management. Also there was a great economic depression in the outside world and physicists were two a penny. I'm afraid we put the defunct tube in a cupboard and waited, hoping and occasionally arguing, that we might be allowed to tackle this problem. However, we did then know that a tube of this kind would work though we did not accurately know why or how well.

As Tedham and McGee were proving to themselves the viability of an all-electronic camera, EMI had reached a stage in their official television research where an electronic receiver combined with mechanical transmission could be shown to the BBC. Shoenberg wrote to Noel Ashbridge, the BBC Chief Engineer, on 25 November 1932:

> I have tried many times to get you on the phone but I have failed miserably. I would like to give you a private demonstration of the results so far obtained by us, both in the transmission and the reception of television. In my humble opinion, they would be of quite considerable interest to you.

It was the first approach that EMI had made to the BBC and Ashbridge visited Hayes on the following day. He reported:

> The method used differs considerably from the Baird system, in particular three times as many lines per picture are used and there are twice as many pictures per second. The apparatus is developed only for the transmission of films and I am informed that the development of the system for studio transmission might not be very easy.

Ashbridge viewed a film of the Changing of the Guard on a 5 by 5-inch cathode-ray receiver. The picture signals were generated by C. O. Browne's mechanical transmitter over a distance of two miles by ultrashort waves.

> The quality or reproduction can be compared with the home cinematograph but the screen is smaller . . . although these pictures give a measure of entertainment value, they are hardly likely at the present stage of development to command sustained attention over long periods. On the other hand they represent by far the best wireless television I have ever seen and are probably as good, or better, than anything that has been produced anywhere else in the world.

EMI wanted the BBC to establish a service by September 1933 but, whilst Ashbridge was impressed he was not convinced and felt that EMI, only offering a 'film' service, were beginning to use 'Baird-like rush tactics' in an attempt to beat the commercial opposition. As the BBC were already transmitting the Baird 30-line system, Reith, fearing adverse publicity, suggested to EMI that they keep their research and the BBC interest in it quiet. That the EMI management didn't abandon television completely at this stage was the result of the dedication of Isaac Shoenberg. McGee:

> To advise his managing director and the board of directors to go on with television, as he must have done, required courage. I believe that it was in the next five years that Shoenberg showed his strength of character, his tenacity in the face of difficulties and, above all, his belief that a team of competent scientists and engineers, given adequate facilities, can be expected to produce a useful solution to a technical problem. He demonstrated that profitable scientific research was practical in industry.

In July 1933, Zworykin finally published his account of the iconoscope and as a general statement of the principles of electronic television it was excellent. But Zworykin was niggardly over detail. He gave nothing away to potential rivals, hiding his intentions behind bland phrases like 'special device', 'new principle' and 'unique type'. But it showed that the iconoscope and the tube made by Tedham and McGee in secret were basically the same. McGee:

> (it was) a momentous step forward . . . it finally convinced our management in September 1933 to allow us actively to take up this aspect of television research.

For the first time EMI contemplated the development of an all-electronic system. Progress in the initial stages was slow and frequently the result of informed guesswork – 'by guess and by God . . . many things were so new we just had to feel our way.' Yet, despite the fact that EMI in the financial year 1932–3 had made a ludicrously low profit of approximately £300, research premises and research personnel began to grow. At its height the team, including men in the workshops, consisted of over one hundred people, two thirds of them working on television, and whilst mechanical television work continued, the emphasis shifted to the electronic or, as it was then called, 'light electrical engineering'.

The laboratories were divided into departments with G. E. Condliffe as overall head and included circuit research, design of camera and receiver, system engineering, aerials and transmission, mechanics and optics, valve research, research into the chemistry of fluorescent materials, of photoelectricity and of the cathode-ray tube as both receiver and transmitter. Research overlapped; the physical proximity of one team in one room to another team in another room meant that no one was working in isolation and all were familiar with progress made in every department. It made for a togetherness, a cohesion. McGee:

> We felt that if television was to fail, it would fail over our dead bodies. It was a curious dedication, almost an addiction, but there it was. And people were prepared to work weekends, late at night, without the slightest complaint.

In charge of research into cathode-ray tubes was L. F. Broadway who joined EMI in May 1933 from Cambridge. His first job was to improve the vacuum in the cathode-ray tube. Broadway:

> So the first thing we really had to do was to get some faster pumps made and process the things more rigorously than was done with thermionic valves and, in those days, cathode-ray tubes were processed one at a time and evacuation would take several hours per tube. And the related point was that we had to construct electron guns which were made of materials which could be degassed in vacuum.

Broadway's second job was to produce a commercially acceptable television screen – 'the fat end of the CRT.' In 1933, the screen was produced by a fluorescent material called willemite. It produced a picture that was various shades of green and white instead of black and white which was 'an obvious limitation.' So research had to be done on developing new types of fluorescent material as well as increasing the size of the display screen from 7 inches square.

> So we were beginning to expand the CRT research group to deal with the problems which had to be solved before we could get an acceptable display

device which could be made in reasonable quantities to be put into the newly designed television sets. And it's curious, looking back on it, that at that time we believed the CRT as a display device was only an interim measure. We didn't really believe that this huge vacuum envelope, a cumbersome sort of thing, would last.

As the team learnt more about the stresses involved in glassware, the size of the CRT gradually increased until the screen was 12 by 15 inches and white. These screens were placed in the earliest sets vertically so that they faced upwards into a mirror placed in the lid and the viewer saw the picture as a reflection. Broadway:

> Then we were all scared stiff of the danger of implosion. C. S. Agate, the chap responsible for receiver design, asked me to come and see him one day. I went in and saw on his desk a magnificent CRT, 12 inches in diameter. I won't mention the manufacturer's name but the glass was quite thin and he looked at me and said: '*That*'s the way to make CRTs. You don't want those awful heavy things that you lot have been making. Look at this, quite light, thin glass etc.' I said, 'I'd as soon stay in this room with a time bomb on my desk as that thing – I'm going.' So I pushed off and the next morning there was no tube on his desk and his office was littered with bits of glass and various bits of tin from the electron gun. So I didn't hear any more about that one. But if half a dozen of those things had blown up and wrecked somebody's sitting room that would have put an awful crimp in television generally.

The electrical circuits for Broadway's hard cathode-ray tubes were done by E. L. C. White. Later, White and Manifold designed the circuits to provide the synchronising pulses between the transmission tube and the receiver.

To provide the experimental transmitter to test the broadcast potential of the new system, EMI asked Marconi for a low-power transmitter capable of transmitting on 6.8 metres wavelength and a bandwidth suitable for television of 120 lines, twenty-four frames per second. But as television technique progressed in one department it had a knock-on effect in every other – including the transmitter built by Marconi's Ned Davis:

> They wanted signals from the transmitter and others didn't want signals from the transmitter, they wanted something else. That was one of the great difficulties until Blumlein came along. He was a real genius. He was capable of co-ordinating all sections.

Alan Blumlein, in charge of all circuit research and development, was, even more than Shoenberg, the man who provided the day-to-day cohesiveness. Bernard Greenhead:

> He could converse with the transmission engineers and make useful comments and then go through the vacuum physics side, again adding useful comments, right the way down through the design and studio and eventually finish up in the workshop. So he was a man of great ingenuity. He was the power over the whole system.

And that system depended, probably more than anything else, on providing a successful television camera. McGee, who took over sole charge when Tedham became ill, had learnt little from Zworykin's published paper. McGee:

> In particular the crucial question, how to make the mosaic, was left unanswered. We had already tried one method successfully, the use of a stencil mesh, but it held out little hope for high-definition pictures with the meshes available. So, to begin, for the first twelve tubes we used the obvious method of ruling a silver layer evaporated on to a mica sheet.

With help from Broadway on improving the vacuum, and White and the circuitry team providing a head amplifier, scanning generator and appropriate operating voltages, McGee, almost two years after making the first experimental tube, was able to get a presentable picture out of tube No. 6, on 24 January 1934. The first demonstration of all-electronic television was given to the EMI Chairman, Mr Alfred Clark, on 29 January. The pictures were greatly inferior to those produced by the EMI mechanical system which had now reached 180 lines. Davis:

> A few people in white coats looking like ghostly figures walking about and we were staggered with this. The mirror drum was so good and this looked so fluffy.

The new tube had comparatively low photosensitivity and it also produced a distortion known as 'shading' which caused excessive brightness in some parts of the picture and too much darkness in others. Shoenberg could, again, have killed electronic television. He didn't. The poor-quality pictures 'had excitement because images actually moved while you were watching.' Tube construction continued and reasonable tubes were being made by February. On 5 April 1934, Tube No. 14

> . . . was so much better in sensitivity and picture quality that we were able to direct the very experimental Emitron camera through the window of the laboratory and show the first direct 'Outside Broadcast' daylight picture to be achieved in the UK.

During the spring and summer, Blumlein, Browne and White concentrated on the circuits to drive the tube and to devise a process to overcome the 'shading' signals by creating artificially generated signals known as 'tilt' and 'bend' which would give uniform quality to the picture on the screen.

Klatzow worked to improve photosensitivity and colour response. He solved the latter by accident. McGee:

> He had left a young technician, Hodgson, to prepare an experimental photocathode while he was away for a short holiday. When he returned he found Hodgson very apologetic because he had bungled the experiment. However, on examining the failed tube Klatzow found to his astonishment that a silver-silver oxide-caesium photocathode had been formed which had a good visual sensitivity but very low infrared response. It took Klatzow quite a long time to find just what had been done by accident and to repeat it in a real tube.

Shortly after the first camera had been made, EMI designed a system of electronic television with six camera channels – four Emitron cameras and two telecine cameras, and built it on the ground floor of the research department. Here, in a small studio, a girl from the office 'would walk around and smile' for the studio cameras whilst a standard film projector ran its images in front of another camera to form a telecine machine. To connect the cameras for testing and demonstration, the company made the first multi-camera cable, 60 feet long, then 200, then 1000 feet. The Emitron camera was set free and the standard demonstration for influential visitors, especially from the BBC who were the sole potential market, was not only to show them pictures from the studio and from telecine and then to wheel the camera to the window that overlooked the Grand Union Canal but to run a cable and camera down to the canal bank itself and pick up all the activity of boats and light on the water. For D. C. Birkinshaw, who visited Hayes for the BBC on 18 April 1934, the significance of the difference between EMI and Baird was enormous:

> A picture not produced by mechanical means. No whizzing discs, no mirror drums, silence, lightness, portability. It showed the way things were going. It was quite easy to see, even then, that the Baird system couldn't eventually lead anywhere because television would have to follow the lead of sound radio and do outside broadcasts and there was no way that I could see that anything so far invented or projected by Baird could ever do an outside broadcast. And to my mind that had always been the chief stumbling block of his system.

In January, EMI had told the BBC it didn't want to provide a transmission system. In May it changed its mind and a new company was formed – Marconi–EMI, with the intention of winning both the receiver and the transmission business. On 20 May the *Sunday Chronicle* headlined '£10,000 at Stake in Television War' but the invention of the electronic camera, the Emitron, went unnoticed by the press. Compared with Baird's open door policy EMI were accused by the press of keeping their doors firmly closed. Broadway:

> From the laboratory to the outside world, security was of a very high order . . . it was a commercial enterprise. You didn't go broadcasting your information all over the place.

Bairds, however, were fully aware of the competition from EMI if not its exact nature. Baird wrote personally to Sir John Reith on St Valentine's Day, 1933:

> This company is virtually controlled by the Radio Corporation of America – 27% which, as you know, is virtual control – which surely controls quite enough of the world's communications without the home of British broadcasting taking it under its wing. I take it that the policy of the BBC is to explore fully the possibilities of *British* television before it gives encouragement to a company which is not entirely free of foreign domination.

Still smarting from RCA's objection to his broadcast licence in America, Baird wrote to the Prince of Wales accusing the BBC of 'crushing a pioneer British industry' and giving 'secret encouragement to alien interests.' Echoes or leaks of these accusations reached the press. *Era*, in November, accused the BBC of 'launching America's television invasion on the world' with 'a scheme to flood the world with millions of cheap sets' and concluded that 'the BBC is, on the whole, a danger to national interests.' So was EMI, in effect, an American subsidiary? McGee:

> It has been said that the Emitron (made at EMI) was a straight copy of the iconoscope (made by the RCA) and that we at EMI were largely dependent on know-how from the latter company. One reason advanced for this is that the tubes look similar. Now I can state categorically that there was no exchange of know-how between the two companies in this field during the crucial period 1931 to 1936. And with regard to the similarity of the tubes it would be clear to anyone with a minimum of technical perception that, given the situation as it existed at that time when we did not know how to make an efficient transparent signal-plate or photo-mosaic, there was no other way in which such a tube could be constructed.

Shoenberg had, in fact, been offered a contract by RCA for the Americans, in return for suitable payment, to do EMI's research for them. Shoenberg had turned them down. Zworykin:

> Two engineers, one of them Broadway, came over in 1933–4 in our laboratory for three months with the order to see all our work. I later mentioned this to Shoenberg. You know what he told me? He said that he couldn't get anything from RCA. It's all developed originally in Britain. I say 'How about Broadway and the other fellows who were in my laboratory for three months?' 'They are fools,' he said, 'they didn't bring anything.' He was joking about fools because Broadway was one of their best men.

Broadway:

> I would think we did a lot better in the technological area than RCA and Zworykin. McGee and EMI owe nothing to RCA and only in 1936 did the two companies sign an agreement for a complete exchange of patents and information. And that was quite a triumph because here was the mighty RCA coming to EMI on an equal footing.

Baird's practical, as opposed to verbal, response to the competition from EMI was to continue with the mechanical system but increase the lines from 30 to 60 to 120 and to transmit pictures from film. Percy:

> As far as telecine went we were inspired by German success. They built a 120-line film scanner which was very effective and Jacomb, who went to Germany very frequently, brought the idea back. We built a replica at Long Acre and it worked beautifully. A disc scanner and a little arc lamp that gave a 120-line picture. And, for the first time, we used a cathode-ray receiver so that eliminated any sort of noise at the receiving end, of motors and things. There was first a little green tube for laboratory purposes with green fluorescence and the first picture I saw was Mickey Mouse. We were very excited. I thought we're getting somewhere now.

A demonstration was given to the BBC and the Post Office in April 1933. It was judged inferior to the 120-line mechanical picture generated by EMI. Baird wrote an apology to Ashbridge:

> Naturally the receivers do not yet show the perfect picture as there is still work to be done on the reception side before this stage is reached. I may add also that the results shown you were not up to the best we can do, as, in order to keep faith with you, I rushed this demonstration through.

By July 1933, the company had moved from Long Acre to premises in the South Tower of the Crystal Palace. Here, under the direction of Captain West, ex-Chief Engineer of the BBC, lines were increased to 180 and transmission made over ultrashort wave. Ashbridge was given another demonstration of pictures from film and, this time, studio scenes as well.

> The picture was made to appear about 12 by 18 inches in size by a large water lens placed in front of a smaller picture. The living objects consisted of an announcer, a woman playing a violin and a man giving a lecture on various forms of architecture with diagrams. I considered the demonstration of living objects disappointing. There was, of course, more detail than in the case of 30-line television but the general appearance of the face was unnatural, and it had a greasy appearance.

In an attempt to solve the problem of poor studio pictures Baird turned to his experience of transmitting pictures from film. Percy:

> We knew we could transmit film so why not take a film of the studio action and then process it quickly. Maddest idea I ever heard of. Absolutely crackers. I can still get hysterical over it. It was another German idea and they had, of course, in their typical efficient way, got it working quite well but we never did.

The system was called the Intermediate Film Technique. In 1933 it was even considered by EMI and rejected as impractical. Alan Lawson joined Baird in November with the idea of producing this process, which involved a film camera placed directly on top of processing tanks and, as the camera filmed, the negative film came straight into the tanks where it was developed, fixed, washed, and, still travelling in large loops over rollers was scanned, while still running through water, by a Baird telecine machine. The film, transmitted as negative, appeared on screen as positive. The theory was good but the practice wasn't. Lawson:

> We were experimenting with various types of emulsions and ended up with a low contrast film specially made, from Kodak. 35 mil. film split down the middle to form $17\frac{1}{2}$ mil. . . . the developing business we got down to a fine art, somewhere between five and seven seconds in the developer. The problem after that was the fixing, which takes a much longer period. We were using the traditional hypo but this was still taking far too long and Banfield, one of the men in charge, said with a bit of trepidation, 'Well, there's only one thing that we can do to speed up fixing, and that is cyanide.' Cyanide, of course, is very dangerous but we eventually got that process down to fifteen or twenty seconds . . . So we were getting magnificent pictures. To this day I think the pictures we got were better, at that time, than anything EMI were producing out of anything. But our big problem was sound . . . we finally decided to go for a single system, the soundtrack on the same piece of film as the picture and that decision must have been made somewhere around 1935.

But even if the Intermediate Film Technique could be made to work successfully, it could not provide genuinely 'live' pictures, nor could it work outside a studio. Baird was forced to think electronic, 'although,' he wrote to Ashbridge, 'I do not think it by any means supersedes mechanical.' Percy:

> We read press reports of various demonstrations and leaks from America and we got mixed up with a man called Farnsworth who had an alternative electronic system. It was a rotten system but it *was* electronic and it *did* produce pictures. We had every sort of opportunity and if the Baird board had been on its toes it would have sent somebody to America, found out about electronic television and said either we pack up and just make receivers or we team up with somebody who knows how television's going to work. But nobody did.

Zworykin:

> Philo T. Farnsworth did very good work but the only thing he was lacking was storage. He didn't have storage. Because he got the electronic image on his large photocathode and because he then deflected all the image across the aperture where the storage should have been. For storage facility you have to have the mosaic.

This scanning system, lacking storage, was shown at Crystal Palace. Percy:

> Camera and everything. Dead silent, no wheels, no discs. Marvellous except that the picture was sausage shaped. Despite all his efforts he never got it straight. It had the most tremendous distortions.

'Magic Electric Eye' said the *Sunday Referee* but 'magic' it simply wasn't.

In the summer of 1934, the government set up the Selsdon Committee, consisting of representatives from the Post Office, the BBC and the government. It was chaired by Lord Selsdon, its brief being to investigate the possibility of providing a high-definition television service to replace the low-definition 30-line already in operation and to recommend the system of transmission. Bairds faced investigation by the committee with a television armoury that included a 30-line mechanical system using the flying spot; an Intermediate Film Technique at 180 lines, mechanically scanned; and a telecine system for transmitting films, also mechanically scanned and, at 240 lines, working well. In reserve was the possibility of using the Farnsworth electronic system – if it could be made to work. Marconi–EMI, the most likely alternative to Baird, had a 240-line mechanical system that still only showed film and an electronic system that was still in embryo. When the committee began to take evidence, Shoenberg called his entire team into the office. Davis:

> It was the most dramatic moment in the whole of television development. He said, 'What we're going to do, in this competition, we're going to offer 405 lines, twin interlace. And we're going for Emitron. We're going to give up mirror drum scanning, we're going on the lines of the electronic camera.'

McGee:

> I consider it the most courageous decision in the whole of his career. Remember

that this meant a 65% increase in scanning rate and a corresponding decrease in scanning beam diameter in the cathode-ray tube and nearly threefold in the signal/noise ratio of the signal amplifiers. The cynic may say that this was a piece of gamesmanship to overwhelm our competitors but . . . it was the decision of a man who, having the best advice he could find, and thinking not merely in terms of immediate success, but, rather, of lasting, long-term service, decides to take a calculated risk to provide a service that would last.

The detailed design of the entire Marconi–EMI system was done in the space of one brainstorming weekend by Blumlein, Browne and White but the Marconi–EMI management seriously questioned Shoenberg's decision. He was told that failure would bankrupt the company. It was a tremendous responsibility for Shoenberg but he went ahead with the determination and fervour of a religious crusader.

The Selsdon Committee reported on 5 January 1935 and Lord Selsdon, as Postmaster-General, broadcast on the wireless:

This afternoon, in the House of Commons, I announced the most important decision of the government on the subject of television, that latest miracle of scientific achievement which is now arousing so much interest. Broadcast television can perhaps best be described if I ask you to imagine that in the centre of your present wireless set there was a little square of glass on which you could now see me, as I sit here in the studio at Broadcasting House. Whether the picture would add to your enjoyment it is not for me to suggest. However, it is proposed that two television systems of High-Definition Television should be tried at the London Station.

He concluded:

You will be glad to know that there is no suggestion of an increase in the ten shilling fee for the Broadcast Listener's Licence.

The committee defined high-definition television as 'not having less than 240 lines per picture with a minimum picture frequency of 25 a second.' Of the companies investigated, including GEC, Ferranti, Scophony, Cossor and Plew TV Ltd, both Baird and Marconi–EMI were selected. They were to operate a regular transmission via the BBC on a week-on, week-off basis for a trial period of six months.

The press anticipated the start of the new series.

Television 'Looker' was the term coined at the television inquiry to describe one who 'looks in' to a television broadcast. There must be a better designation.

The *Daily Express* announced a competition. The *Daily Telegraph* provided some of the answers:

television observer, teleseer, tele preceptor, telvist, televist, audobserver, audoseer, audovist, invider, telegazer, telespector, visioner, visualiser, beholder, opticarious, Bairder, ingazer, teleite, telescriber, viewer.

And assured its readers that:

the television receiver is not in the least dangerous once the elementary fact is grasped that it must not be tampered with internally when in action.

'Is television a menace to the halls?' asked *Variety News* (7 Feb. 1935). 'Can television see into your home?' asked the *Daily Express*. 'Will television sterilise the population?' McGee:

> Very early on I was given the task to check whether the X-rays produced by the electrons in the cathode-ray tubes would be injurious to health. Well, I was confident that the effect would be negligible but we had to produce cast-iron evidence to counter the propaganda that we believed was being put out unscrupulously by the Baird company.

On 11 September 1935, the BBC, after 1500 programmes, closed its 30-line television transmission. There was a chorus of press protest. 'Television Blow from the BBC. Mr J. L. Baird, television pioneer, told the *Daily Mirror* last night, "It will mean that thousands of sets will become obsolete."' Not obsolete, countered the BBC, it will just mean that, for a time, there will be a 'non-visual service'. Had the 30-line experiment been worth it? Bridgewater:

> As a technique, 30-line television was something of a blind alley but it was still television and, whatever the number of lines, if you're doing television some of the arts and practices are the same. We all knew that our 30-line wasn't the be-all and end-all of television and we spent a lot of time thinking about the deeper technical problems of television of the future – the number of lines, resolution, bandwidth, amplifiers – whilst in practical terms, at Broadcasting House, we were learning the basics, the groundwork. Campbell, for example, with his photocells and mixer panel was only anticipating lights and lighting controls that we were to have later on. And I think we evolved a knowledge of the ways shows are done. Robb really extended us within the limits of the system and, although what we did was merely 30-line, it was by no means inappropriate for what we had to do when we came to Alexandra Palace.

6g The dancer Laurie Devine in a black and white cut-out mask, 9 November 1932

6h The Pantopuck Puppets, 19 October 1932, in *The Villain & the Heroine*

6i Sally the seal arrives for a television performance, Broadcasting House 1932

6j Boxing demonstration by Freddy Baxter and Teddy Lewis, 22 August 1933

6k Acrobatic dancers Ada and Eddie Caros, 7 November 1932

6l Adeline Genée and Anton Dolin in *The Love Song*, 15 March 1933

6m/n *(Above left)* The Balalaika Orchestra, 11 October 1933 (photographed in the light from the 'flying spot'). During their performance, the wooden steps they sat on broke and had to be held together by studio hands. *(Above right)* Sandy Powell and Frank Larden in a comedy sketch, 'The Caretaker', 19 June 1933

6o Josephine Baker, 4 October 1933. Scenery, costume and floor had to be in sharply contrasting black and white

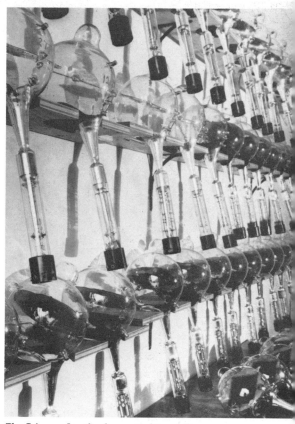

7a Bernard Greenhead with prototype Emitron camera. It had no viewfinder

7b Lines of cathode-ray tubes at the EMI factory at Hayes

7c/d *(Above left)* The Intermediate Film camera and processing gear in the Baird studio lab at the Crystal Palace, 1934. *(Above right)* Two frames from film made by the Intermediate Film process. The actress is Alma Taylor and the soundtrack is the white stripe running down the far left-hand side

7e *(Top left)* A.A. Campbell Swinton

7f *(Top right)* Eustace Robb, Producer of BBC 30-line

7g *(Middle left)* Cecil Madden, Programme Planner and producer of *Picture Page*

7h *(Middle right)* Gerald Cock, first director of BBC Television

7i *(Left)* Isaac Shoenberg, Research Head at EMI (in later years)

8/9a *(Above left)* Douglas Birkinshaw, the first BBC TV chief engineer and the man responsible for the conversion of Alexandra Palace into the world's first high-definition television station. The mast and transmitting aerials (vision above: sound below). *(Above right)* Bebe Daniels and Ben Lyon anchored to the Baird studio floor in *Starlight*. Producer Cecil Lewis. Studio B, 3 November 1936

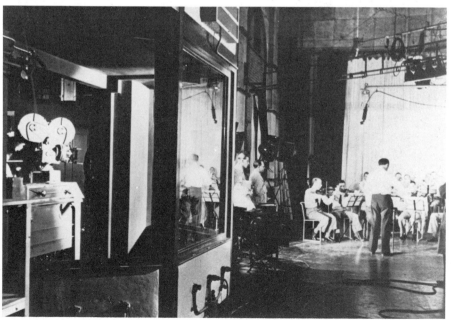

9b Studio B. The Baird System: showing the 'Intermediate Film Camera' behind the glass window

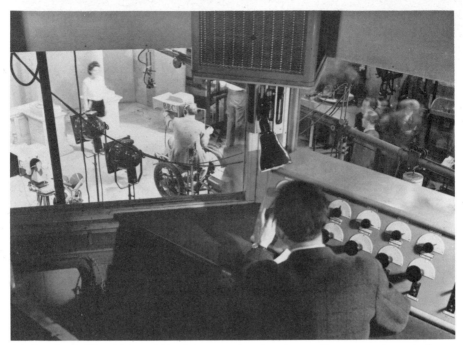

9c Studio A. The Marconi–EMI system: showing the studio as seen through the glass window of the producer's elevated control room

9d *Café Cosmopolitan* showing the three Emitron cameras, on left, on right and, mobile, in centre. The cameras are now fitted with viewfinders. Studio A, 11 February 1937

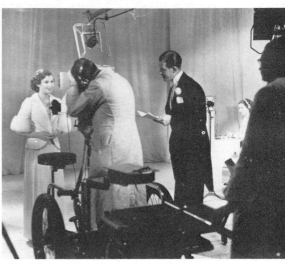

10a *Picture Page* (Afternoon edition).
Leslie Mitchell interviewing. Joan
Miller at the switchboard

10b *Picture Page* (Evening edition –
which meant evening dress). Leslie
Mitchell interviews Dinah Sheridan

10c The knife-throwing Denvers in *Variety*, producer Cecil Madden, 24 October
1936. Curtains provide a very basic backdrop

8

ALEXANDRA PALACE
February 1935–November 1936

Ally Pally, thus named by Gracie Fields, was not the BBC's first choice for a television station but it had three advantages. It was high up, already built and available. The Selsdon Committee had given the BBC just eighteen months to prepare itself for regular high-definition transmissions and so, with time at a premium and with little money to spare, the Corporation decided that it was cheaper, easier and quicker to convert an existing building than to build from scratch. The Alexandra Palace, near Wood Green in north London, was built as an entertainments venue in 1875. Campbell went to see it:

> I found an old tyre, no roof, no doors and could see the sky. The smell of cat in the old banqueting rooms nearly made me sick and the whole thing looked the most dreadful mess.

In the absence of anything better, the BBC hired the two floors and tower at the south-east corner. Conversion of the building began immediately under the control of Douglas Birkinshaw, engineer-in-charge:

> It was my job, along with Terence MacNamara, to design the London Television station. Determine the size of studios, the areas required for everything, write down everything we wanted. It was a mountain of work and we had to overcome all the difficulties ourselves. There was no convenient article or book we could refer to. It was, after all, the first major television station in the world.

As well as the premises, the BBC provided the facilities like the sound transmitter, the mast and the aerials. The competing companies, Baird and Marconi–EMI, provided the rest of the equipment.

The total floor space was nearly 32,000 square feet and on the ground floor were the transmitter rooms which included the Marconi–EMI and Baird vision transmitters and, between them and used by both, the BBC sound transmitter, plus a room for viewing film, a restaurant and kitchen. On the floor above were the studios. From the staircase, the main corridor ran the length of the building. First on the left was the Marconi–EMI studio. It was 2100 feet square and 25 feet high – tiny compared with the 1960s' Studio 1 at BBC Television Centre, which is 10,800 feet square and 40 feet high. The studio was soundproofed with sheets of asbestos, ceilinged with building board and floored with black lino. Two sets of curtains, one white and the other black, provided for 'an interchange of backgrounds'. Slung across the centre of the studio was a special lighting bridge which could, if required, accommodate spot and flood lights similar to film lights and, on the studio floor, were outlets for more lighting and microphones and a lighting control board. High up at one end of the studio was the plate-glass window of the control room with a panel to control sound and vision, monitor screens and desk for the producer in charge. Next door to the studio was the Marconi–EMI telecine room.

Further down the corridor on the left was Baird country; the Baird telecine room, followed by the Baird spotlight studio which housed the spotlight scanner and then the Baird control room facing into the Baird studio. The studio was exactly the same size as EMI's but laid out quite differently with the larger stage facing the little projecting glass-fronted room that housed the Intermediate Film camera. Each studio, after the intolerable heat of earlier studios, was fitted with proper ventilation.

On the opposite side of the corridor were dressing rooms, a band room, rooms for make-up and costume, a green room for performers and a shaft for lifting scenery from the terrace below. In the south-east tower on the third floor, with a view across the Alexandra Palace racecourse and most of London as far as St Paul's and the Surrey hills, was the office of the Director of Television, offices for the producers and, above them, the television mast.

The design of the mast was based on the experimental mast built for EMI at Hayes. It sat 215 feet above the tower and was tied into it by 50-foot steel bars at each corner, and 17 tons of concrete. The total height above sea level was 606 feet and it carried, at the top, aerials for both sound and vision. Birkinshaw:

> The aerial is much less interesting to the ordinary person than the television camera but it is just as tricky and can land you in as much trouble. The whole thing is a highly mathematical business which had to be worked out in great precision. We originally thought we might get reliable reception from about twenty-five miles from Ally Pally. Well, we got fifty-five miles and we got

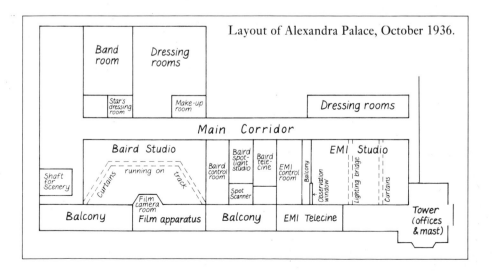

Layout of Alexandra Palace, October 1936.

reception from much greater distances if the viewer could get his aerial high up. The signal was received in Manchester and there were the usual cases of freak reception from the Continent. The vision, of course, was the novelty but the sound quality was superlative. Every bit as good as modern UHF. Now the reason for this was that you can't broadcast vision on anything but a short wave and so, as the domestic receiver must be able to receive sound and vision together, we naturally put the sound up on the available wavelength and the bandwidth was miles more than you need for sound. It was like driving down a motorway one mile wide. The vision went out at forty-five million vibrations per second and the sound at forty-nine and a half million and because of the requirements of vision, sound simply benefited.

The top of the mast looked rather like the spokes of an umbrella with two tiers of eight arms hinged and radiating and, between the arms, the wires of the aerials. The whole mast was designed to move in the wind several inches out of the perpendicular and was 'proof against the heaviest gale', except the gale in the winter of 1936–7 when the wind got under the arms of the umbrella and blew them shut. The wires were twisted together in an impossible tangle and transmission, until they were untangled, was impossible. Birkinshaw:

> Now, normally, if you want to do something on the aerial, you must select a calm day. You don't do it in the dark in a gale. But the strong principle underlying BBC engineering is that the show must go on. So, I thought, I must go up and make my own impression as to whether it's safe and, if it is, I'll ask the riggers if they're willing to have a shot at repairing it. So that I could see what I was doing, I asked Campbell if he could mount a group of 8-kilowatt spotlights on the roof and illuminate the mast from top to bottom. Which he did. And there it was, standing out like a beacon all over north London. And I began to climb. Two hundred and fifteen feet with the wind clawing at me and the rain dashing against me. It was the most frightening experience I've ever had in my life and we lashed the aerials so that it could never happen again.

In the spring of 1936, Birkinshaw selected his team of technicians:

> I was allowed to go anywhere in the BBC and invite any engineer to come and be a strong and dependable ally in this great adventure but I felt obliged to say to them that they were going out into the unknown because, as there hadn't been a high-definition television system before, we had no one else's previous experience to go on.

Among the team were Campbell and Bridgewater from 30-line days, both appointed Senior Maintenance Engineers whose job was to familiarise themselves with the new technology and pass on the information to other recruits, and Herbert Baker and H. F. Bowden, senior transmitter engineers. Birkinshaw:

> These two dedicated characters had the problem of finding out how the transmitters worked; finding out how to keep them working; finding out how to assure they delivered their maximum power and quality. Their world was as important as the more spectacular studio side because you could bring the whole programme to the end of the transmitter and then see the whole thing blow up.

They had to inspect and adjust the transmitters and spot any sign of incipient trouble because in a transmitter you have very high electrical pressures and you want to watch what's going on in case you have a bang.

The life of a transmitter engineer could be dangerous:

The transmitters were water cooled and, of course, when water gets out with a high electrical voltage present, it's not very funny. Nor, late at night, is the face of a rat poking round the modulator. But that was underground life at Ally Pally.

In March 1936, the two companies began to move in their equipment:

The most sophisticated, well-thought-out equipment began to come from EMI. They designed their equipment with a technical subtlety which can only be really appreciated if you're a dyed-in-the-wool engineer. Baird's equipment was beautifully made, too, but they tended to obtain their scientific results by the brute force application of electrical components and principles. They would use what you might call electrically cumbersome ways of arriving at a result whereas the EMI would do it neatly and most ingeniously resulting in less cost and less space taken up.

The two companies both issued general descriptions of their systems. Bairds stressed their 'remarkable filming equipment' which was 'perfect in every detail' and claimed 'the whole installation, with typical British thoroughness, is built as solidly as the electrical installation of a battleship.' Marconi–EMI once again emphasised the 'flickerless' nature of their picture and, in a broadside at Bairds' Intermediate Film Technique, the ' "Electric Eye" which enables scenes and events to be picked up direct as they occur, in contradistinction to other systems in which it is necessary to photograph the subject before it is televised.' And, to counter Bairds' jingoism, stated, 'The Marconi–EMI system is an all-British commercial product ahead of any other world development.'

The Baird equipment was easy for the BBC team to understand as Bridgewater and Campbell had had working experience of some of it, but not the EMI. Birkinshaw:

I realised that my team would not be able to make head or tail of this. It involved doing tricks with electronic equipment the like of which had never been seen and over the next couple of years I set myself to unravel the EMI mysteries in detail and wrote a book which records how the whole of the EMI system is constructed and operated. It was styled, not by myself, but by others, the famous 'Black Book'.

The 'Black Book' became the BBC engineers' technical bible and because so much of the equipment was so new that it was unpatented, the whole team were under oath not to allow any secrets to leak from one company to another, 'which, I can tell you, was a considerable strain.'

During the period from March to August 1936, equipment was tested and understood; cameramen, none of whom had even worked film cameras before, were recruited and trained; transmitters were fine tuned. Birkinshaw:

An awful lot of finishing touches had to be done on site which couldn't be done in the laboratory. So there was a hive of activity on the transmitters, in the studio, all the way up the mast to the aerials. It was very tiring but exciting. I know I lost half a stone in weight. I know Blumlein was supervising a very difficult job on the EMI transmitter one evening and he was so tired he keeled over and cut his head quite badly. We had to get the doctors in. We were working a regular fifteen-hour day.

Appointed Director of the Television Service (D. Tel. – the BBC loves initials) was Gerald Cock, ten years with the Corporation and its first director of radio Outside Broadcasts. He had previously made a living prospecting and mining in America, was an explosives expert, managing director of a film company and Hollywood ranch owner. Birkinshaw:

> Cock was a most likeable man with an active and imaginative mind. Although extrovert and very persuasive to get what he wanted done, but in the nicest way possible, he inspired us all.

Eustace Robb, who had made as great a success of 30-line as it ever could be, was overlooked and resigned.

Cock, like Robb, was an innovator. He determined that the BBC should make strong links with the entertainment world, come to an agreement with the film producers to work together, saw an increase in 'actuality' and 'topical' programmes and prophesied that 'much of the present painfully acquired broadcast technique is bound for the scrap heap.' The mandarins at Broadcasting House were scared:

> In my opinion, the present plans of the Television Director are too ambitious. With his characteristic keenness and enthusiasm, he is planning to start a service at a level which I feel need not be reached for some months after the actual date of the start of regular transmissions.
>
> (Cecil Graves to Charles Carpendale, 26 March 1936)

Nevertheless, most of Cock's ideas were approved. They included ideas for a television orchestra, programmes with an emphasis on personalities from the press, theatre, sport, news and excerpts from old and new films.

As Birkinshaw assembled the engineers, Cock assembled the production team – productions manager: D H. Munro; producer in charge of programme planning: Cecil Madden; producers: Cecil Lewis, Dallas Bower, Stephen K. Thomas; assistant producer: George More O'Ferrall; music director: Hyam Greenbaum; film assistant: L. G. Barbrook; stage managers: Peter Bax, Harry Pringle; wardrobe and make-up: Mary Allen; administrator: Leonard Schuster. It was a behind-the-camera team recruited in equal proportion from radio, film and the theatre. For people in front of the camera, the BBC advertised:

> The BBC is conducting a search for Superwoman. She must have super personality, charm, tact, a mezzo voice and a good memory. She must be as acceptable to women as to men. She must photograph well. She must not have red hair and must not be married.

The reason why only blondes and brunettes need apply was because of the continuing worry over red sensitivity. It was thought possible that a red-headed girl might televise as a girl with no hair at all. However, despite the exclusion of red-heads and marrieds, there was a riot of interest: '5000 want one Job' (*Daily Sketch*, 3 Jan.); 'TV Beauties Storm BBC' (*Era*, 8 Jan.); 'Search for Twin Paragons goes on. Personality, Pep and Patience wanted' (*Evening News*, 5 May). The actual number of written applications received for the job of female announcer was 677 and of hostess 445. The winners, who, it was decided, would be called announcer hostesses, were Elizabeth Cowell, 'a true brunette with soft brown eyes and a lively face which one would call chic rather than beautiful', and Jasmine Bligh, 'niece of Lord Darnley and descended from Captain Bligh of the *Bounty*. Serious and dignified. An auburn blonde, statuesque, really beautiful and queenly.' Bligh:

> They wanted to know what our legs were like. Now we never showed our legs on television so, instead of saying 'Miss Bligh would you raise your skirt slightly', they made us climb up three steps and get onto a table where, no doubt, they discovered what they wanted to discover.

Jasmine Bligh had first heard about television from well-connected friends one weekend at a house party. Bligh:

> I looked upon the whole thing as an enormous joke but as I was out of a job I applied. I knew I was photogenic, I knew I could speak the King's English, I'd had four years in the theatre and I knew I could cope with people. That was about all and, eventually, I was put on the short list of twenty. We had to do a test which consisted of announcing three programmes in French, German and Italian; memorising a fifty-word telegram and being questioned on it; answering general questions and then showing our legs to, amongst others, Miss Freeman who was in charge of all female staff at the BBC, Sir Charles Carpendale and Lord Reith.

The short list was reduced to four and the girls were screen tested at the EMI studio in Hayes. Broadway:

> They were a bit jittery to say the least and I didn't think Jasmine was so good at first. She appeared rather starchy and not forthcoming. Elizabeth seemed to exude a little more charm but this was a part of announcing that took time to develop. Television announcing was not the same as radio announcing – a disembodied voice – nor the same as acting where you can expect an audience reaction. They had to realise that they were putting on a show for a family in a sitting room and talking to them personally. Television was a new medium with an identity of its own. They had to discover that and, from an artistic point of view, they were starting from basics just as we had done with technology.

Elizabeth Cowell:

> I remember Jasmine and I were finally told in Broadcasting House in April that we'd got the job but we wouldn't keep it if we told anybody at all.

Bligh:

> For three months they didn't know what to do with us. We spoke into various

microphones in various studios at BH; we had our photographs all over the papers for days – eighth wonder of the world for a week, and then, finally, they felt they had to present us to the public and we appeared at St George's Hall with Geraldo and his band and we announced three musical items in front of an audience of five hundred people. We were both so nervous we had to be given sal volatile to get us on the stage.

Cowell:

> Frightfully little pay but it was gorgeous to get it and £25 a year dress allowance so we could dress only the top half. What happened below the waist was nobody's business.

Bligh:

> Under contract for six months at a ridiculous salary, £300 a year, and the evening dresses wardrobe bought for us were appalling – two shirts, two skirts, two evening dresses and two evening blouses to last a whole year. If we'd been allowed to advertise, which, of course, we weren't, we could have been dressed by any model house in the world – instead, grey worsted skirts, little polka-dot blouses, terrible organza evening dresses. But we were young, pretty, I was twenty-one and Elizabeth was twenty-two and it didn't really matter.

The girl announcers were taken to Alexandra Palace in the summer of 1936 – with Leslie Mitchell. 'He-Man Hunt Stumps BBC' (*Daily Sketch*, 19 May); 'TV Adonis Found' (*Daily Mail*, 22 May).

Leslie Mitchell had made a guest appearance with Dame Marie Tempest on the Baird television system short-wave demonstration at Selfridges in 1932. He had been an actor and then gone into radio, occasionally announcing television programmes for 30 lines in the basement of Broadcasting House. But he was not the first choice for 'Television Announcer. Second Class. Temporary.' Among others, Robert Donat had been approached but he'd refused and when the *Daily Mail* printed Mitchell's photograph and announced his appointment, he was a little surprised:

> Nobody had told me. And there was my office full of press people asking questions. So I phoned up the great panjandrum himself and he said, 'Ah, well, Mitchell. Ah. Ah. Well. I think the best thing I can tell you is that you're under consideration. No. We haven't asked you.' So I told the press people they'd got it all wrong and I made a brilliant joke – 'Much Adonis About Nothing' – but nobody really took it up. And because there was no real money attached to the job and no one important would do it, it was experimental in every way, I was able to take the chance on a job that I hadn't applied for.

There were more problems over clothes:

> I had a scene with one of the governors. He said: 'I gather you're being a little difficult about clothes, Mitchell, but you look all right to me.' I said, 'Sir, I know, but we have to wear make-up and I've discovered the lights are very strong and, if you'll forgive me, one perspires rather a lot and, unless you buy good clothes, they won't stand up to it and I don't think one can afford to keep on buying

clothes.' He said, 'Well, I tell you what we'll do. We'll pay you £50 in advance on salary. Will that help?' I said that would be fantastic and went straight to Moss Bros. Soon after that I was described in the press as the best-dressed man in the BBC. But I'm not so sure that was a compliment to the BBC.

During the summer of 1936, engineers, technicians, producers and performers worked together to get the two television systems working smoothly for the official opening of the service in November. The first test transmission took place on 12 August, the picture of a chequer board and the sound of a mouth organ, but the unexpected call from Cock to provide a test transmission for the Radio Show in late August was the real stimulus that everyone at Alexandra Palace needed. Like the prospect of imminent death, it concentrated the mind wonderfully. Jasmine Bligh was taken ill with appendicitis, Elizabeth Cowell caught a serious chill and the Baird Intermediate Film Technique refused, initially, to work at all. It also demonstrated the hostility of vested radio interests determined to prevent television from being a success. *Morning Post*, 31 Aug. 1936:

> Sabotage attempt at Radio Olympia . . . Tin Foil 'wad' to Stop Television . . . Apparatus now under Guard.

Daily Worker, 31 Aug. 1936:

> . . . obviously the work of someone with an expert knowledge of the mechanism concerned . . . believed to have been acting for rival trade interests . . . considered to be the work of the same hands that produced a number of previous and hitherto unsuspected incidents which include the mysterious burning out of a transmitter and the finding of a dead mouse wedged in the equipment.

But the show went on – *Here's Looking at You*, twice a day, every day, for two weeks, live from the studio and film from telecine, alternating on a day-on, day-off basis between the two systems. It showed that the engineers, in Birkinshaw's phrase, 'were more prepared for regular television than we cared to admit'. But it also showed, not surprisingly, the technical limitations of the two systems, especially Baird, and the inexperience of the production team and the performers. Birkinshaw wrote a long report to Gerald Cock on 5 September which, in turn, became the basis for Cock's report to the Deputy Director-General on 7 September. Only two copies of this document were made and both were marked, in Cock's own hand, 'secret'.

It commented that lighting was poor and, whilst sound reproduction was good, there was a 20% loss of picture quality between transmission and reception. There was a request for more staff and more space:

> programme facilities are impossibly cramped. It is a fair analogy to imagine the whole evening's sound broadcast programme, rehearsals and performance, allocated to one Broadcasting House studio.

He noted that it had been extremely difficult to get satisfactory films from the movie-makers; that there was a definite limit to the number of times a programme could be repeated and that 'watching television is still a strain on the attention.' Items should be kept short, about ten minutes, and 'between each, comparatively long, restful intervals, carefully devised, may well last up to five minutes,' (the germ, here, of those interminable 'potter's wheel' interludes and gentle rushing streams that punctuated the television of the 1950s). Moreover:

> the theory that 'anything' will do in the early days of television, due to curiosity about the medium as a scientific achievement, is mistaken. It is almost certain that television will be judged entirely on its programme value in competition with other available entertainment.

In contrast to the excitement surrounding the experimental transmissions to RadiOlympia, the official start of the BBC Television Service, on 2 November 1936, was something of an anticlimax. Even the press, for the time being, seemed to have lost its enthusiasm. The *Times* announcement was tired and ponderous: 'The moment long seen afar off by eyes of faith, has come at last.' The opening programme reflected the tiredness – it was called simply *Variety* and was almost a rerun of *Here's Looking at You*. Eric Coates wrote a Television March and Adele Dixon sang a song:

> A mighty maze, of mystic magic rays
> Is all about us in the blue
> And in sight and sound we trace
> Living pictures out of space
> To bring a new wonder to you.
> The busy world before you is unfurled
> Its songs, its tears, its laughter too,
> Conjured up in sound and sight
> With the magic rays of light
> To bring new enchantment to you

This was followed by comedian dancers Buck and Bubbles, Chinese jugglers called the Lai Founs and the Television Orchestra. It was preceded by the Official Opening Ceremony. The platform party consisted of the BBC Chairman, the Postmaster-General and the chairman of the Television Advisory Committee. They were part of what the newspapers termed 'television history in the making' and they were part of it twice as the ceremony was televised first in the Baird system, Bairds having won the toss, and then repeated for Marconi–EMI. For the Baird transmission, the platform party was joined by the chairman of Bairds who was substituted for the Marconi–EMI transmission by the chairman of EMI. It was an official opening for official people making official speeches. Leslie Mitchell tried valiantly to unstiffen the proceedings:

> One of the first things I managed to establish was that you couldn't read a proclamation every time you appeared in front of the television cameras. Much as one would like to look fairly royal, it was a bit silly to unwrap the long sheet of print and start reading out what you had to say. So I refused absolutely to read

the opening announcement. They said: 'It's been sat on by the BBC for several weeks.' And I said: 'Well, it may have been and I'm sorry.' And I tore it up. I knew that we were opening the following day and I doubted if they could get anyone to replace me – but I did suggest they should try – but they didn't and I did announce without a script and the only thing I was really scared about was that I should say 'The Most Paster General'.

The Times thought Mitchell's performance most successful but, in contrast, the performance of the non-professionals was awkward and stilted and what they had to say was boringly predictable; Mr R. C. Norman, BBC Chairman:

> We of the BBC are proud that the government should have decided to entrust us with the conduct of the new service. We are very conscious of the responsibilities which that decision imposes upon us . . . the foresight which secured to this country a national system of broadcasting promises to secure for it also a flying start in the practice of television. At this moment the British Television Service is undoubtedly ahead of the rest of the world. Long may that lead be held. You may be assured that the BBC will be resolute to maintain it.

Chauvinism on such occasions is natural. But was the claim true? Was the British television service ahead of the rest of the world? *The Observer* concurred and called the service the 'first of its kind' and stated that 'observers from the United States and Germany . . . have stated without hesitations that the BBC's service is definitely better than anything to be seen elsewhere.' (1 Nov. 1936.) The *Daily Telegraph* pointed out that neither Germany nor the USA 'has built a station intended to transmit high-definition pictures to the home.'

As well as Britain, there were seven other countries actively involved in television. In 1936, the Swedes were testing on ultrashort waves and both the Dutch and the Italians were experimenting with the electronic iconoscope. The Russians and the French were already on air with low-definition television similar to the BBC 30-line experiments. Moscow broadcast regularly at night and Paris, to public viewing rooms, on Sundays. In addition to their low-definition system of 60 lines, Paris was also using a mechanical system of 180-line high definition. But most advanced were the Americans and Germans.

The bubble of the American mechanical television boom of the early 1930s had burst. The Americans, for the most part, had replaced their low-definition system with an all-electronic one – but with no public television service. The cause of the delay was partly because of patent rows, between RCA and Farnsworth for example; partly because rival firms could not agree on transmission standards; but mostly because of the way America proposed to finance its new broadcasting service – with commercials. 'Thus,' wrote L. Marsland Gander in the *Daily Telegraph*, 'the system America has created exacts its penalty. Television may be almost technically complete but it is not yet a commercial proposition.'

The Germans, on the other hand, had a thrusting service which had begun on 23 March 1935. Reich's producer, Eugen Hadamovsky, in a formal ceremony in Berlin, launched 'the world's first regular television service.' (That is, of course, if you discount the BBC's 30-line service launched in 1932.) Transmission was on 180 lines at twenty-five pictures per second mechanically scanned. Pictures were provided by film or, from the studio, by the 'indirect method' which was the same Intermediate Film Technique Baird was using at Alexandra Palace. Later, in 1936, as Hitler increasingly saw television as an instrument of propaganda, the Germans introduced three electronic cameras (Farnsworths) to supplement the IFT and to cover the mass spectacle of the Berlin Olympics. But transmission remained on 180 lines. Programmes consisted of a weekly newsreel, studio performances and excerpts from movies and documentary films. Test transmissions for manufacturers took place in the morning and afternoon and each evening there was an hour-and-a-half-long programme from 8.30 to 10.00: a total, in 1935, of thirty-one-and-a-half hours' transmission a week. There were few private television sets and, in a country faced with rampant inflation, these were not bought but given by manufacturers to influential people. The rest of the public in Berlin watched in public viewing rooms.

Whether Britain was the first to establish a high-definition regular television service depends on the interpretation of the terms 'regular service' and 'high-definition.' Bridgewater:

> A complete high-definition service isn't just the number of lines, it's how else the picture looks and if it flickers. I would say that the combination of 405 lines and fifty fields a second makes the British all-electronic system the first acceptable high-definition service.

Birkinshaw:

> If you consider that 180 lines is a high-definition television then the Germans were first. And if you don't, then we were first.

As the BBC officially opened its service, John Baird, the man who had established low definition, the man whose name in Britain was synonymous with television, the man who, according to the press, 'The BBC Forgot', sat in the body of the studio, furious at what he regarded as another deliberate slight.

9

THE TWO SYSTEMS
November 1936 – February 1937

In August 1936, the difference between the Baird and Marconi–EMI television systems was not immediately obvious to the viewer, nor to the press. 'At the moment,' said *The Economist* (29 August 1936), 'there is little to choose between them.' And *The Observer* thought 'the rivalry has been the very best thing possible for television in this country.' It was not an opinion that was shared by the engineers and producers who worked at Alexandra Palace. Dallas Bower:

> It was absolute folly to have two systems. Bairds was a bench operation still in the laboratory.

Cecil Madden:

> Working in the Baird studio was a bit like using Morse code when you knew that next door you could telephone.

Gerald Cock, in his secret memo of 7 September 1936, held the same opinion:

> It is quite evident that (quality of transmission apart) the Baird Spotlight process and probably Intermediate Film, are unsatisfactory and inflexible. It is certain they will increase the cost and difficulty of the service severely with results that will not be justified in picture quality . . . the telecine is good, but it would be self-deception to anticipate eventual success for the Baird system unless some equivalent of the Emitron is forthcoming.

The only real equivalent was the Farnsworth camera – still in the laboratory, and Baird's only means of transmitting 'live' pictures from the main studio was by Intermediate Film (IF). This process, improved from 180 to 240 lines, successfully televised the Baird section of the official opening ceremony but the problems of the system were inherent and too numerous to solve. Mitchell:

> I'd come straight off stage and gone round to see myself on film in the control room. It was possible to do this because of the 54-second time gap between the time I was filmed and the time it took for the film to be processed and transmitted. And there was a picture of a little man with bow legs and bowler hat and I said, 'What the hell's that?' And they said, 'It's you Leslie – it got mauled up I'm afraid.' So I wasn't terribly impressed.

The IF machine was 6 feet tall and housed in a special unit that thrust onto the floor of studio B like a large bay window. Jim Percy was the Baird engineer in charge:

It was more or less grouted into concrete and, from its little glass hut, glared out at three different angles. And that was it. You couldn't wheel it. You couldn't raise or lower it. You could hardly do anything with it. The thing was quite inflexible.

Practising on the machine against the time when it might have to be operated by the BBC was BBC cameraman John Bliss:

Baird's camera had a turret of lenses so at rehearsal I would follow the action through the camera and decide, with the producer, what lenses to use. I didn't shoot any actual film because it was too expensive. We used 1000-foot rolls of unstandard $17\frac{1}{2}$ mil. – known as 'slit down 35 mil.', and the problem was loading the film in the dark. You had to take the core, the centrepiece, out of the roll and substitute a Baird core and put it into the camera magazine without dropping it. But thousands of feet of film were dropped on the floor and ruined.

Alan Lawson was the regular cameraman for Bairds:

I would say to the producer, 'This is the picture you're going to get. When the artist comes to that position, if you want a close-up, this is what it will look like' and he could look through the camera. He could operate the camera, it didn't really matter, and I would swing the lenses and he could see what he would get.

Bliss:

The producer would tell me what he especially wanted and what to avoid but during the performance you had to follow the action the best you could. There were no monitors for you or the producer to see what you were getting. You were on your own. You memorised the producer's script and hoped you were getting what he wanted.

Lawson:

It's exactly the same as making a film. The producer assumes he's getting what he said he wanted.

The only difference between using a film camera for 'live' television and for making a film is that, with television, you are stuck with what you get first time. There are no retakes. Madden:

You had absolutely no camera mobility at all. You were tied down to a specific set-up and all you could do was swing the turret on the camera. It meant you simply had to stay in one fixed long-shot position and come into the action by swinging the turret head – and swinging in full view of the audience who, on the home screen, saw a blur.

Lawson:

It wasn't a terribly flexible system. You couldn't do any tracking, you could only pan and all we had was a turret with four lenses and you spun the turret when you wanted a close-up. The picture disappeared and then reappeared as a close-up and that's how it would appear on the screen.

Madden:

> So it didn't make for any degree of flexibility at all and it was further limited in so far as you could only shoot to the capacity of the film magazine, 1000 feet, which was very unsatisfactory from a programme point of view. It wasn't a practical proposition at all.

Lawson:

> You had twenty minutes' worth of film and that was it. That was the length of your show. So we never did any full-length plays on intermediate film.

The machine was incredibly noisy and made performing difficult and, even when it was running smoothly – filming, developing, fixing, washing, transmitting – it was difficult to keep it that way. Processing with the cyanide was variable: one moment the picture was light, the next it was dark. Dirt got stuck in the disc holes, pieces of gelatine spooled off the film, jammed in the scanning gate and masked or mauled the transmitted picture, and, as the film was still scanned wet, underwater, bubbles appeared on the film and swelled and distorted the image. The water was necessary in order to keep the film lubricated and prevent it from snapping and the film was scanned through an optical glass in the telecine machine. But, because the picture and soundtracks were on the same piece of emulsion, sound had to be produced underwater too.

Lawson:

> We were constantly bugged by the uncertainty of the soundtrack. Because it was scanned underwater, the perforations on the film used to bring down air bubbles and you'd get one of those fixed in the sound gate and you got a motor boating effect. Pfft. Pfft. Pfft. You'd blow it, kick it, everything to get rid of the air bubble and it would be all right for a while, then another bubble would come down.

The sound on screen was, on occasions, 'not unlike gurgling bath water.'

The machine had such an insatiable thirst that, on one occasion, it emptied all four storage tanks on the Alexandra Palace towers and ground to a halt.

Percy:

> The announcers spent most of their time apologising for breakdowns because everywhere you looked down the long chain of fifty-four seconds, you had disaster staring you in a hundred places.

Disaster and danger:

> A lot of us were standing on a wet floor with 10,000 volts running through the machine; the cameraman was hanging over the Nipkow disc spinning at 6000 revs a minute and if you absentmindedly sipped some of the cyanide fixing fluid which splashed on the floor, you were dead for a certainty. Liz Cowell generally trailed her long frock into it and had to be hosed down quick so, as all this was happening in the cramped little scanning room, you can say rehearsals and transmissions were always exciting.

Mitchell:

> The IF was a racket and I was so sorry for the Baird boys standing on their

131

head, sopping themselves with water, trying to get new development. It really was awful to watch them and the strain on them was appalling.

Birkinshaw:

Baird set his staff an impossible task of making a good practical television system out of the wrong principles.

Lawson:

It was a hell of a long way to crack a nut.

Bairds could have improved their system and solved many of their transmission problems if they had opted for a time lapse of ten minutes instead of one but, as 'television' and 'immediacy' were synonymous, that was an option not open to them. It also denied them the opportunity of offering recorded programmes. Percy:

The film was wound up wet on a spool and then stored so, when things did work properly, you had a film of the complete programme that could be sent out again even in a year's time.

This was done occasionally, but only as an experiment. However, with hindsight, there is no doubt that Baird's Intermediate Film technique was, in Jim Percy's phrase, 'the grand-daddy of all canned television programmes'.

The Baird Spotlight Studio was for announcements and the occasional solo performance. It was the 30-line system increased to 240. The disc was about 3 feet in diameter and had a very big arc lamp which shone through a hole into the little studio to illuminate the announcer. The reflected light was, as usual, picked up on batteries of photocells. When in focus the picture was sharp but grainy and there were the usual mechanical problems of dirt in the disc holes, heat from the incredible amount of light and the lamp was liable to burn out. And it still only transmitted head-and-shoulders pictures and required the subject to remain accurately positioned. The celebrated New Zealand tenor Peter Dawson was already into the first verse of 'The Road to Mandalay' when he was stopped in full view of the audience and asked, as arranged, to sit down. Munro:

The rehearsal was all right but when it came to the transmission, to my horror, we couldn't see Dawson's face. We only saw from the neck downwards. So we had to fade the thing out and I went into the studio and said: 'Mr Dawson, you were told to sit on the stool.' 'But,' he said, 'there was a lady in the studio.' The lady was Elizabeth Cowell and, being a gentleman, Dawson stood up – and cut his head off. That was the Spotlight Studio.

As in the old days, the performers had yellow faces and blue lipstick and sat on a backless music stool staring at the spotlight. Mitchell:

It was a terrifying ordeal. Kneeling beside you were two studio attendants and when the light came on through the orifice in the wall, it was very bright and flickering – straight into your eyes. Then one of them would give you a nasty jab in the kidney on the left – that was the signal to smile, and the other would give an even nastier jab in the right kidney and this was the sign to talk, which I usually did. The whole ordeal, as well as being painful, was monotonous. And, one evening, the call-boy came round and said: 'Mr Mitchell. Mr Mitchell. Spotlight Studio. Spotlight Studio.' And I shot out, went in, sat in this seat in the dark, was jabbed, stopped smiling and said: 'Well, that's all we have for today and I'm delighted you were able to be with us and hope you'll join us for tomorrow's transmissions.' And the whole place erupted in flames: people shouting: people running down the corridor and in through the door shouting: 'What the hell are you doing Mitchell?' I'd discontinued the programmes before they'd begun.

The grainy pictures from Spotlight were always recognisably different from the IF pictures they were supposed to match and using Spotlight and intermediate film in the same programme caused time problems. Campbell:

> You spent much of your time cuing things with a stop-watch to make sure you'd started the IF programme fifty-four seconds before the Spotlight had ended – because of the IF time lapse – and if you got it wrong there would be a nasty limp with nothing on the screen.

Baird's hope of replacing both the IF and the Spotlight system with a viable electronic alternative to the Marconi–EMI Emitron rested with the Farnsworth camera. But this became less and less a realistic proposition. Although Bairds had had the Farnsworth for a year, it was still in an experimental state and had only one trial at Alexandra Palace. It was operated by John Bliss who, because the camera had a poor viewfinder, had to press his face close to a black cloth that was the only barrier separating him from several thousand volts and instant death. In the event he was deafened only by loud bangs and suffered a burnt ear. Percy:

> The Farnsworth was a supreme desperation sort of thing and we brought it up to Alexandra Palace in the last days when everything else was going wrong. We showed it to people, everybody laughed and we took it home again.

Lawson:

> I think the rest of the Baird group rather laughed at this rather Heath Robinson thing of Farnsworth's. It was certainly very erratic. It never seemed to work the same twice.

But the Baird system was not all disaster. Intermediate film was an adaptation and extension of their telecine technique. It failed because of the method and quality of production and not because of the quality of the telecine machine itself. Percy:

> On film we could beat 'em – even on 240 lines at twenty-five frames a second. Although I say it myself, our telecine pictures at Alexandra Palace were very very good and much better than theirs.

Telecine – the method of showing 'cine' film by 'tele' vision, was Baird's most successful operation and one that he'd worked on since about 1930. Despite the occasional black lines across the telecine picture, the result of dirt in the disc holes, Baird telecine pictures were of very high quality. Percy:

> With our straightforward scanning device with no electronic storage, nothing except a photocell, we had a perfectly square, plain, beautiful, clear picture. By comparison, in the early days, the EMI telecine was really shocking, bloody awful.

All that EMI could do to provide a telecine picture was to try to adapt one of their electronic studio cameras and point it at the gate of a standard film projector with the film travelling at the rate of twenty-five frames a second – the same rate as television pictures are built up. If the film was bright then the pictures were reasonable. If the film was dense then they were terrible.

Although the Marconi–EMI telecine was a weakness in their system, the system itself was their strength because, unlike Baird's, it was complete, it was standard, it was integrated. It also worked. Percy:

> After the first week, although EMI had trouble with their telecine, the studio stuff was great and, unlike us, they never really broke down. And the first time I saw their picture in their control room – the camera was pointing out of the balcony window over London and smoke was rising from the Muswell Hill chimneys – the thing was so peaceful, so calm, no noise, nothing at all that I thought, 'Well, this is it, you know, pack up and join the navy.'

There were four Emitron cameras – lighter than television cameras have ever been since and comparatively portable. Three were in regular use in the studio and the other was spare. Two of the cameras were mounted on 'iron men', iron pedestals which could be raised or lowered by turning a handle, and on top of which was a panning head on which was mounted the camera itself. One of these cameras was positioned centrally in the studio to cover the main action and was made completely mobile by being mounted on a film dolly, a simple run truck, that could be pulled and pushed around. The other camera, to cover the action 'in the wings', could be moved, with difficulty, on four small castors. The third camera, mounted on a tripod, was more or less fixed for the announcer but, after a week, was replaced by another iron man to make mobile the entire camera complement. Although flexibility in the early days was more theoretical than real, it was built into the system and increased production values enormously. The edition of *Picture Page* transmitted on the opening day, 2 November, on the Baird system was a static, visually unexciting show restricted by the IF technique to two basic shots from virtually the same angle. The first *Picture Page*, transmitted as a test on 8 October on the EMI system, was, in comparison, fast moving and visually interesting because of three cameras offering several different shots from several different angles.

With Bairds, the action had to come to the camera. With EMI, the action could still come to the camera but, and this was the crucial difference, the camera could go to the action. With Bairds, the system dominated the producer. Madden:

> In the Baird studio, you could only do your producer's work at rehearsal and then, during transmission, just had to sit back and wait.

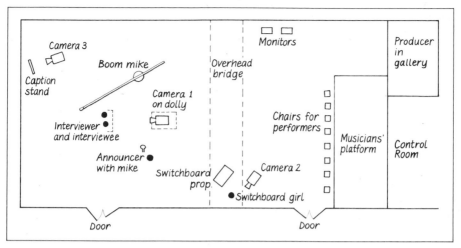

Alexandra Palace EMI Studio, January 1938, arranged for *Picture Page*.

With EMI, the producer could dominate the system. *The Times* explained his role:

> The producer is the linchpin of every item and his control tower, separated from the stage by darkened plate glass, is the most significant place in the studio, for it shows the technical complexities and the difference between television and other forms of entertainment – stage, screen, or sound broadcasting. The producer sits next to the window, looking at two frames. One frame shows the image in course of transmission: on the other he can switch the field of vision of any camera on the set. Beside him sits the production manager, whose functions are similar to those of a stage manager in the theatre (the stage manager of television is on the set taking notes). In front of the producer sit the sound engineer controlling total output and the sound mixer selecting and cutting it. Behind him is the key man, the vision-mixer. The platform also holds the sound engineer as a roving wing forward, another man in charge of the gramophone and a junior engineer logging the programme.

> (*The Times*, February 1938)

Apart from an increase in the number of picture monitors, the separation of sound and vision into different rooms and added sophistication all round, the studio gallery was to remain essentially the same in fifty years' time. But the EMI system was not without problems. The lack of a proper viewfinder on the camera was a serious drawback: a focusing spyhole, perfectly adequate for a camera under test in a laboratory, was quite useless in the studio and the problem was only solved when EMI constructed a viewfinder that had to be clapped to the camera side. The fact that the image seen by the cameraman remained upside down and back to front was something to which he quickly adapted.

Another useful refinement that was missing from the early cameras was a light that would indicate which of the three cameras was 'live' or, indeed, whether a camera was on or off. The cue for a performer to start talking to a particular camera was given by a thumbs up sign from the cameraman. Occasionally the signal wasn't given at all or, when it was, could be misinterpreted by the uninitiated. Mitchell:

> Robert Speight was playing the Archbishop of Canterbury in Eliot's *Murder in the Cathedral* and he said, 'Leslie, I can't tell you how I loathe you for bringing television into my life. It's the most terrifying thing I've ever done. When are we on?' And I said, 'Wait a minute, it's coming up in due course' and the cameraman stuck his thumb out. Robert thought he was making a rude gesture and gave him an Admiral's signal back. And that was the first sight the audience had of the Archbishop of Canterbury. Made a striking beginning to any programme.

Performers were instructed not to make other elaborate gestures, especially in close-up. Dinah Sheridan:

> You never turned your head sideways otherwise your nose would stick out like Pinocchio and no gestures straight towards the camera; in fact, no gestures at all because if the camera was slightly out of focus it would cause the image to balloon.

Other problems included fading, camera matching, red sensitivity, and the seemingly continuous problem of 'tilt and bend'.

Fading between cameras was slow but not impossible. It only became a problem when producers wanted to fade fast and so asked the system to do something it wasn't designed for. However, producer demand often led to technical improvement. Over a period of months, the BBC and EMI engineers reduced the eight-second time lapse that had wrecked Chilton's leap in *Here's Looking at You* to four, to about two, though the 'cut' was not finally achieved until after the war.

Camera matching was a problem caused by the fact that each camera tube was handmade and so differed from every other tube in colour response, sensitivity and length of life. In practical terms this meant that when they were new or just returned from the laboratory after being reconditioned they were particularly red-sensitive; red clothing seemed to disappear along with red lips, red props, red anything and caused problems for make-up, costume, design, and the engineers.

In addition, one camera picture might be bright whilst the picture from another camera might be much less bright and cause the picture brightness on the home receiver to be constantly changing. And, whilst some tubes might last 200 hours, another might last only ten and begin to die during a transmission. Mitchell:

> You'd get a tired camera which would suddenly give you grey hair without your knowing it. Or a flower would turn suddenly white.

'Tilt and bend', the electronic phenomenon that caused the picture to 'shade' across the display screen from light to dark, was a problem that the EMI laboratories had worked on for three years. It was still not solved but methods to control shading were built into the system. 'Racks', named because of the racks of equipment involved, controlled each camera's performance.

There were five knobs for each camera – one for camera matching and four for 'tilt and bend', two 'tilt' controls (frame tilt and line tilt) and two 'bend' controls: each control feeding in black to overcome bright sections of the picture or white to overcome dark. Bridgewater:

> You stood or sat sideways to this bank of equipment and turned the knobs and looked to the right to see the screen and the results you were producing on your monitor. And once you'd neutralised tilt and bend, the brilliance was wrong so you turned another knob to bring it to the right level. And then, if the picture changed at all, or the lighting, or you changed to a different camera, you, or another engineer, had to turn your hands to a different lot of controls for that second camera. There was a lot of operational know-how to be acquired and it was always difficult and was, in fact, never fully overcome with that design of Emitron.

Although the Marconi–EMI system rarely broke down completely, it was often a close-run thing. One play, produced by Dallas Bower, began transmission with four cameras. Greenhead:

> The first camera broke down and while I was trying to repair that, the second one broke down and then the third one so that poor old Dallas was left with one camera. Gradually we got the others back into action but all this was going on while the programme was live and that really gets the adrenalin working.

And replacing the camera tube was not easy. Bridgewater:

> You had to change the tube inside the camera and the tube didn't just drop into place like putting a lamp bulb into its socket. It was a very dangerous operation and we were terrified of breaking these tubes which were reputed to be insured for £600 each. They came from EMI in very large crates in a bag in the middle attached by springs all round to the sides of the crate so that they were suspended. And you brought the crate into the studio, right up to the camera and then very gently lifted the tube out, held it until somebody took out the old tube and then the new one could be put in.

Tubes were hired by EMI to the BBC, not sold, and at the outset there was great difficulty in maintaining supply. It was a hand-to-mouth existence where Greenhead would return tubes to McGee at the factory for reconditioning whilst, at the same time, new tubes were made on an embryonic production line. The new tubes were put on test and 'Cat's-Eyes' Watson checked the results:

> I could see better when I went round at night time: which tubes were failing, which had failed and which would go forward and eventually we got a better vacuum and a better coating on the tube and failures became less and less.

Frequently, new or reconditioned tubes had to be raced to Alexandra Palace in the afternoon for broadcast use that evening but it's McGee's proud record that throughout the period of broadcasting from Alexandra Palace 'we managed to avoid a single occasion when a programme was not broadcast because of tube failure.' But there were plenty of other causes of breakdown. Bridgewater:

Breakdowns are written on my heart. They could occur at any time during transmission and usually did. The main transmitter valve could go; the connections on the camera could fail; the camera cable, subject to heavy mechanical stress, could become loose, even snap; the vision control equipment could fail or the resistors could overheat and because everything was so new there were no spares, no back-up equipment. So we often had to use soldering irons which frequently caused as many failures as they repaired.

By comparison, technical problems with sound were minimal. Sound was familiar, vision was not and on many occasions engineers worked much of the night and all of the morning, right up to transmission and even beyond, to get the system as fully operational as it could be. Despite the breakdowns, despite all the tensions and frustrations associated with the new medium, the unanimous verdict of engineers, producers and performers was that the Marconi–EMI system was better than Baird's. Greenhead:

It was obvious to all concerned that the inflexibility of the Baird system, from the Intermediate Film technique, cutting into the actual telecine unit and then cutting into the little interview studio, meant that it couldn't go on like that, compared to a complete flexible, all–electronic system which could fade or switch from studio to film to OB and back again. To us it was only a matter of time.

On 30 November 1936, within a month of the Official Opening, the Baird premises at the Crystal Palace were consumed by fire; offices, workshops, equipment, spare parts. Baird wrote in his autobiography: 'It occurred at the most awkward possible time and interfered seriously with our transmissions from the BBC.' Alan Lawson:

It was devastating really. It took the stuffing out of the Baird Company completely. That was really the end. It was probably fortunate for them that it did happen. They may have recouped some of their losses. I don't know. But all the back-up had gone. All one's stores, all one's work back-up had just gone up in smoke.

But worse was to come. On 6 February 1937 it was announced that the television service would continue on the Marconi–EMI system only. Mrs Baird:

John took this blow philosophically. What else could he do? I don't think perhaps he expected anything else. He was very upset but he didn't show it very much because by then he had his own laboratory built in the house where we lived and he had two assistants working on colour and telescopic television. He was always terribly interested in his own work.

Despite the slump of Baird Company shares on the Stock Exchange, the end of transmission was, for the Ostrer Brothers, owners of the company, a blessed relief. Transmissions had done nothing but lose the company money and it was now free to concentrate on the manufacture of television sets and the future of big-screen television in the cinema. For the production teams and engineers at Alexandra Palace, if their hearts were with Baird, their heads were with EMI.

Whilst they had sympathy for the Baird technicians they had no regrets at the demise of the system. Madden:

> It had been like playing with clockwork when we'd already got electricity. The bloody thing just wouldn't work. We couldn't get rid of it quickly enough.

Even the Baird technicians had to agree. Jim Percy had been with Baird for eight years:

> There was no stopping the advance of that flickerless, tireless, inertialess electron camera. We lost because we were backing a horse that could not run. . . . People have suggested that we lost because of the Crystal Palace fire but the fire had nothing to do with the failure of the system. It occurred when we were about to be chucked out anyway. It was a very Wagnerian end. A nice end. A sort of firework display.

Baird's participation at Alexandra Palace had cost Baird and the BBC a great deal in money, time, effort and emotional energy. Should Baird have been allowed to compete at all? Percy:

> The Television Advisory Committee were mad. They'd seen both systems and anybody who had any modicum of sense would have said, well, for crying out loud, tell Baird he's had it. They were technically incompetent.

Birkinshaw:

> If it had been merely a technical decision, I think the country might well have started with the EMI system alone. But with Baird, after all the publicity they'd received and after all the prestige he got, rightfully, for being the first person to produce a television picture, it would have produced a terrific political row not to have had Baird in on it.

The Selsdon Committee didn't publish their private deliberations, only their report, and on the technical merits of the two systems they merely stated that both 'had operated experimentally over wireless channels for some time past with satisfactory results.' But the kind of political as opposed to technical discussions they must have had was presaged in the Private and Confidential minutes of a meeting between the BBC and the Post Office as early as 21 April 1933:

> 'In conclusion, Mr Phillips said that the Post Office were afraid that if the Baird Company were prevented from installing high-definition equipment, questions would be asked in Parliament and in the Press which would be difficult to answer and the Post Office mainly, and the BBC to a lesser extent, would be blamed for the inevitable bankruptcy of the Baird Company. The latter would be bound to distort the facts leading to the decision to install another maker's apparatus. The Post Office wanted to protect themselves against any such trouble, and this was the real reason for their anxiety that the BBC should afford the Baird Company, rather than any other firm, facilities for research in television of the high-definition type.'

Mr F. W. Phillips, Assistant Secretary, General Post Office, was later a member of the Television Advisory Committee chaired by Lord Selsdon. His view, expressed forcefully eighteen months before, was the view that prevailed. The decision to install the Baird system at Alexandra Palace was entirely a political one.

The Baird Company was finally placed in the hands of the receiver in 1939. Baird himself spent much of the war working on television systems for 3D colour and, on 14 June 1946, was demonstrating big-screen television at the Classic Cinema, Baker Street. He died four days later. He was 58.

Baird was a man who had a childlike delight in making things work, a man who had almost as much pleasure from getting a note from a toy nightingale as he had from achieving Noctovision. Dora Jackson (Baird's secretary, 1932):

> He had a lot of people go down to his house at Box Hill and he wanted to impress them with the nightingales. But they only sang when they felt like it so he said to me, 'Do you think you can get me an artificial nightingale?' I wasn't surprised at anything he could ask for . . . so I went to Selfridges and they gave me this little tin can and Baird set it on top of this lovely board-room table blowing frantically and nothing happened. Then he got hold of a carafe of water and poured some into the can, blew it and this beautiful note came out. He was absolutely delighted. Little things like this pleased him intensely.

He was a man obsessed by the notion of invention. Dora Jackson:

> He used to dictate masses of provisional specifications . . . used to get very enthusiastic about things – the chaps would go and build machinery, experiment a bit, then he'd go off in another direction.

He was a man who was, in the words of his own son, 'the last of the inventors to work alone in an attic.' He was not helped in his work by his need for publicity nor by his city friends interested in making a quick buck out of television, but Baird ultimately failed because he was a mechanic and not a scientist.

He was slow to recognise the importance of ultrashort waves. He was even slower to recognise the need for cathode-ray tubes and an all-electronic system. He could have overcome his lack of scientific knowledge by employing academic consultants, by employing scientists straight from university, by collaborating with another firm. He did none of these things. He hugged his invention tightly to himself and by the time he had neither the money nor the expertise to continue and was approached in 1932 by Marconi, the Ostrer Brothers turned Bairds down. Baird wrote:

> If we had joined Marconi, we should have been with this combine, not against it. Our policy of facing the world single-handed was sheer insanity.

Baird produced 178 patents. They show, says Professor Burns, 'that he was a most sound and capable inventor', but opinions about Baird's television achievement range from the vitriolic: 'a fraud . . . an inventor who didn't invent anything,' to the condescending: 'a crank but a charming man'; from the frank: 'a man with the ingenuity to overcome problems that didn't exist,' to the poetic: 'a man of vision,' to the pixillated: 'the father of television.' There are other opinions. P. P. Eckersley, the former Chief Engineer of the BBC who rejected Baird in 1928, wrote, thirty years later:

> Baird is to be honoured . . . among those who see past immediate technical difficulties to the eventual achievement . . . he had that flair for picking about on the scrapheap of unrelated discoveries and assembling the bits and pieces to make something work and so revealing possibilities if not finality.

Jim Percy worked with Baird from 1928 to 1937 and, later, was a government consultant on underwater radar:

> He was right at the end of the mechanical age. He thought in terms of wheels and sprockets and devices that spun round. He really wasn't with the electronics age at all. He hardly knew how a cathode tube worked. He hadn't got the technique, he hadn't got the knowledge, he hadn't got the genius. But he created a demand because he proved that television worked even if it worked badly. He accelerated the television age. If it hadn't been for Baird shouting and yelling and putting his crude 30-line pictures all over London, we wouldn't have had television in this country before the war. He demonstrated that television *could* be done if not the way it *should* be done.

Tony Bridgewater worked with Baird from 1928 to 1932 and was Chief Engineer of BBC Television from 1962 to 1968:

> His contribution was to show the possibility of television. To get it going and to get it known, to interest the BBC. He was a stimulus, a catalyst and, as a personal achievement of course, it was pretty stupendous to get it going at all.

There are three giants of television in Britain – Campbell Swinton, Isaac Shoenberg and John Logie Baird: Swinton, the man who conceived the all-electronic system; Shoenberg, the man who led the team that turned Swinton's conception into reality; and Baird, the man who gave television publicity and provided the first picture. That Baird clung to his mechanical system was his mistake and his personal tragedy.

10

TELEVISION COMES TO
LONDON (1)

A lot of people wanted us to open small and do tiddly little items and I said: 'This
is absolute nonsense. The thing to do is to open big. To open as you really intend
to go on.' Go for bust. Really show them what you can do – fast.

(Cecil Madden)

Cecil Madden, Programme Organiser, was a member of the Programme
Board, the group of men who decided what programmes should be done. The
board met weekly and its other members were Gerald Cock, Director of
Television; Leonard Schuster, his administrative assistant and money man;
Douglas Birkinshaw, engineer in charge; and Donald Munro, Production
Manager:

We had to have as much variety in our output as possible in order to interest the
public. To achieve a balance in the week's programmes.

In the first week the programmes included a ballet, a play, several talks which
ranged from a bus driver describing how he'd made a model of the *Golden Hind*
out of matchsticks, to the artist John Piper describing pictures and sculpture
from forthcoming exhibitions; numerous demonstrations which included
champion Alsatians, zoo animals, prize chrysanthemums and boxing; several
variety and light music shows – Bebe Daniels and Ben Lyon in *Starlight*; the
BBC Dance Orchestra directed by Henry Hall with the 'Three Sisters', Molly,
Marie and Mary, and *Cabaret* with singers, a comedian and an impressionist,
plus British Movietone News and 'in co-operation with the Air Ministry, a
chart will forecast the weather'. It was a programme mix taken over largely
from radio except that the emphasis was, naturally, on the visual and not the
verbal – the demonstrations and the ballet would not have been done on the
wireless. Madden:

It was all a scary rush at the time and was probably the weakest run we ever did
but it was as good as we could do, remembering the limitations – especially of the
Baird studio.

The week proper began on Monday night after the afternoon's Official
Opening. It began with a programme announcement from the Spotlight Studio
and ended with the filmed British Movietone News from telecine but the major
offerings were *Picture Page* and the BBC's first filmed documentary, *Television
Comes to London*:

In this film, specially taken for the BBC, viewers are given an idea of the growth of the television installation at Alexandra Palace and an insight into production routine. There will be many shots behind the scenes. One sequence, for instance, will show Adele Dixon as she appears to viewers in the Variety at 3.30 this afternoon and will then reveal the technical staff and equipment in the studio that made this transmission possible.

(Radio Times, 2 November 1936)

The final sequences of the film were directed by Dallas Bower and filmed by James Carr, but the man who started the film was the 'film assistant', Bill Barbrook. Major Barbrook, retired army officer and friend of Gerald Cock, was the head and only permanent member of the BBC Film Unit. It was rumoured that he'd got the job because he had his own film camera and his first attempt at film documentary was, in its execution, decidedly home movies. Munro:

Bill had been up on the roof of Alexandra Palace while the mast was being built, filming the construction. No sound of course. He had the film developed and then came down to my office in Portland Place and said: 'We've got to get music for it somehow.' I went through the library and got out Dvořák's *New World* symphony. So there we were in this tiny little office about 12 by 10 feet, Bill with a hand projector churning out the film he'd shot and me with a portable gramophone trying to fit it in. We projected onto the wall, too, there wasn't even a screen. That was more or less how we began at Alexandra Palace. Improvisation.

It was a modest film, only fifteen minutes long, but it was in the documentary tradition of John Grierson who had recently completed *Industrial Britain* (1933) and *Night Mail* (1936). It was a tradition that the BBC was, after the war, to continue with thousands of filmed documentaries; a tradition that helped distinguish the British movie industry from Hollywood's and which was to help distinguish British television from American.

As significant in terms of its own future and the precedents it established was the main 'live' offering of the evening, *Picture Page.* A visual version of radio's *In Town Tonight*, it was devised and edited by Cecil Madden and produced by George More O'Ferrall. Billed in *Radio Times* as 'A Magazine of Topical and General Interest', it was exactly that – 'a magazine which would be topical and interesting and really could have anything in it that we wanted.' Munro:

It was an extremely simple programme from the production point of view. There was no scenery, just an interview programme – but it was entirely personality. There'd be one thing in each programme that would interest at least one member of the public, even if it was a performing dog.

The show opened with a boy bugler from HMS *Warspite* standing against a Union Jack background and accompanied by a signature tune, 'Red, White and Blue', played on record by the Jack Hylton Band. A picture book, on which was engraved the show's title, slowly opened, the pages turned and the music changed to 'Song of Surrender', the personal signature tune of Joan Miller who, smiling in white smock, was revealed seated at her telephone switchboard with earphones on her head and telephone plug in her right hand. She spoke to an imaginary caller:

> BBC Television. This is the switchboard of *Picture Page*, a topical magazine introducing visitors, types and personalities. You want to see who? Miss Kay Stammers? . . . Just one moment, Miss Stammers is coming into the studio now.

Joanie juggled her plugs and:

> You're through. You're looking at Miss Kay Stammers, the celebrated tennis player.

And the camera panned, as it was the Baird system, to find Stammers with Leslie Mitchell in lounge suit, for the afternoon, or evening dress for the evening, ready to begin the interview. 'You're through. You're looking at . . .' became television's first catch phrase. The programme was transmitted twice on the same day each week, was thirty minutes long and had as many as eight interviewees all introduced by Miller at the switchboard. The device of the switchboard was brilliant in its simplicity. It provided programme identity, programme continuity and, whilst the switchboard itself was a dummy, when the EMI system was in use the headphones were real and provided a vital link between Miller and the programme director in the EMI studio gallery. Miller:

> Sometimes when I was about to put a guest through, I would hear the director's voice saying, 'Sorry Joan, that camera's broken down, we can't go through yet. Keep talking.' And so I became an expert ad-libber. In fact I think Leslie and I were the best ad-libbers in London. Finally, the director would say, 'All right. Go through Joan.' And I would announce the guest and always had to say, 'You're through. You're looking at Pipe Major Matthews. The bagpipes man from Trafalgar Square.' Or 'Harry Haines, the muffin man.' Or 'The Pearly King of Blackfriars, Mr and Mrs Tinsley,' or 'Pam Barton, the golf champion.' There were hundreds and hundreds. But sometimes they'd tease me and say we'd broken down when we hadn't – just to see how well I could talk.

Miller was a young Canadian actress who had come to London in 1934, understudied Greer Garson and, introduced to Cecil Madden, had been asked to write for him. She produced a heavy article on voice culture:

> 'Oh,' Cecil said, 'but I wanted something for a variety show.' I asked him to let me try again and that was how I wrote my first comedy sketch, 'Grand Hotel – Good Morning', where I was supposed to be a very tough American switchboard girl, quite different from the *Picture Page* girl, but that put the idea of the switchboard into Cecil's head. And when, on the first day of the show, I came into the studio and asked him what I should wear he looked round and his eye lit on the technician's overall and he said, 'Wear that.' And that's how I got my white coat.

Improvisation again, and so, too, were Miller's announcements. She was given her script first thing in the morning by Madden, wrote her own lines only to change them on transmission as breakdowns occurred or subjects were introduced into the programme at the last minute. But always the same ending:

No. I'm sorry. There's nothing more today. Call again next Thursday. Goodnight everybody. Goodnight.

And 'Red, White and Blue' played over the credits. Madden:

> She was a good actress. Very resilient. She was an unknown but we wanted to make our own stars if possible. And with Joan, we made a star.

The first real 'star' of television.

> Dear Madden,
>
> I would like to drop you a line of congratulation on your *Picture Page* last night. I thought it was simply excellent. Indeed, it gave the impression of a big show, the standard of which you would not be able to keep up.
>
> Although personal opinions in the matter of what are and what are not good items are usually valueless, I would like to say that the fellow telling the ghost story was probably the best item (he was extremely well lit). Next, I would put the costers and K. Stammers. Jim Mollison looked as if he were suffering from 'having had several' but was, of course, of interest from the publicity point of view . . . anyway, my hearty congratulations on an excellent show.

The memo was signed by R. T. B. Wynn, the Chief Engineer of radio, and praise from radio, who were highly critical of the upstart television service, was praise indeed.

The *Picture Page* transmitted from the Baird studio on 2 November 1936 and billed as 'first of a series' was, in fact, the second. After the test transmission to RadiOlympia in August the entire television service was ready for off. Their sense of frustration at not being able to continue was shared by the correspondent of the *Daily Telegraph* who argued that, to maintain interest in television, 'it is essential that some regular schedule of tests should be adopted immediately.' More specifically, he argued that, for a regular service, 'animated lantern lectures, footling interviews and unexciting variety turns will not be good enough. Novelty appeal will soon pass. What then?' The BBC's answer was a series of hour-long test transmissions from 1 October which culminated in the first edition of *Picture Page* transmitted on the Marconi–EMI system on 8 October. The *Daily Telegraph* critic was elated:

> *Picture Page* . . . was a brilliant success. It set up fresh standards in television entertainment and presentation. Production, for the first time in direct television, approached cinema standards of efficiency, with the essential difference that no 'cutting' or retaking is possible. . . . Mr Cecil Madden, the editor, and Mr George More O'Ferrall, the producer, have found the secret of successful television programmes – human interest, a rapid tempo, frequent 'close-ups' and no overcrowding on the small screen.

On the show were Squadron Leader Swain who had just regained the world altitude record for Britain and 'showed watchers the special suit he wore and the visor he cut open to get air'; John Snuggs, 'the street performer known as "The Troubadour"'; Mrs Flora Drummond, the suffragette 'who wore the regalia that in 1908 earned her the title of General Drummond'; Ras Prince Monolulu, 'the racecourse character', and a sixteen-year-old model called

Dinah Sheridan, 'discovered' on the train from Kings Cross to Welwyn Garden City:

> I was studying at that time at a stage school in London and my sister and I and a lot of other students used to catch the 5.10 train home every night. We were almost like a club and woe betide anybody else who got into our carriage. And, one day, a poor benighted man got in, sat in the corner and suffered as we flicked cherry stones all over the place. When I got home the telephone rang. My mother answered it and came and said, 'There's a man says he's the one who was sitting in the railway carriage and would like to speak to you.' And I thought, 'Oh, God, he's going to complain about the cherry stones.' But, no. He said, 'My name's Leslie Baily. Would you like to be on television?' He got three guineas for getting me and I was paid two guineas for being got.

Picture Page, unlike a radio programme, was only assembled on the day and frequently late in the day. This in itself was a television breakthrough and made the old radio hands nervous. Madden:

> We did it by a series of scouts who were sort of journalists. They had to produce the person, contact me and ask whether I wanted whoever it might be – some famous novelist or someone who had just arrived in town, and I'd look at the balance of the programme and would say 'yes' or 'no'. It was a day and night job, of course, a few phone calls back and forth in the middle of the night to say that someone was on a plane. And a scout, by bad luck, might have only one item whilst another might have five or six. But it worked out and my little team of scouts were marvellous.

Amongst them, as well as Leslie Baily of *Scrapbook* fame, were Mary Benedetta, S. E. Reynolds, John Gardner, Dorothy Cannell and J. E. Cannell, a former scout for *In Town Tonight* who wrote, 'London characters for television are found by chance meetings, walks through markets and leisured exploring of byways. They must have exceptional intelligence and, above all, a good memory to face a scriptless performance before half a dozen dazzling lamps.'

Scripts were written by the scouts and handed to interviewer and interviewee. Sheridan:

> I had to learn it. It was absolutely cut and dried. But I wasn't allowed to hold a script as you do in radio. I had to learn it entirely by heart, which wasn't very easy and I do remember the producer saying to me, 'Now loosen up a bit, relax, don't sound so studied.'

On 9 December, Leslie Mitchell interviewed the pianist Eileen Joyce. It is a classic of unlooseness:

> *INT.*   Well, Miss Joyce, we're very pleased to see you back in England again. Did you enjoy your Australian tour?
>
> *E.J.*   I enjoyed it very much indeed, but you know I really went there to have a nice long holiday and see my people.
>
> *INT.*   Instead of which you never stopped playing.
>
> *E.J.*   Yes, three public concerts which were broadcast, every week. I was so busy I was five days in Sydney before I caught a glimpse of the harbour!

146

	And in New Zealand I didn't even see a Maori – or the hot springs.
INT.	Anyway, we heard you had a wonderful reception out there.
E.J.	Yes, it was rather overwhelming. You know, it was a funny thing in Australia, my concerts were packed with women and most of my fan letters were from women. The men weren't a bit interested. They just weren't musical. But in New Zealand all the fan letters came from men and they were mostly men in the audience.
INT.	How amusing. But which of all the many places you went to did you like the best yourself?
E.J.	Tasmania by far. It was like fairyland. I shall never forget drifting down the Tamar river in the early morning with forests each side of us and everything perfectly still.
INT.	It sounds lovely. And now you're here Miss Joyce, won't you please play us something?
E.J.	Yes. I'd love to. Well now, what about playing you that attractive Viennese waltz by Friedman. I played it a lot in Australia and they seemed to like it very much out there.
INT.	Oh yes. Please do. What is it called?
E.J.	It's 'Viennese Waltz No. 3' by Friedman and arranged by Gartner.

There followed a three-minute recital. Mitchell:

> Nobody had ever had to interview people in front of cameras before. Nobody could tell you what to do – they didn't know. To have to say something interesting at all costs to an unknown number of people through the camera was a terrifying beginning. One had no idea whether one was being good, bad or indifferent; whether one had said it properly; whether it couldn't have been better expressed; whether people were saying, 'What a fool. What's he up to?' There was no sympathetic urge coming out of the audience. You were talking into a void and exposing your lack of talent. I was absolutely paralysed with fear. And people said, 'You talk too much Mitchell.' Of course I talked, I was nervous and when somebody stopped talking I knew the show had to go on. So, the technique I employed was the technique I was taught at school. Be polite to strangers, be helpful, be interested, listen – as well as talk. I was confused by having to cut the interviews down to seconds but I had one advantage. I was enormously interested in other people as well as myself, in the reactions of people and I have enough sympathy not to be beastly to them. And I gave them confidence fast and they relied on me. And then, to try to inject some spontaneity, I played my only dirty trick on them which was to ask them the questions in a different order from the one we'd rehearsed, to make them think about what they were saying. Otherwise they'd just say 'yes'.

By January 1937 the scripts for interviews were, as Mitchell's experience and technique improved, less and less formalised. Mr J. E. Lewis, Captain of the English Amateur Soccer team, had six questions put to him, four of them unscripted, and he was left to answer entirely for himself. Mitchell:

> I took a very nasty, unwarranted decision, that I would do the interviews as far as possible with nothing except an indication of what they were going to talk about. Outstanding points that I shouldn't forget. I came to the conclusion that it was possible to do better without a written script and I still think so.

Mitchell's technique, born of experience on *Picture Page*, became the standard technique for the television interview. Mitchell became popular, another home-grown 'star' for Madden. But Mitchell, officially a BBC announcer, was requested to follow the BBC radio precedent and remain anonymous. At one point it was suggested that Mitchell, whilst doing his interview, should remain out of vision.

> I had a note from someone important saying, 'In future you will be known as "the male announcer".' I was so angry about this because I didn't think it was necessary to point it out as the other two were very female. So I arranged that anybody I interviewed from then on should say: 'As Mr Mitchell was just saying. . . .' And nobody could stop them and I became known as Mr Mitchell. I'd got an identity.

By April 1937, the show had reached its fiftieth edition. During that period, and giving an indication of the voracious appetite of the new medium, Miller had introduced and Mitchell interviewed 430 men, 230 women, twenty-five boys, seven girls, five accompanists, one horse, three monkeys, a parrot, a mynah bird, a cat, five dogs, a rat, twenty-three mice, Guy Fawkes, a tailor's dummy, the ghost of Alexandra Palace and a silkworm. 'The most consistently successful of all television programmes,' said the *Daily Telegraph*. 'It gets better and better.' After the eightieth edition *The Observer* agreed: 'Full of interest . . . not a dull moment. It always gives us two or three items of more than usual interest but this time every shot was a bull's-eye. Particularly good were the Bantu university professor and the taxi-driver who had just returned from a trip to John o'Groats.'

As the show stretched into its second year, deadlines became tighter. Mitchell:

> The characters would turn up and you wouldn't know who they were or what they were. For example, I interviewed a woman – English, but a funny little thing, and I said to her, 'I gather you've been in China quite a long time?' And she said: 'Yes, I have.' And I said: 'And you've come back after a long time? What were you doing?' And she replied, 'Oh, I was teaching.' And as she spoke there was this terrifying bond springing up between us because she was helpless and I was anxious to be helpful and I asked her the only thing I'd been told about her. I said, 'I gather you sing "Onward Christian Soldiers" in Chinese. May we hear it?' And she did and I said, 'That was absolutely charming, thanks.' What nobody had told me was that that little woman had taken four hundred people over the Chinese mountains and had films made about her – Gladys Aylward.

The decision to interview the rival skippers of the Oxford and Cambridge boat race was taken after *Picture Page* had actually gone on air and the two men were rushed by car from the West End to Alexandra Palace to become the last item in the programme. Madden:

> The regular producers all looked on *PP* as a slightly backward step because they wanted to do whatever they were engaged for – plays or music. And to have to do *PP* they didn't much like so all the other chaps were always applying – production assistants mostly – and it trained them. It trained the whole staff

because everybody was watching everybody else and saying, 'Well, I could do a bit different, or better.'

Film became a regular ingredient, a clip being used, for example, to introduce a famous tennis player or racing driver, but better or worse visuals from experimenting trainee producers couldn't damage the basic format. *Picture Page* remained the 3Ms show – Miller provided the charm; Mitchell, the professional expertise and, now scriptless, the spontaneity; and Madden maintained the invention and provided the essential enthusiasm. And, because the show was live from the studio, there was always the excitement for the viewer of anticipating the unusual, the unexpected, of things going wrong. Mitchell:

> Cecil had invited onto the programme a lady elephant and her three children. They came up in the lift, a pantomime in itself, and stood in a row facing the main stage on which a lady soprano gave her all in a rendering of something with very high notes in it. And when she reached the top note, Mum looked at her children and then started to pee and all the children started to pee too. This is not necessarily very peculiar but we had a small number of guests invited to watch the show. They were right behind the elephants on steel chairs with no protection. And they were awash, all sitting with their feet up on the chairs trying to get away from the flood.

Animals were a regular safety net for *Picture Page*. Mitchell was successively chased by a cheetah, almost raped by another in full view of the cameras – 'What a fool I am,' said the owner, pulling the animal off, 'he's never been mated, you see' – and badly frightened by a python. Mitchell:

> I was a little conscious of the fact that it was looking for a tree to bash me against but I showed it to the cameras and then moved over to the lady beside me and she suddenly shrieked, 'Oh. Oh,' and I couldn't think what it was, but the python had done all it knew all down the lady's feet and shoes and ankles and the woman was a foot deep in whatever the python was getting rid of. And I said, because I couldn't think of what else to say, 'I'm terribly sorry.' And she said, 'Isn't it funny. They only do it every three months. It would be tonight.'

The unexpected and the unpredictable were not confined to animals.

> I was interviewing somebody in another part of the studio when Cecil came up, waited until there was a pause, and then whispered, 'Can you interview the Grand Vizier of Morocco?' I finished the interview and then said: 'What did you say?' Cecil said: 'Grand Vizier of Morocco. He's here for the Coronation.' I said, 'Does he speak English?' Cecil said he didn't know and left. And I was left at the wrong end of the studio. I couldn't see where the young man was; no idea what language he spoke and had no Spanish and only schoolboy French. So I decided the thing to do was to brazen it out. And I went in search of him and there he was sitting with a scimitar in a very magnificent carved chair they'd found for him and a long beard and all the Eastern fittings. He looked at me, smiled and I looked at him, my eyes crossing as the cameras came over and I asked him in French whether he would like to say a few words on television. And he said: 'Ha. Ho,' and some other gobbledegook. So then I motioned to the cameraman, got

him over to my side and said to the viewers: 'His Excellency asked me to convey to viewers his deep appreciation of the kindness shown to him on his visit to London where he is, of course, for the Coronation and he's found the experience of being on television most interesting and thanks you all.' And then I went in search of Cecil whom I was going to kill. And he said: 'What the hell went on? Did you go mad or something?' And I said, 'Well, it was a bloody silly thing to ask me to do. The man didn't even speak English, spoke no French. Nothing. I was left to make a bloody fool of myself.' Cecil said: 'Several times he said to you, Leslie, "Voulez-vous posez moi la question?" ' I said, 'He certainly didn't say *that*, whatever else he said.' And I've never quite forgiven Cecil and he's never quite forgiven me. But that was half the charm of live television – what goes slightly wrong. And people liked it because they saw me getting out of difficulties I imposed on myself.

Not all interviewees were animals or jokers; not all interviews were unserious. Among the heavyweight personalities were musicians Henry Wood, Wilhelm Furtwängler, John Barbirolli, Dame Ethel Smyth; actors like Tyrone Power, Ray Milland, Leslie Howard and Charles Laughton; writers W. H. Auden, George Bernard Shaw and James Thurber; photographer Frank Capra and doyenne of the theatre Lilian Baylis. Even after two hundred editions, the reviewers were still marvelling at the show's 'unfailing vigour': 'and not the least amusing turn was Leslie Mitchell interviewing himself with the aid of a gramophone record.' L. Marsland Gander, in the *Daily Telegraph*, commented:

> *Picture Page* is the oldest television programme still going strong and it has the youngest arteries of any. Perhaps the first *Picture Page* in October 1936 will one day rank in history with Marconi's first transatlantic transmission for it marked the beginning of television as a serious rival to other entertainments. I shall remember that opening programme as one of the outstanding events of a lifetime.

Over forty years later and with the benefit of hindsight, Gander could still see *Picture Page* in much the same way:

> It was all slightly amateurish by comparison with the modern product but *Picture Page* was really and truly remarkable at that time. A tremendous triumph and achievement.

So why was it so successful? *The Listener*, after the hundredth edition, wrote:

> . . . the real merit of the idea is that it gives us a succession of little shows so brief that even if some items are not so entertaining as others, they pass too quickly for us ever to grow bored.

Fifty-six editions later, *The Listener* wrote again:

> The fact remains that a great many of those who compose television's audience are known to like their mental diet supplied to them in small mouthfuls; they are like very young children who must be fed spoonful by spoonful. So while the greater part of the programmes sent out from Alexandra Palace consist of good wholesome meals, there are certain periods allotted each week in which the entertainment is regularly spoon-fed.

In July 1939, still in *The Listener*, Grace Wyndham-Goldie wrote what was to be the programme's pre-war obituary:

> . . . part of its success is due to its extreme superficiality, to its refusal to demand any sort of concentration and to the fact that standards by which it is ruled, and they are applied to Cabinet Ministers and performing elephants alike, are a mixture of news value and entertainment value. Now *Picture Page* is one of the few topical programme series which reflects English life. So the dangers of these standards and of this superficiality are obvious enough. Should they be avoided by altering *Picture Page*? I do not think so. But I do think that we should have more programmes which are equally topical but which are ruled by other standards and which reflect English life from an angle less superficial.

She concluded:

> *Picture Page* is, in fact, a kind of high-speed television circus. There's something of everything and nothing for long.

Picture Page was the most popular regular programme on pre-war television. In terms of the development of television production in Britain, it is important because, with its signature tunes, its catch phrases, its speed and variety, it established a pattern whereby its philosophy of 'something of everything and nothing for long' became the hallmark of every successful daily magazine programme ever since.

In the first years at Alexandra Palace, television transmission was limited to ten hours a week – two hours a day, an hour in the afternoon from three to four o'clock and an hour in the evening from nine to ten o'clock. There was no transmission on Sundays. The programming emphasis, if there *was* an emphasis, was on entertainment. *Here's Looking at You*, the BBC's first television show, was a variety show. The first programme on the opening afternoon was called, simply, *Variety*. Saturday nights on television became a variety ghetto. Madden:

> We had such frightfully good entertainment available to us. There were shows going on in all the London nightclubs and a great deal of money was being spent. Henry Sherek ran the Dorchester cabaret which had troupes of girls coming over from America with wonderful routines, very fine band parts and stars changing all the time. The Music Corporation of America had the Grosvenor House; Cochran ran the Trocadero. There was a cabaret, an artist or two in every place – Quaglinos, the Windmill, the Ritz – everywhere. Of very high class. The sort of people we really wanted and so we were able to draw on a great deal of ready-made entertainment without having to do an awful lot of rehearsing ourselves. And, in most cases, we were able to engage bands and conductors as well.

Capitalising on the available talent, Madden produced *100% Broadway*, in which every artist was from the USA or Canada:

> I remember one comedian in particular, David Burns, and when I went back to New York, years later, there he was with Carol Channing in *Hello, Dolly!* The talent was so very good – there hasn't been such talent since.

Another light entertainment show was *International Cabaret*, reviewed by the *Daily Telegraph*:

> Sherkot, the silent comic, was once again highly amusing in this bill but I like none of his other efforts so well as his goal-keeping to orchestral accompaniment: it is a classic among burlesques.

Also on the bill were the Knife-Throwing Denvers. Madden:

> Most of these Saturday-night shows were now an hour long and so you would need two or three hours' rehearsal during the day – particularly if you've got the Denvers – and I've never forgotten one Saturday when Cock said to me: 'Cecil, you've got those knife-throwing Denvers again!' And I said: 'Yes, they're very good. They're the best.' And he said: 'Well, it's very dangerous. I don't want the newspapers having a scandal you know and it would all be your fault.' He'd really got me scared that there would be an accident and so, in some panic, I went down to the door where the artists were arriving in one of our coaches that brought them from Broadcasting House and the girl had a terrible bandage on her foot. And I asked them, 'How did that happen?' 'Oh,' he said, 'we've been sleeping a bit rough lately.' So, I thought to myself, 'You haven't booked the top act.' Anyway, when we got into the studio, I said to him: 'Look I get very worried by your throwing all these things at rehearsals because, after all, you're going to do it all again at night and we all know where you're going to throw it.' They always start with the knives and end up with the hatchets. And I said to him: 'I'd much rather you didn't do it at rehearsal, just show us the positions so I can get my cameras lined up.' And he said: 'Oh, I must do it. I have to do it. I can't not do it. I've got to have the practice.' I was frightfully worried there'd be an accident and Cock would say 'I told you so' and I'd get the sack.

In the event, there was no accident but the irony, for the home viewer, was that the act could hardly be seen at all. The *Daily Telegraph* (3 April 1937):

> Unfortunately, on the small screen, the act is not so terrifying as on the music-hall stage. Dextrous knife work is necessary to show off the hair-raising thrills of knife throwing round the human target. However, when it comes to the spectacle of throwing choppers blindfold at one's wife, concealed behind a sheet, perhaps television is merciful in its imperfections.

Programme allowance for all shows for the entire week was just £1000. It was intended to pay for artists and writers and William Streeton, the booking manager, informed all producers that no star could be paid more than £25. Madden:

> I said 'That's ridiculous. How are you going to get the best people in the world for £25?' and he said, 'You've got to cut your coat according to your cloth,' and rang off. And the next call came from Sophie Tucker, the great American-Jewish star, and Sophie said: 'Cee-cil, I gather you're running television programmes. Ted Shapiro and I would like to be the first American stars to be on your programme. Is that OK?' So I said: 'Sophie. It's OK.' Then she said: 'But I've heard a rumour that nobody's going to be paid over £25.' Now Sophie was playing two shows a day at places like the Palladium as well as appearing at the Grosvenor House and the money she was making was tremendous. However,

there was prestige to all this and I said, 'Well, Bebe and Ben are very anxious to be the first.' And she said: 'Tell you what. Ted and I are two people. We'll do it for £40.' And she duly did.

Fortunately for television, television itself was a draw. Production Manager, Donald Munro:

> It was amazing the interest theatre and film people showed in this new medium and a great many of them gave their services free, weren't paid at all. They'd get expenses and perhaps a car would be sent for them. That's all.

As well as Sophie Tucker there was Joe E. Brown, Larry Adler, Adelaide Hall, Fats Waller, Carroll Gibbons, Gene Autry, Maurice Chevalier, Elisabeth Welch, Ivor Novello, Beatrice Lillie, Stanley Holloway and an up-and-coming Vera Lynn plus the older hands who had already appeared on 30-line television like Arthur Askey, George Robey and Gracie Fields. Munro:

> Gracie had organised a trip with a special train from Wakefield to bring a lot of old age pensioners and gave them a day out in London. They were given a 'Yorkshire' tea in the great hall at Alexandra Palace and we had Gracie in front of the screen to do an act. Didn't cost us anything. She was there anyhow.

Stars who'd made their name on radio, like Jack Jackson and his Band, began to work on television:

> *Jackson:* Ladies and Gentlemen, I can't tell you how thrilled we are to be working on this television programme.
> *Cooper:* We're thrilled to be working on any programme.
> *Jackson:* This is Jack Cooper folks, and, as you can see, he's not a bit shy although he comes from very shy parents. In fact, if his parents hadn't been quite so shy he might have been three years older! What are you going to sing?
>
> (script of *The Show Goes On*, 13 Nov. 1937)

As well as using established stars, television began to make the names of comparative unknowns – like Cyril Fletcher:

> I lived quite near to Alexandra Palace in Friern Barnet and very frequently things would go wrong there – there'd be a thick fog and the bus wouldn't go from Broadcasting House and reach AP in time and they'd ring up and say: 'Cyril, we need you for ten minutes.' And I would go and do ten minutes of the odd odes and they kept a special little coat for me there, a sort of bandboy white evening dress.

The experience of performing on television could be quite traumatic. Fletcher:

> It was all very difficult because all over the floor were enormous cables which you kept tripping over and so you were placed in a particular position. Perhaps your first sketch would be nicely placed in front of a camera where the studio audience could see you but your second might be placed in some horrible little corner where the studio audience could hardly see you at all. So, they might hear a few strange voices coming from that corner but as for them appreciating the comedy, the glorious little piece of comedy you were doing – impossible. For a comedian,

audience reaction is essential and when there's no reaction possible a lot of people began to appear a little unfunny on television.

Another young man beginning his career was 'and Partner'. Nick Long Junior and Partner were appearing at the Grosvenor House. Long was a tap dancer who needed a break between routines and began to employ a young comic to cover his intervals. 'And Partner', speaking English in Cairo and Istanbul to an uncomprehending audience, devised, in desperation, an audience participation act that involved him saying a word twice and getting the audience to repeat it. It became his stock in trade and it was 'and Partner' who shared an Alexandra Palace dressing room with Cyril Fletcher:

> I thought he was marvellous in front of the camera – and he was so miserable. He said: 'I've come all this way from America and they don't understand me. They won't stand for it.' His name was Danny Kaye.

Even Mr Middleton the gardener was drafted into cabaret. The *Daily Express* (23 March 1938) reported:

> Mr Middleton has been forced almost into this new departure. Because, for months now, that very celebrated humorist Nelson Keys has been 'taking off' Mr Middleton in televised cabaret performances. Mr Keys appears in mildewed slouch hat and a decrepit coat saying, in a depressed voice, 'These thistles are doing nicely today. Add a little fish manure at the earliest opportunity. So nice for the neighbours.' A few days back Cecil Madden wrote to Middleton saying – wouldn't he like to get his own back. And Middleton, to everyone's surprise, agreed. He will be featured as Nelson Keys taking off C. H. Middleton. And he will carry a dead cat . . .

Keys usually appeared in the appallingly named *Tele Ho!* 'One day,' said the *Daily Mail*, 'the literature of television will include "An Anthology of Television Titles" – a glittering record of producers' attempts to give each programme an original touch at the outset,' and cited *Café Continental, Coffee Stall, Queue for Song*, and *Time to Say Goodbye*.

There was an exuberance, a freshness about television because it was new and because it was live. Anything could happen – usually on *Picture Page* but not always. Ivor Novello was booked for *Composer at the Piano*. Madden:

> He appeared at Alexandra Palace and sat down at the piano and suddenly coachload after coachload started arriving at the front door. People emerged in their, well, hundreds. And we said to Ivor, 'What's all this?' 'Oh,' he said, 'I'm getting a little help from my friends.' He'd brought the entire cast of *Glamorous Night* from Drury Lane – at his own expense.

Experience taught that whilst anything might still happen, certain ground rules could make it less likely. For example, don't book an act you've never seen; don't quarter performing sea-lions in dressing rooms with bath as it frightens the actors and, if you have birds in bird shows, hold on to them. Madden:

> A toucan got out of somebody's hand and flew up to the lighting bridge. And when anybody crawled along the bridge to get it all it did was to move away and

go on making those dreadful noises. Hours of rehearsals went by and they still couldn't get the toucan down and we had to open the evening with it still up there – making those frightful noises all through the tenderest love scenes of the day's play.

Experience also taught that certain forms of light entertainment were ideal for the small screen. The Jacquard Puppets, Scott Gordon's Marionettes and Colin Gray's Glove Puppets were the precursors of Andy Pandy, Muffin the Mule and the Flower Pot Men. Ideal, too, were cartoons. *Cabaret Cartoons* was a monthly show in which Harry Rutherford stood in the wings and drew the act performing for the cameras. He worked quickly under countdown instructions from the producer in the gallery and finished his sketch at exactly the same moment as the performer with an exact copy of the performance.

Combining the two techniques, the drawn cartoon that animates as a puppet, were the film cartoons from Walt Disney. Disney approached the BBC in 1936 when the entire film industry was opposed to television and the Corporation were desperate for films of any kind. Disney offered two Mickey Mouse cartoons a day – one for each transmission. At a stroke, Disney had not only broken the unofficial embargo and provided the BBC with quality material but, unawares, had solved a problem that at the time was of paramount concern – the problem of turn-round time. With two separate items in the studio for each transmission and, for various different reasons, only one studio available, it was essential to have a film break after the first studio item in order to prepare the studio for the second. Fifteen minutes was essential for 'turn-round'. The filmed News provided ten minutes, Disney now provided the extra five. There was no formal contract between the parties. Madden:

> We had a special relationship, the BBC and Walt Disney – and still have – long after he's dead. And nobody ever knew what debt we really owed him.

Almost fifty years later, Disney is still going strong on television – along with magazine shows, variety and all the rest of light entertainment. But, between 1936 and 1939, almost equally strong on the box were drama, opera, ballet and talks.

11

TELEVISION COMES TO LONDON (2)

Once we'd got the Opening over – with its Variety show and *Picture Page*, I was very anxious to do three things in the first week – a full play, a full opera and a full ballet. And it seemed impossible that we'd get all three. We got the play *Marigold* from the Royalty Theatre with the whole London cast. We got the Mercury Ballet – Madame Rambert has always been available and wonderful and offered her ballet. And the third thing, the most impossible of all, was an opera. Now who would have thought that there was an entire opera getting ready for Covent Garden which, for some extraordinary reason, had got held up and the dates changed? It was an English opera by Albert Coates, called *Pickwick*, with very big stars and this whole production was lying about waiting to be given a date for Covent Garden. We got them in first.

(Cecil Madden)

In 1936, there were only five producers for the whole television output. In addition to Cecil Madden who, as well as being programme organiser, produced variety programmes, there was Cecil Lewis (talks); George More O'Ferrall (drama); Stephen Thomas (music – including ballet and opera) and Dallas Bower (opera and film). Thomas had had theatre experience with C. B. Cochran and Sir Nigel Playfair and Bower had produced and directed a film version of du Garde Peach's well-known radio play *The Path of Glory*. These 'famous five' were soon joined as de facto producers by stage manager Harry Pringle and the man with overall responsibility for wardrobe, make-up, scenery, design and staffing, the production manager D. H. Munro. Although each producer was contracted to produce programmes for a particular programme area, in practice they had to cross borders and produce almost anywhere.

Providing the most obvious 'balance' to the light entertainment output was Talks and, after Cecil Lewis left the BBC in 1937, they were the responsibility of the first woman television producer, Mary Adams. (By 1939, there were still only two women producers amongst twenty men.) Talks, for the most part, were 'Home Service serious'. Amy Johnson, the aviator, Rebecca West, the writer, or J. B. Priestley, the dramatist, appeared, for ten minutes, 'Speaking Personally'. Commander King-Hall and Leslie Hore-Belisha gave the background to current events and, although some of these talks could be little more than visual radio, they were all conceived for television.

John Hilton illustrated his talk entitled *The Declining Population* by means of charts and diagrams – to have a baby in the '30s was an act of patriotism – and

John Piper in *Eye of the Artist* introduced the work of a 'young, unknown sculptor, Henry Moore', by having a piece of sculpture in the studio. And it was the imaginative approach of Mary Adams that called for a studio filled with gas cookers wrapped in bicycle tyres to enable Kenneth Clark to demonstrate the art of the Surrealists.

Peppering the memoranda of Talks Department were the terms 'high', 'middle' and 'low' brow. Whilst Clark and Piper were 'highbrow', certainly 'lowbrow' were the talks designed for the do-it-yourself addict, often involving Jasmine Bligh as a passive onlooker or actual hod-carrier. They weren't especially successful. The *Daily Telegraph* complained (24 Nov. 1936) of the boredom of watching a man for half an hour explaining how to replace a broken windowpane. But these talks quickly developed into more entertaining features where much of the enjoyment came from the personality of the presenter.

Cooking and gardening, both televisual, became popular viewing and Marcel Boulestin, the Television Cook, and Mr Middleton, the Television Gardener, both 'firsts' in a long and continuous line of television cooks and gardeners, became extremely popular personalities. So, too, did David Seth-Smith, the Zoo Man. And television became quickly aware that the 'performer' is as important in 'talks' as in variety and that who presents a subject is as important as the subject presented.

'Talks' were comparatively easy and cheap to produce; much more complex and expensive was 'Drama' which, after light entertainment, was the biggest area of production. Madden:

> The basis of television has got to be something which really involves the writer and I coined a phrase, 'a play a day', and, in those three pre-war years we actually did a play every single day. Which is quite a thing.

In two and a half years, BBC Television produced a total of three hundred and twenty-six plays, all 'live' from the studio. They ranged from Shakespeare to Sheridan, from Shaw to Synge and St John Ervine. Two hundred and sixty-seven were British, twenty-seven of them by J. B. Priestley, 'who was most interested and came and chatted and had tea on numerous occasions in the production office', and fourteen were specially written for television. Although the bulk of the drama output came from cut-down versions of the classics or abbreviations of current successes in the West End, and rarely lasted more than thirty minutes, not all plays or productions were 'safe'. Dallas Bower put *Julius Caesar* into modern dress as Hitler was strutting the stage of Europe. Eugene O'Neill's *All God's Chillun*, about a black husband and white wife, is controversial now and was even more controversial then. And few European or American television stations today would put on the Habema Theatre's full-length productions of *The Dybbuk* and *Uriel Acosta* – in Hebrew.

Lured to Alexandra Palace, not by the money – there wasn't any – but by the opportunity to do plays that they might not have the opportunity of doing elsewhere, were many of the leading performers of the day. Greer Garson, mammoth star of the West End, came to perform Sheridan's *School for Scandal*, Shaw's *How He Lied to Her Husband* and an enormously ambitious

157

production by More O'Ferrall of Flecker's *Hassan* which included the original Delius music. Robert Speight did *Murder in the Cathedral* and Ralph Richardson did a now forgotten play by Priestley, *Bees on the Boat Deck*. Trevor Howard, James Mason, Michael Redgrave and Sybil Thorndike were happy to learn new parts or even to recreate present successes for the sake of the new medium. Laurence Olivier and the great Australian actress Judith Anderson were appearing in Lilian Baylis's production of *Macbeth* at the Old Vic. Baylis offered the play, directed by Michel St Denis, to television. Madden:

> She banged on the door of Olivier's dressing room at the Old Vic during rehearsal and said, 'You're all going up to Alexandra Palace to do television.' Olivier was absolutely mad. 'I'm engaged,' he said, 'to do *Macbeth* in your theatre and nowhere else.' However, none of us were really daunted by this and More O'Ferrall was sent to do the presentation; Streeton was sent to do the contracts. He rang up Judith Anderson – a very difficult actress. He said: 'I understand you're going to be our Lady Macbeth?' 'What,' she said, 'gives you that idea?' 'Well,' he said, 'we will send a shooting brake to Broadcasting House for the artists to take them to Alexandra Palace so they don't have any trouble.' 'Trouble!' she said, 'I've never heard anything so disgraceful. The idea of Lady Macbeth in a shooting brake? *If* I come, which is very unlikely, I shall take a taxi from where I live: I shall go to this place in north London and you will be on the doorstep with money in your hand and you will pay the taxi. Otherwise I really don't see how you can do *Macbeth* without Lady Macbeth.' Then Lilian Baylis died. She actually died and I think if she hadn't died there would have been a blow-up and it wouldn't have been performed. But, as everybody respected her memory it became possible for everyone to make the gesture. Olivier came. Anderson came. Cruikshank came. And a wonderful cast and production. The whole of *Macbeth* for – £75. 'Total', it says on the contract, 'to include certain props.'

The first play presented was *Marigold*, on 5 November 1936, a 'Scottish comedy of rare charm by L. Allen Harker and F. R. Pryor'. It starred Sophie Stewart. It wasn't a new production but merely a representation by George More O'Ferrall of 'scenes from' the West End original. It lasted a mere twenty-five minutes but, although it was a theatre production, the actors were not allowed to give just a theatre performance. On 3 November *The Times* had complained of the 'broad gesture' affected by certain BBC announcers and continued:

> Now, more than ever in ordinary broadcasting, the television artists will have to remember that their audience is not the public one of music halls and theatres, but of the average private house.

The actors in *Marigold* were shown how to contain their performance and be conscious of the camera close-up. In this they were helped by the restrictions of the Baird system – one camera, always in the same position, and few close-ups – but for the actors in the first play done on the Marconi–EMI system, *The Tiger*, on 23 November, the problems were greater. Here the actors had to cope with three cameras. They needed to be aware of which camera was taking the picture, which might be taking the close-up, be in exactly the right prearranged position to deliver a particular line as well as delivering it in a natural but, for them as stage performers, wholly *un*natural way. Here was a whole new technique of acting – a technique different from stage, different from film, different from radio which first had to be evolved and then learnt. A process that made Robert Speight 'so frightened I can't even talk' and Greer Garson 'absolutely scared to death'.

Mitigating against good performances was the short amount of time available for rehearsals. Bower:

> We were always up against this frightful problem of inadequate rehearsal time and one could easily find oneself going on the air with the last act of a play, for all intents and purposes, technically completely unrehearsed. One would just shoot it off the cuff. It made for the most terrifying strain. Beyond belief.

Alexandra Palace was actually on air for only two hours a day but the same areas used for transmission had also to be used for every other necessary activity – routine maintenance of equipment as well as rehearsals for cameras, lighting, scenery, costume and, of course, actors and producers. For the benefit of actors, early rehearsals of a play were taken either at Broadcasting House or the BBC Studios in Maida Vale – but it wasn't enough. An abridged version of *Othello*, for example, had only two hours' rehearsal in the studio – almost half of which was taken up by marking the positions of the actors with yellow chalk on the floor. The actual camera rehearsal of the play was limited to little more than the hour that the play was going to take to perform and the actress playing Desdemona, whilst she knew her lines, had never seen a camera or stood on chalk marks before. As a result, said *The Times* (5 Feb. 1938):

> She had little enough time to learn how to act 'into' the camera or master the art of two-dimensional gestures. (A lovely movement of appealing arms stretched towards the camera misses its effect if the arms leap out of focus into the semblance of marrows.)

In March 1938, with the advent of television on Sunday, regular performances were given by Birmingham Rep. They did a new play each month and, on the second Sunday of each month, beginning with Shakespeare's *Henry IV Part I*, the entire production was transferred from Birmingham to Alexandra Palace where duplicate sets were waiting for it. Drama expanded further with the introduction of serials and comedy series. The first serial was *Ann and Harold*, starring Ann Todd, and the first comedy serial was the unprepossessingly titled *Percy Ponsonby's Progress* which featured Charles Hyslop. But the main achievement of BBC television pre-war drama was to have produced, with little experience and less money, so much and of so high quality, to have made television drama important and to have achieved 'a play a day'. Madden:

> But on no account have a play on Guy Fawkes' night. The studios were not soundproof and the locals all used to come up and throw in their squibs and crackers to bust up our production. They just loved doing it.

Ballet had been part of television ever since Tony Bridgewater's sister balanced on a table in Baird's dark studio at Long Acre. Now, eight years later, it was to become an even greater part, and for the same reason – ballet is quintessential television: vision and sound, movement and music. It was television's good luck that the start of the service coincided with the first great flowering of an English ballet tradition. Marie Rambert, trained by the maître de ballet of the Diaghilev company, had founded her own ballet school in London at the Mercury Theatre. Her aim was to train English dancers and English choreographers and the performance in the first week of television in the Baird studio began with a work by Frederick Ashton to music by Peter Warlock. The rest of the twenty-five-minute programme was more traditional but had an explosive effect on Marie Rambert's rival. Madden:

> I was immediately rung up by Lilian Baylis, 'What's all this about the Ballet Rambert? I've got the best ballet in the world. The Vic-Wells. You can have my ballet as much as you like. Ninette de Valois, the administrator, will fix up all the details.'

Job was the first Vic-Wells ballet. It was televised on 11 November:

> The dancers were almost overcome by heat. They rehearsed and gave two performances on the same day under terrific lights and by the end of the evening the temperature on the steps leading up to heaven rose so much that the unfortunate barefooted angels ascending and descending thought they must be heading for the other place.
>
> (Mary Clarke, *The Sadler's Wells Ballet*, 1955)

Job was followed by twelve other ballets which included *Les Patineurs*, *Carnaval*, Ashton's *Checkmate*, Ninette de Valois' *Rake's Progress*, Walton's *Façade* with Walton himself conducting, and dancers like Fonteyn, Helpmann, Ashton, the company that was to emerge as the Royal Ballet.

At least a dozen ballet companies appeared at the Alexandra Palace – Franco-Russian and American as well as British: the Ballets Russes de Monte Carlo and Buddy Bradley's Sepia Chorines as well as the Covent Garden Royal Opera House ballet and an incredible line-up of world-famous dancers, including Markova, Baronova, Toumanova, Dolin and Fokine. Many of them were produced by Donald Munro:

> The early days consisted of the Vic-Wells people doing things like *Façade* and *Carnaval* – very straightforward. The Russians were rather more ambitious and one of the most interesting programmes I ever remember doing was a completely unscripted, unrehearsed programme of the Russians at rehearsal. Just a bare studio with one or two odd bits of scenery and Arnold Haskell, the famous ballet critic, in front of a studio monitor to do a running commentary. The cameramen were in certain positions: one on a low tripod, one overhead in the gantry and another on a tracking dolly and it was shot completely off the cuff. I think it was one of the most successful programmes I ever did.

The press agreed. 'Most admirably produced,' said the *Daily Mail*. 'The air of informality was highly refreshing and well sustained.' 'One of the most successful television programmes so far broadcast.' 'The kind of experience one can only get from television.' And it continued:

> In television, as in painting, the art of composition within a rectangular frame plays a vital part. When we are watching a film the projection is too big for us to notice very vividly whether figures and background are well composed. But on the smaller television screen, composition affects our appreciation of the picture more than we may know. The television producer must handle his subject almost as though he were working on a canvas, though his task may be harder because he is dealing with living figures and changing patterns and forms.
>
> (*The Listener*, 7 July 1937)

For Munro, the choice of picture was instinctive not intellectual:

> I'd see an attractive picture on one of the cameras and I'd say to the vision mixer, 'I'll take that one.' And we'd go over to it.

Ballet was as fortunate in its producers as the producers were in the ballets and their performers and, by the summer of 1937, ballet, according to *Radio Times*, had 'established itself firmly as an important part of the more serious side of television programmes.' So, too, had opera – if not quite so successfully.

There was no tradition of opera-making on television and no strongly emerging national opera company that television could easily draw on. And, because it lacked the movement of ballet, opera was not so suited to the small television screen. *The Times*, reviewing Albert Coates' new opera, *Pickwick*, on 14 November 1936, dismissed it as having little more than curiosity value:

> These doll like marionettes let forth at us immense voices while the orchestra had to be content with a comparatively modest place in the background. Then, too, owing to the small area of vision, the drama is inevitably cramped.

In other words, the studio as well as the television screen, at 10 by 8 inches, was too small, the singers didn't know how to project for the cameras and the sound engineers hadn't learnt how best to place their microphones to give the correct balance between singers and orchestra. The review continued:

> But when the experiment of broadcasting opera is likely to be repeated and when adjustments are made . . . it will be possible to get something of the stage action as well as the music into operatic broadcasts. Even then it will remain, as all broadcasting still is, merely a substitute for the real thing.

Pickwick was produced by Dallas Bower:

> I didn't regard it very seriously, frankly, because it wasn't an original production of mine – it was somebody else's production and we simply took it and broke it down and put it onto the stage at Ally Pally and reduced it all slightly, necessarily, because the stage was so much smaller, and there you were.

The transmission lasted twenty-five minutes and the orchestra was conducted by the composer.

In the first year of television opera, productions were small scale – mostly of chamber opera like Blow's *Venus and Adonis* or eighteenth-century ballad opera like *The Beggar's Opera* by Gay. But as confidence mounted so producers attempted 'proper' opera which culminated in the most elaborate pre-war production, the entire Act 2 of *Tristan and Isolde* billed in *Radio Times* as 'a masque to the music of Wagner': a 'masque' because the production attempted to overcome the perennial problem of finding singers who both look the part and can sing. It was a problem peculiar to opera and exacerbated by television where the closeness of the camera destroyed any illusion that a young boy was anything other than a plump, middle-aged woman. Stephen Thomas had found a solution in his production of *Hansel and Gretel* at Christmas 1937, where he employed actors to mime the actions to the singers' out-of-vision sounds. Jane Vowles sang Gretel and a child actress, Muriel (*Doctor in the House*) Pavlow, played her. It was extremely successful. Bower used the same trick with *Tristan* on 24 January 1938. Basil Bartlett and Oriel Ross had their actions choreographed by Anthony Tudor whilst Walter Widdop and Isobel Baillie sang. That the production was only a qualified success was not the fault of the device. Lionel Salter commented that it was 'one of the least eventful acts in all opera and one which later producers hesitated to produce at all.' Bower, experimenting, deliberately matched his direction to the pace of the action – or, rather, inaction. Whereas a modern production might average five shots a minute, Bower used only one every two minutes, that is just thirty-six shots on a sixty-four-minute transmission, and the final result was, visually, funereal.

Opera producers had a remarkably heavy workload. Stephen Thomas produced, in June 1937, Act 3 of *Faust*; Act 3 of *La Traviata*; Gay's *Damon and Phyllida* (twice) and the next month repeated Gay on 13 and 15 July, and produced Alfred Reynolds' opera *Derby Day* no less than four times: a total in two months of four different productions and ten performances. Whilst some operas were presentations of stage productions, others were productions especially for television and, for Christmas 1938, the BBC commissioned the first opera specially designed for television, Spike Hughes' *Cinderella* with Gwen Catley as Cinders. Altogether, in two and a half years, thirty operas were produced on television – twice as many as today when, overall, television time is twenty times as great. It was a phenomenal achievement much mocked by the boys in light entertainment. Their especial target was the sophistication (or pretension) of Glyndebourne which, in Harry Pringle's *Cabaret Cruise*, was 'sent up rotten'.

Accompanying the opera and ballet as well as variety and even *Picture Page* was the Television Orchestra – perhaps the most versatile orchestra ever assembled. Bower:

> I remember one evening when in the first part the orchestra accompanied a splendid cabaret entertainer called Hildegarde and in the latter part accompanied Piatigorsky playing the Haydn cello concerto. And Piatigorsky, Hildegarde and I returned to London in the car and Piatigorsky was absolutely staggered. He said: 'I find this really quite extraordinary that such an orchestra can take on this degree of difference in what it's doing over a period of two or three hours. Quite extraordinary.'

When Gerald Cock was looking for a man to assemble an orchestra for television, he consulted Adrian Boult. Boult recommended Hyam Greenbaum. Greenbaum had been second violinist in the Queen's Hall Orchestra under Henry Wood when he was just sixteen. He played in the Brosa Quartet, was pianist for Diaghilev, was musical director for C. B. Cochran's revues and for the recording companies Decca and Vocalion. His wife was the harpist Sidonie Goossens:

> He was such a talented musician, everybody respected him. Willie Walton and Constant Lambert came to him for help all the time. I've got it written on one of Lambert's scores where he says to 'Bumps', 'I think you wrote more of this work than I did.' He and Willie Walton would sit up all night long writing music for a film that Willie couldn't get on with and they'd work at it together. I would feed them with coffee and benzedrine to keep them awake. He was behind all the musicians of his day but he always wanted to conduct symphony orchestras.

Greenbaum was able to hand-pick his own players: mostly orchestral players like the leader Boris Pecker but good showmen, too, like the drummer and percussionist Gilbert Webster 'who could do all the stunts with cymbals and drumsticks' and a young viola player called Eric Robinson. A total of about twenty-five musicians were augmented for large-scale opera after it was discovered that the orchestra was too small for *Pickwick*. Bower:

> Coates was extremely amusing because we were absolutely horrified when 'Bumps' and I looked at the score. We found all sorts of things we couldn't manage. We went and saw Coates and he said: 'Oh, I don't know. Doesn't matter in the slightest.' 'But, Mr Coates, there's a contrabassoon.' 'Oh my dear fellow, leave it out.'

Greenbaum was a perfectionist: a man who became increasingly irritated by the day-to-day demands of the less serious side of television; a man whose real interest lay in orchestrating and playing Pergolesi's opera *La Serva Padrona* or Busoni's *Arlecchino* or Puccini's one-act *Gianni Schicchi* and not in providing a backing group for light entertainment. The television orchestra was a symphony orchestra which, on most days, was asked to behave as a dance band. Munro:

> They could do everything. They did Pogo the Horse, three beeps and a bump but could play Wagner beautifully. Antal Dorati who guest conducted congratulated us on our very fine orchestra. And he wasn't the only one. But what equally amazed me was that a television orchestra had been approved at all in the pre-war days. It cost a bit of money and Broadcasting House cut back on everything else. An orchestra must have seemed a luxury but maybe radio thought an orchestra was the kind of civilising thing that television should have. And this one was exceptional. The same orchestra would split up and do jam sessions.

Eric Wilde and his Teatimers was formed by Dallas Bower from the main body of the orchestra. It was led by Wilde, the orchestra's first trumpet, driven by Gilbert Webster's drumming and soothed by Eric Robinson's second instrument, the guitar, and performed on afternoon television in front of a huge cardboard cutout of a teapot. In an era of great dance bands it was one of the best bands around. Bower:

> Greenbaum was a remarkable man and a superb musician. Had he lived there's no doubt whatever he would have become one of the Number One conductors.

But Greenbaum died a frustrated and disappointed man at the age of 41 from an illness that was aggravated by overdrinking. He was perhaps television's first alcoholic casualty.

Not all music on television was supplied by the television orchestra. Other orchestras gave performances – the BBC Symphony, Henry Hall and the orchestra of Lou Stone when, on 21 May 1937, from the enormous stage of the Coliseum to the tiny confines of the Alexandra Palace studio was transferred, cast, chorus and musicians, the entire Rodgers and Hart musical *On Your Toes*. But the action, of course, had to be confined. The studio simply wasn't big enough.   Lack of space at Alexandra Palace was as big a problem as lack of time. Jonah Barrington in the *Daily Express* described another transplanted show, Cochran's *Round and Round*:

> The efficiency with which the producer Donald Munro put over a full-size cabaret in a studio several sizes too small left me gasping. Cochran's young ladies had to crawl under wires to their places, there was not enough room for a large orchestra, no room whatever for an audience. Picture it. The floor a mass of cables. One small space under glaring hard lights for the artists. Everybody not being televised out of the room to save space. Jasmine Bligh motionless before the camera – every facial feature etched in glaring relief. Someone blows a whistle. Confusion subsides. Bligh starts speaking. The young ladies danced in. Miraculously they did not tread on each other's toes. Snappy, singing, juggling, toe-tapping. Show runs like clockwork – and with only ninety minutes rehearsal. Under-staffed, short of money, short of rehearsal, short of space – yet Alexandra Palace has a big lead over Broadcasting House for entertainment.

'Lack of space and time,' wrote *The Times* (5 February 1938), 'has severely hampered the efforts to transform television from an ingenious toy into serious entertainment.' For some productions, the restrictions were monumental. Bower:

> It was an absolute nightmare. There wasn't enough room for anything. Everything was always bursting into the passage. There was no room to move. It was very difficult indeed – particularly for ballet.

The *Radio Times* commented on the compression forced on the Vic-Wells ballet production of *Le Spectre de la Rose*, 24 September 1937:

> Had Petroff's leap been on a Covent Garden scale he would probably have been out of range of the cameras and he certainly would have hit the walls of the studio very hard.

It was also very difficult for opera where the orchestra was at one end of the studio and the principal singers at the other and cameras, lights and microphones in between with the chorus frequently concealed behind the set. It was not possible for everyone to follow the conductor's beat and so an assistant conductor had to be stationed strategically to relay the signal. Lionel Salter:

> This involved his darting from one side to another so as not to be always in the singers' eye-lines (at all costs they should not be seen to turn their heads or eyes aside), leaping over cables and other obstacles and remembering camera positions so as not to get into shot, even conducting prone through a fireplace on one occasion – all the while casting frantic glances over his shoulder to check unanimity of ensemble with the conductor.

In the first three months of transmission there was, in effect, only one operational studio – either Baird or Marconi–EMI. With the demise of Baird, an extra studio became available for rehearsals but the Baird studio was not immediately converted to the EMI system and, as late as January 1938, a whole year after Bairds had ceased operation, the Baird equipment was still in position. As productions became increasingly ambitious, space – even utilising both studios, one for production and one for rehearsals – was still not enough, especially when almost two-thirds of one studio was occupied by the orchestra alone. Birkinshaw:

> The area of the studio was 2100 square feet. It was not enough for them. They even went out to use a corridor, placing palace guards and barricades at both ends so that nobody could come along. And even into a dressing room taking the cameras that were mobile on long leads. But I got the feeling that even if we'd given them the Albert Hall they wouldn't have been satisfied.

In the autumn of 1938, the old Baird studio was refurbished and refitted with Marconi–EMI equipment. It was no longer an annexe to Studio A but a fully operational, electronic studio in its own right.

With two studios available, there was twice the space and twice the time for rehearsals as well as the opportunity to use both studios at once. Bower's production of *Tristan* was the first, with the orchestra and plump singers in one studio and the miming actors in the other. Munro used both studios in vision for his production of Acts 1 and 3 of the Vic-Wells *Sleeping Princess*, 25 March 1939:

> We used the two studios for continuity – there was no space in just one studio for a complete change of scene. Act 1 was done in Studio A, Act 3 in Studio B – with no interval.

It also enabled Munro to use models and combine them with live action:

> In the *Sleeping Princess* there's a transformation scene, walking through a forest, and it was done with a tiny little model of the princess asleep in her bed. We had a fixed shot on the model and then superimposed the live action – using the two studios simultaneously. The models were in A and the action in B. It was all experimental and it came off.

It was a device described in *The Bystander* as 'an innocent deception that saves the producer from constructing cumbrous and expensive scenery.' In 1933, in the literally dark days of Studio BB at Broadcasting House, two dancers like Genée and Dolin could scarcely be seen in picture together. Now, six years later at Alexandra Palace, *The Sleeping Princess* showed sixty dancers in vision supported by eighteen players of the Television Orchestra. It was an indication of how television and television ballet had expanded and progressed.

Since February 1937, when the Baird system was dropped, producers no longer had to concern themselves so much with the limitations and vagaries of the technology but were free to concentrate on the kind of picture and the kind of production they wanted. They were free to plan, to plot, to evolve procedures, to learn the possibilities of the new medium. Bower:

> We were intensely ambitious, there's no doubt whatever about that and as it was something entirely new there were no procedures at all so that we had to establish procedures very early on. Before we arrived there were no people at the BBC who had had any experience really, certainly not of the cinema and very few in the theatre and such planning as had been done at Ally Pally was entirely in terms of a curtained stage – a theatrical as distinct from a film approach.

The 'theatrical' shooting method devised in a hurry by Cecil Madden for *Here's Looking at You* where the cameras processed down stage as a succession of curtains opened to reveal the next variety act was not, on his own admission, the way to make television. 'It was never used again.' Nor was it possible to adopt a film approach as film and television were essentially different. In film, one camera records the entire action which is then repeated and recorded by the same camera from different angles but with the Marconi–EMI system of television there were three cameras operating simultaneously, producing 'live' pictures of the same action from different angles. It was the responsibility of the producer in the gallery to select which picture he wished to transmit in order to create a smooth but varied progression of visual images. It was an entirely new concept and needed an entirely new approach. Bower:

> Everything had to be planned and what Thomas, Munro and I decided to do was to lay out everything that was to be done, ahead, exactly as René Clair or Hitchcock designed their films on paper. This was done in the rehearsal room and then, having done that, the entire crew was told the shooting scheme and before we went onto the studio floor the camera and sound crews knew, theoretically, exactly what they were going to do. But, by virtue of the fact that it was 'live' there were certain restrictions in what you could ask any given cameraman to do. Could he, for example, get into one position from the one he was in previously in time to give me that close-up? Particularly as we had only three cameras it meant a good deal of hard arithmetic on paper and the need for very careful timing.

The evolved shooting procedure was to have the main camera covering the main action on the main set and which would be front on, whilst subsidiary action was covered by the two other cameras shooting 'grotto' shots at right angles and at both sides of the main set. The technique was used brilliantly by Munro in his first version of the ballet *Checkmate*:

I had great belief in presentation, that one should present a programme, not just shoot it and I thought there's only one way – have somebody playing chess. So we had four people round a chess board – people closely connected with the ballet like Arthur Bliss and Ninette de Valois – playing a dummy game. And, while they were playing, the announcer was explaining what was going to happen. It was just used as an intro and shot on a side set by camera 4 before we went to the main action of the ballet.

The effect was tremendous: 'magnificent presentation', 'really polished broadcast'. Immediately the shooting procedure became standard, producers began to experiment. Bower:

Pirandello's *Henry IV* was the first production that I did which involved a complete reversal shot. 180 degrees. That is very much something of the cinema and I had to use a four-sided set for the complete reverse otherwise I'd be shooting at my own cameras.

On Your Toes, 21 May 1937, was the first time in such a fast-moving production that the producer did long shots of the general action and then cut in with close-ups. *Dancing Times*:

The cameras were excellently placed taking first long shots and then close-ups to show the over-emphasised hand, wrist and head movements conceived in the best Balanchine 'tongue in cheek' manner.

Madden did much the same thing with his Denvers knife-throwing act:

I had a camera behind him, one in the middle and a camera at the receiving end so, from the audience's point of view, it really was an exciting act because the knife seemed to be coming at you.

The standard method was being modified to allow the camera to reveal the action in the most effective way, for ballet in particular. Munro:

We placed a camera overhead and a camera as near as possible to ground level, to get foot shots. One example was in the *Sleeping Beauty*. Fonteyn comes right down, bends down on one knee, and a low camera was put there, already marked out with chalk exactly where she had to come – and that camera was only used for that one shot. But it was dramatic. And that low camera became a thing in constant use in ballet productions.

In other forms of dance, too. Madden:

I developed a technique of my own of taking the cameras right off the iron men and putting them onto a low tripod, and I used to make the cameraman lie flat on the floor . . . hands upwards so as to take rows of chorus girls from the feet up.

Even static action could be imaginatively shot. Sidonie Goossens was asked to play her harp at the top of a ladder:

That was Dallas Bower. I remember that very well – this very rickety platform about 6 feet off the ground and just big enough to hold me and the harp so that I could be shot from low down. It seemed highly dangerous and, of course, I had to memorise the music as there wasn't room for a music stand.

167

Bower:

> It wasn't really very dangerous: it was a perfectly safe 6-foot-high rostrum – however –

Goossens and Fonteyn combined to give recitals. Munro:

> Margot was on the main stage, the dance arranged by Freddie Ashton as she wouldn't do anything unless he did the choreography, and Sid was on a little side set with her harp. Always trying to experiment, I superimposed the picture.

The effect was to see Fonteyn dancing through the harp strings:

> It wasn't planned. Just came out of the blue. We were learning all the time, you see, and something inside me was picking up all the things that one could do.

The same sort of effect was devised by Madden for *Cabaret Cartoons*:

> What I wanted to create was something that was pure television – wasn't theatre, wasn't radio, wasn't variety, wasn't anything but real television and the cartoonist Harry Rutherford not only ended up with an exact reproduction of the act he'd been sketching but, as he and the act finished at the same time, we superimposed the two and got an exact double – his drawing supered over the face of the performer. It wasn't anything you could do in any medium except television. It was pure camerawork and electronics.

Superimposition was used to create triple images, especially of dancers, and, occasionally, the screen was split into four. The programme was called *Fugue for Four Cameras*. It was a ballet devised by Stephen Thomas and choreographed by Anthony Tudor – one of his first ballets written specially for television, and was danced by Maud Lloyd. The action was covered by four cameras – each one of which had three quarters of the frame masked off so that only one quarter of each camera was used. It was this quarter that contained the single but complete image of Lloyd. When the four quarters from the four separate cameras were, electronically, put together, it produced a composite television picture in which Lloyd danced in quadruplicate. Munro:

> It didn't quite come off but it was one of our experiments. You had to try these things out on the public and it was the only time we ever did anything like that.

As technology improved certain techniques became easier. As Birkinshaw improved the time it took to 'fade' between cameras so the 'fade' became an artistic effect rather than an embarrassing necessity – as in the infamous dance leap in *Here's Looking at You*. The *Evening Standard*, reviewing the *Sleeping Princess*, noted:

> The mechanical devices used to enhance the fairy-tale atmosphere were on the whole most successful, particularly the fading in and out of the Lilac Fairy on her mysterious arrivals and disappearances.

The 'fade' was used again with great effect in the second version of *Checkmate*. *Dancing Times*:

> . . . a heavy feeling of impending drama was given by the fading out of the lifted

arm of one of the Players into the enormous arm on the backcloth which in turn was faded into the actual chess board scene.

From the outset, the producer was not limited to pictures from the studio but could generate pictures on film from telecine. The first time that studio and film were used together as a deliberate device was in Munro's variety show in April 1937, where film was used to introduce the Paris–Londres cabaret from Grosvenor House:

> But it was done at Alexandra Palace. And as a prelude to the performance I thought, right, we'll get hold of some film and we'll have an aeroplane supposedly taking off from Le Bourget coming over to London. The programme began with Elizabeth Cowell sitting in the studio in front of a dummy TV set and, on the screen, the title of the show: *Paris–Londres*. It faded from that to film of an old Imperial Airways plane lumbering across the Channel to England. And in the studio we had contrived a section of the plane. The film showed the plane landing, the doors opening and the steps being put into position. At that precise moment I cut over to our replica in the studio and the Grosvenor House girls came down the steps and went into their cabaret act.

Popular Wireless commented:

> This is something that cannot be done in any other form of entertainment and it should be cultivated by the television staff . . . Actually it was something more than film and studio combined for recordings were also introduced. In fact, I think Mr Munro can claim to have introduced a unique type of entertainment.

Film was again used as a prelude to the opera *Pagliacci* and was introduced as part of the action in the play *The Tiger*. Clemenceau is sitting in a seat saying 'There will be war' and immediately there was film from telecine of shell bursts faded quickly into the studio action and out again. Madden:

> It made it frightfully effective. Whereas in the Embassy Theatre, which is where we got it from, you couldn't do that. This is where television added a dimension that was so valuable. That made it something unique.

From film of shell bursts, Dallas Bower in *Emperor Jones* went one better. He needed a scene of Jones padding through a muddy field, a close-up of feet going in and out of mud. It couldn't be done in the studio so he pre-filmed it himself and later introduced it into the studio action. Madden, in *International Cabaret*, linked his items with film of an express train, faded back into the studio to a railway signal which then dropped to reveal the title of the next act and finally faded to the camera covering the start of the act itself. George More O'Ferrall in a play about the relief of Mafeking in 1937 used a combination of 'just about every camera and telecine'. Greenhead:

> He spent quite a lot of time on a photomontage sequence from telecine to be used at the end of the play to describe Mafeking's relief. As the sound of the guns blazed away there were marching feet and the soldiers on telecine going into battle. Then, from the studio, a poster was rushed up to the camera, then back to more film and George said: 'OK, fellas. We'll go and have a meal now. It's going to be all right.' So, precisely at eight o'clock the play starts and we come right to

the end of this great photomontage sequence – the war at its crescendo, drums rolling, guns banging away, posters being rushed up and down – never heard such a cacophony. And George is looking at all this and when it comes to the great pièce de résistance – the record, with all the sound effects, began to run out. So the sound man gingerly faded out and the vision mixer thought, 'What do I do?' So he faded out and George jumped up and said 'Bloody marvellous. Bloody marvellous.'

For the producer learning his craft under the severest restrictions of time, space, money and technology and, as the shows were 'live', with only one chance to get the transmission right, the actual process of production could be a nightmare. Bower:

> The awful gnawing pain in your tum as you went up that ladder to the gallery has to be experienced to be believed. Particularly if you felt you weren't adequately rehearsed for the end part of your play. You not only had all the other requirements to attend to – timing of fades, timing of mixes, the necessary titling, any gramophone records you were using, all had to be cued in but, if you weren't properly rehearsed you had to give the cues yourself, make absolutely certain the cameramen were with you completely and, of course, cue in and out of telecine. Absolute nightmare.

Munro:

> You were transmitting, say, camera 1; your next shot was on camera 2, then from the script which you'd worked out in advance, you could see that you wanted camera 3 set up at a certain angle. So you OKed 2 on the preview monitor and you called out to the vision mixer, 'I want to preview camera 3.' He'd set that up and you'd say, 'That's fine. 3. Stand-by. I'll be coming over to you later.' There was no great bank of monitors, one for each camera as there is today so that you know everything that is happening. You only had the transmission monitor and the preview monitor, and in anything complicated the producer was doing a running commentary all the time through his microphone not only to the cameramen on the floor but to his stage manager on the floor and to the vision and sound mixers in the gallery. Must have been bedlam. But it worked. It didn't always come right but it did in nine cases out of ten.

As it did with *Le Spectre de la Rose*. Munro:

> The costumes were missing. They didn't turn up for rehearsal so we couldn't rehearse. Eventually they arrived just in time for the transmission and, Campbell having roughly done the lighting and a few positions been marked on the floor, we put the thing out completely unrehearsed. And Cyril Clark, a member of the orchestra, said to Hyam Greenbaum the conductor, 'That was a very short rehearsal.' 'That wasn't a rehearsal,' said Greenbaum, 'that was the bloody transmission.' But you can only get away with a thing like that once.

In September 1937, Grace Wyndham-Goldie wrote a review in *The Listener* which marked a significant breakthrough in television production:

> Last week was for me epoch making. I watched Mr Thornton Wilder's one-act play *Love and How to Cure It* in the viewing room at Alexandra Palace. Now I

admit that viewing at Alexandra Palace is a very different matter from viewing in one's own home. The screen there does not have the hysterics as it occasionally does in private houses from a mixture of 'interference' and inexpert handling. And there is, too, an atmosphere of tension and excitement – very like that of a first night in the theatre – which undoubtedly works on the nerves and heightens appreciation. But even allowing for favourable conditions *Love and How to Cure It* was still an immense advance on previous plays I have seen . . . the picture certainly was not perfect; its edges had a hazy, out-of-focus look and the individual shots had not the posed certainty which made parts of *Hassan* and *Murder in the Cathedral* pictorially satisfying. But . . . for the first time I found it possible to become absorbed in the story and forget the difficulties of the medium.

It showed that the progenitors of that medium were rapidly learning their business. The engineers were learning how to improve picture quality and, more important, the producers were learning how to use their equipment and techniques without their effects becoming obtrusive. Six months later, in the spring of 1938, *The Times* reported:

Today pictures are not only brighter and clearer . . . but the technique of presentation has been learnt and we no longer feel that the producer is wrestling with an unfamiliar and wayward medium.

Producers continued to experiment, continued to improve but, by the summer of 1938, they had done more than learn how to handle the new medium. Bower:

We took ourselves pretty seriously and what we did was important to this extent that, as there had been no real television previously, we set the norm and established procedures and, as far as I know, the procedures we established then are the procedures in use today.

10d Valerie Hobson and Richard Coleman in *Cabaret*, 5 July 1937. A painted backdrop and increased movement and sophistication

10e Douglas Byng – television's first drag act in *Byng Ho* as 'Doris, The Goddess of Wind', 24 April 1939

10f Danny Kaye and Nick Lang Jr. in *Autumn Laughter*, Henry Sherek's Dorchester Hotel Cabaret presented on 21 September 1938

11a Drama: Bernard Shaw on the set of *How He Lied to Her Husband* with Greer Garson and, seated, the producer George More O'Ferrall, 8 July 1937

11b Ballet: *Les Patineurs* with Margot Fonteyn, Robert Helpmann and the corps of the Vic-Wells Ballet. Producer D.H. Munro, 3 May 1937

11c Opera: *Pickwick* by Albert Coates, producer Dallas Bower, 13 November 1936

11d Serials: Episode One of *Ann and Harold*, a five-part romantic serial starring Ann Todd and William Hutchison, 12 July 1938

11e Demonstrations: Marcel Boulestin, the first television cook

11f Talks: *Experiments in Science* No. 2. Dr Wolfe; Alan Best; Peter the Chimpanzee and Keeper Brown, 21 September 1937

11g Keeping Fit: *Bodyline* No. 4, 16 November 1937

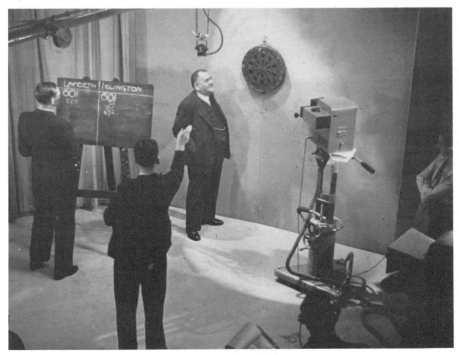

11h Darts: Lambeth v. Islington, 15 October 1938

12a The *Grand Tour*, 7 September 1938, showing the sophisticated use of lighting to model figures: and the penumbrascope, producing shadow scenery

12b Television Tilly, the tailor's dummy used to try out the effect on the camera of colours and materials. Mary Allen, head of wardrobe and make-up; Peter Bax, stage designer

12c The scenery workshop – suits and overalls. The giant teapot was used as a setting for Eric Wilde and his Teatimers. 19 April 1937. (Tom Edwards on left)

12d Realism in a first-class railway compartment achieved by carefully constructed scenery and 'natural' lighting. Desmond Davis and Leonide Zarine in *Vice Versa*, 3 December 1937

12e A deliberately grand and spacious theatre effect for the opera *Arlecchino*, 2 February 1939

13a Archery on the terrace at Alexandra Palace. 'Mrs Inigo Simon takes aim', 19 October 1936. The Emitron camera on the dolly is on an extension cable from studio A

13b Fire-fighting demonstration, 9 February 1938. 'Miss Jasmine Bligh, hostess-announcer, is "rescued" in one piece from the burning palace'

13c The Television Garden in Alexandra Park. C.H. Middleton 'discussing the relative merits of various paving stones', 26 June 1937

13d The first genuine Outside Broadcast. The Coronation, 12 May 1937. Interior of the Mobile Control van parked in Hyde Park. Note picture monitors head height at the far end

13e The Coronation, 12 May 1937. The Royal Coach passing the television camera (on pavement) at Apsley Gate. The cameraman is John Bliss

13f The Lord Mayor's Show, 9 November 1937. The Mobile Control van parked in Northumberland Avenue with two cameras positioned on the roof

12

SERVICES

What happened was you'd give just a preliminary sketch of requirements to Leonard Schuster, the executive concerned with budgeting. An indication of the size of your cast, number of sets needed, wardrobe requirements, props, and you'd be given an allocation and you had to adhere to it quite strictly. You were working within margins of £5–£10 and if you went over, it would be lopped off another producer's allocation. But, if you went under, the saving didn't go straight back into programmes. Not a bit. New door knobs in the ladies loo or something. I was furious over that.

(Dallas Bower: producer)

In 1982 the cost of a single drama production was £150,000. In 1937, the weekly allocation for the production side of the entire television service was increased from £1000 to £1500. Munro:

We had to practically beg finance because the powers-that-be in Broadcasting House were anti-television. It was a question of cheeseparing and here we were lucky in having Schuster who came from a banking family and was a financial wizard. How he managed to get money I will never know. He had a bottomless purse somewhere and whether he got it from the family firm or from Broadcasting House, I didn't ask. It's not impossible it was from his own pocket. I wouldn't be surprised.

The key to success and solvency was careful planning and servicing. Every Monday morning there was a production meeting. Cock was in the chair. A post-mortem was held on the previous week's output – the choice and quality of the productions, the success or failure of their presentation, problems pinpointed, flaws exposed, solutions canvassed for the following week. Birkinshaw:

Technical difficulties arose frequently because the producers were asking the equipment to do what it wasn't initially designed to do. They said: 'Now why can't we do this – why can't we do that?' – thereby putting on the pressure to provide more when we hardly knew what we were doing already.

Proper eyepieces for the cameramen, all cameras properly mobile, longer and better camera cables, 'And they not only wanted more but they wanted it tomorrow.' Demands too on sound, lighting, design, costume, make-up, props – all aspects of television production which developed as the demands of the producers increased and the limitations of the technology were overcome or grew less with the experience of operation.

Sound, in a visual medium, tends to take second place: because of the success of radio it was also, in 1936–7, taken for granted. But the reproduction of sound for television was not merely a question of repeating the methods employed in sound radio. Or, for that matter, the methods employed in film production. In radio, sound engineers could place their microphones where they liked, hang them up, put them on stands, even hold them within inches of an actor's face. In television, of course, none of this was possible. Microphones had to be kept out of sight. In film they had to be kept out of sight too – in a vase of flowers, under a table for the duration of a shot, perhaps for as much as two minutes before they could be repositioned for the next shot. But, in live television, which required the same continuity of presentation as the theatre, microphones had to be out of shot for half an hour. Birkinshaw:

> A great deal of studio experiment went on in order to overcome our problems. We still occasionally used microphones on stands but, for the first time, we had to develop this business of slinging microphones on booms – long poles from which the microphone could hang just above the actor's head and just out of shot of the camera. And, when the boom operator accidentally dipped his microphone into the shot there would be a great cry from everybody in the studio control gallery 'mike in shot' and the unfortunate bloke whipped it out of sight. But we used to get that mostly cleared up at rehearsals.

As well as just hanging from its pole, the boom mike had also to be angled and the angle changed as the actor's position changed in order to prevent the sound from being clear one moment, muffled the next. Boom operating became a highly skilled job and sound, working in tandem with the cameras, grew to be as flexible as the camera system itself.

As sound had to adapt to the needs of a continuous visual performance, so, too, had lighting. In films, lighting set-ups were changed for each individual shot. In the theatre, lighting was a general flood with the occasional use of a spot. In television, it had to be general enough to cover the entire action for a camera long shot but concentrated enough for the camera to come in close on a face which should not be half in shadow – even when the actor moved.

The provision of studio lighting was originally the responsibility of the competing company concerned. Bairds, essentially a film studio with a fixed camera, used film lighting and Mole Richardson equipment. It produced some interesting effects. *The Times*, reviewing a *Picture Page* item, said, 'The lighting especially emphasized the ghostly character of the proceedings.' EMI, on the other hand, were less experienced. Campbell:

> They had not the faintest idea of anything to do with lighting. They equipped us with things called Camden lamps. They were sheet metal; they cracked; they made a noise sometimes like a cannon going off. And you couldn't concentrate the light properly. They were appalling.

Just how poor the EMI equipment was and how poorly utilised was first noticed during the run of *Here's Looking at You* in August 1936. Campbell:

> Everybody had white faces. Everything went flat. It really was dreadful because it was all done from the front. In photographic work you light principally from behind to give depth.

181

The lighting levels required in the EMI studio at Alexandra Palace were, in technical terms, about 250 foot-candles, a considerable amount of light to be obtained merely from stand lamps and an amount which had to be kept even. This was difficult when the power of an individual lamp could not be controlled – lamps were either on or off – and when lamps, as the production demanded, were moved about the studio. It was especially difficult when movement merely produced a proliferation of multiple shadows – shadows cast by a dozen things, cameras, microphones, props, people. As Birkinshaw said, 'As far as lighting was concerned, most of us were rather dim.'

As Bairds had a film lighting man who knew what he was doing, BBC engineers became involved in Baird lighting hardly at all. With Marconi–EMI, however, the lighting responsibility devolved onto the BBC stage managers Peter Bax and Harry Pringle who, amongst their other duties, were to 'see to the lights'. And, as the engineer in charge of the shift, it was the responsibility of Desmond Campbell to check the stage manager's lighting set-up. Campbell, with his background as a professional photographer and his experience of photocells in 30-line television, knew more about television lighting than anyone. Campbell:

> I would go into the studio and say that wasn't in the right place and so on and so forth and it wasn't long before they said, for Heaven's sake, why didn't I do it from the beginning. So I did. For over a year I worked about eighty hours a week because I had to do the damned lot.

Campbell immediately equipped the EMI studio with temporary scaffolding round the walls and scaffolding bars on the bridge overhead. This got some of the lights off the ground and into high positions, as in a film studio, and light, as in normal daylight, could now come mostly from above. The arrangement had the additional advantage of keeping the lighting cables from getting tangled with the cables of the cameras. Campbell:

> When we opened in November we were still running with the Camden lamps in the EMI studio and Mole Richardson in Baird. But, having the gallery built, I was able to use the Camden lamps fairly well. Fourteen feet was the highest you could get a lamp and we used specially made clips that gripped the tubular steel but, whilst the majority were on the bridge now, I still used a fair amount on the floor. In fact I've always insisted on some on the floor, often insisted on one above the camera. But with lamps now behind the artists and beside the artists as well as in front of them, much to everybody's amazement, the pictures were very much better. No one could quite understand it. There was depth where before everything had been flat.

When the Baird studio was closed, the lamps were moved next door. New equipment was gradually bought. What had been temporary in terms of scaffolding was made permanent. Campbell was nicknamed 'The Prince of Darkness' and, relieved of his electronic engineering duties, was officially appointed the first BBC Television Lighting Engineer. Birkinshaw:

> He had a tremendous eye for good scenes in pictures and, whilst the overall result was produced by the producer and actors and scenery and the rest of it, the

attractiveness of the television picture owed an enormous amount to Campbell. He was the chap who first put artistic qualities into the engineering television picture. He was the Father of television lighting.

Campbell had some fifteen lights available to him in the studio and they were positioned at rehearsals. From reading the script and discussion with the producers, he knew the general kind of lighting that was required but 'you lit in the early days as the rehearsal went along.' Mitchell:

> So ignorant were they in the early days that I was asked to sit-in for back-lighting rehearsals and they burnt my hair off. I said: 'I'm sorry, I can't take any more heat' and put my hand behind my head and my hair came off in handfuls.

The lighting set-up devised at rehearsal was repeated for the transmission and, if the programme was to be performed again, the original lighting positions and changes were written down, diagrams made, so that the lighting, too, could be repeated. It was the start of the modern lighting plot. Bligh:

> The immense trouble he took with us. He was determined his girls were going to look as good as anybody and we would have lighting calls – in the morning usually – and if it meant standing for twenty minutes it didn't matter because you knew that when you went out you'd look all right. And, as Elizabeth and I were totally different, she was dark and I was very fair, the lighting was entirely different. And sometimes, because I'd had a late night, he'd come up to me when I was on camera and say: 'Oh, Jasmine, you don't look very good, do you dear?' and would put a thin gauze in front of the camera lens and I'd look wonderful. He was a brilliant man.

Campbell used lights for a deliberate artistic effect in the ballet *Checkmate*. *The Times* reported (16 May 1938):

> The most interesting innovation in the televised version of the ballet was the use made of shadows. Mr. Frederick Ashton was an extraordinary picturesque figure, flanked by the red (chess) pieces who cast interesting shadows on a plain backcloth. Later he was even more impressive sitting on his throne in lonely and terrified majesty, while the menacing shadow of the attacking Black Queen advanced towards him sword in hand. The Queen herself ultimately came into view of the cameras as in the stage production, but this scene gave us something new, a dramatic emotional picture in terms of photography.
>
> (Quoted by Janet Davis)

As lighting developed, so did scenic design, props, wardrobe and make-up. They developed in tandem, reacting to developments in other areas, overcoming problems together and frequently creating together. The penumbrascope was a combination of lighting and scenic design. It was devised by Malcolm Baker-Smith, the design assistant, and was basically a shadow projector. Using cardboard cut-outs huge shadows could be projected on a flat white cyclorama and, using this technique, *100% Broadway* could be performed in front of a backdrop of the Manhattan skyline – black and white and in silhouette but enormously effective. The penumbrascope was used for Marlowe's *Edward II* and Shakespeare's *The Tempest* and, as the Elizabethan dramatists left scenery to the imagination, so the penumbrascope stimulated the imagination to create out of shadows the air of mystery, murder and magic which four-square scenery would have killed stone dead.

Television scenery became the responsibility of the stage manager Peter Bax. With enormous experience of design in the theatre, he was the ideal person to respond to the increasing and changing demands. And, to construct it, was Tom Edwards, the same man who had built the steps for the Balalaika Orchestra in 30-line days. He was not an official member of the design team, merely the maintenance carpenter, but like so many other people in early television, like Bax himself or Campbell, was the man on the spot who did what needed to be done and did it supremely well.

Initially, scenery consisted of a white circular backdrop (a cyclorama) and curtains, but, shortly after *Here's Looking at You*, the curtains were scrapped. They were replaced by a 'unit' set – a set constructed of archways, pillars, etc. which, although fairly solid, could be dismantled and re-erected.

But, as cameras and lights began to roam, scenery needed to be moved more quickly and quietly. It became lighter in construction and, as the cameras roamed even more, the traditional arrangement of backdrop and wings was changed into a set with three sides, as in *The Tempest*, or even four, as in *Tristan and Isolde*, until scenery became as flexible as the camera system it served. But, until the last few weeks, it was always painted a uniform grey. It was the best colour for camera response but was unsettling for novice performers who needed the reassurance of realism.

Sets were furnished by Props under property-master Percy Cornish. Munro:

> Props were nil to start with. They consisted of various staff members raiding their lofts at home, getting any junk they could get rid of, carting it up to Alexandra Palace to become the Prop Shop. I donated a pram. Much to my wife's disgust later on. And, before we got round to buying or hiring stuff, that's how we managed our props. As in other areas, we all mucked in.

In charge of wardrobe and make-up was Mary Allen. One of her assistants was Isabel Winthrope. 'It was Mary Allen who had the flair and enthusiasm to find new answers to new problems.'

Her department worked long hours in cramped conditions at the behest of producers whose words were law – or almost law. Notice of production was usually two weeks, as much as six weeks for a big production. Work schedules were drawn up; a budget agreed but, as usual, cash was so short that wardrobe, although needing to reproduce costume from every historical period, was not allowed to buy a book on costume history. They had to borrow from Broadcasting House library on 'Short Loan Only'. As a result, research was mostly done by the assistant assigned to a programme in the Victoria and Albert Museum, the British Library, local libraries or from wardrobe's own expanding collection of old photographs and prints. However, the accuracy provided by the research could only rarely be matched in the costumes themselves, either because the producer demanded the wrong kind of costume (flamenco frills for a play set in modern Spain) or because, for the professional costume stockists, authenticity and modern commercial viability were not to be reconciled. Isabel Winthrope:

> There was, roughly, 'Middle Ages' – the same type of costume had to do for anything from 1100 to 1500; then there was 'Elizabethan' and 'Eighteenth Century' for which anything would do provided it had panniers.

These costumes were hired, on a rota system to avoid any suggestion or charge of bias, from theatrical costumiers – Simmons, Nathans, Bermans, Samuels, Morris Angel and even Moss Bros. Furs for lush Edgar Wallace crime plays came from reputable furriers. And the costumes were the best that were in stock or the best the production could afford – sometimes the cheapest. Winthrope:

> I've never seen anything so horrible as the men in Roman tunics. They were going around looking as if they were falling out of night shirts.

Very occasionally a costumier would make costumes for a whole production but costumes that weren't hired were made by BBC wardrobe itself – starting with hats and smaller pieces and not always as planned. Winthrope:

> Stephen Thomas was to put on a programme of sea shanties and usually the costumes came up the day before. But this time they didn't come up until just before the show and, quite unlike him, dear old Mr Gillan of Nathans had left out the seamen's 'tarred' boaters. And the only thing we had to hand was buckram – so there were our two seamstresses running up about ten hats. Then we had them sprayed with black paint in the paint shop and put to dry in the boiler room with the result that they came out with wavy brims and looked as if they were about to fly off. But we had to make do and mend things, think up something to replace something else at very short notice.

Like ping-pong balls painted gold and wired on elaborate headdresses for a Chinese item; like a woman's 'two-way' stretch for a man who'd forgotten his jockstrap; like artificial flowers borrowed from Props Department to disguise a too-low décolletage.

The continuing problem of camera colour sensitivity played havoc with wardrobe. Even if all three tubes began the week with the same colour response, by the end of it, one tube could be reproducing red as medium grey whilst another was reproducing it as almost white. Winthrope:

> The worst play of all was *The Cardinal's Candlesticks* in which we had five or six cardinals wearing red cassocks. So you can imagine the different shadings as the actors moved from one camera to another. And, later, we took to making costumes like cassocks in grey, using the same bales of grey cotton used in studio sets. But we used red as little as possible and avoided other awkward colours too. White always dazzled and, in contrast, made people's faces black: and black produced a white fuzz round its edge.

Make-up had a comparable problem and needed to provide a make-up that would cover the entire colour range otherwise, as cameras faded from one to another, faces would fade from natural to pale to almost black. As a result, make-up was a mixture of Max Factor panchromatic and sometimes Leichner stage greasepaint blended together depending on the reading on each camera from the Ilford colour chart that Mary Allen insisted was placed there. Red was avoided for the shading on cheeks and a putty beige was used as groundwork. Eye-shading was brown, occasionally blue. Winthrope:

> With a woman I would start by seeing that her face was completely cleansed of ordinary make-up; see that grease was removed and then start with dabs of foundation which I smoothed over as thinly as possible. If there was some flaw in the actual structure I would try to improve on the shape – if her nose wasn't quite straight I'd use a light shade in a straight line down the bridge. Then I'd do the eyes, draw a line round by the eyelashes enhancing the size of the eyes; if they were rather small I would do a little bit of inserting a lighter shade inside the actual lower lashes. I started in the days when eyebrows were very thin, which were rather awful as they gave women a medieval appearance, so I had to draw in the eyebrows. Then lips, which I always tried to shape naturally but often girls wanted to follow the fashion of the Swansons and Crawfords. They liked to have voluptuous lips whether these suited their faces or not and I would have to do a bit of gentle arguing. And lipstick itself was kept to shades of brown. After all was done, I powdered all over to set the make-up and sponged a matching liquid make-up on neck, bosom and arms. They could have walked out into the street and not caused any commotion.

Which was an advance on 1932–5 or the Baird Spotlight make-up. Make-up for men was similar – just less of it, except that men's beards, however closely shaved, were a camera problem. Experiments were done and a foundation concocted that obliterated the 'shadow'. Make-up and wardrobe were monitored at rehearsals. Winthrope:

> We had to sit in front of a little monitoring screen in the studio – in the most cluttered studios you've ever seen. And we made notes about what changes we might need to make in the dresses and what shades of make-up to use. The actors weren't usually made-up during rehearsal and Mr Campbell, the lighting expert, would often come over and tell us that such and such an artist on such and such a camera would have to be especially dark or especially light.

During transmission, as engineers coped with camera breakdowns, wardrobe mended snagged clothes, helped artists change in double-quick time, and make-up powdered damp brows that shone in the burning lights or did a succession of make-up changes like taking the actor playing Christopher Wren from a clean-faced youngster of eighteen to an eighty-year-old with bad boils in the space of an hour's live transmission using both studios and with only one or two minutes for quick changes. 'Because it was live: it was spontaneous: it added something.' Afternoon transmissions also enabled mistakes to be corrected before the repeat transmission in the evening. Winthrope:

> Now we had a lot of acrobat acts and they were wearing what we would today call bikinis and Gerald Cock rang us up one afternoon and said: 'Navels are showing. You must get rid of them for tonight.' What could we do without restricting their

186

movements? We got some stretchy plaster, stuck it over their navels and gave it the same colour as their bodies and, on the screen, it looked like bruising. I've never seen anything so funny. But navels, like low necklines, were banned on early television.

To prevent this kind of embarrassment and to give wardrobe extra time to test the effect of materials under different lighting conditions, the department had created Television Tilly. Tilly was a tailor's dummy who stood for hours under the hot lights, saving everyone, including Leslie Mitchell, from further burnt hair. Leslie, in gratitude, interviewed Tilly for *Picture Page* – a one-way conversation that ended with a handshake. 'I took her hand to say thank-you and it just came off. It was quite a shock.' However, Tilly was not used to test the lighting effects on couture garments. Munro:

> Fashions were an obvious thing to televise. Interest the ladies who'd get their men to buy television sets. And we had two incredible contacts in those days – Harold Plaister and Ken Afar, who were in the advertising fashion business. There were certain problems to be overcome because no designer's name could be mentioned, but we were able to get regular broadcasts from Alexandra Palace of the latest fashions. Half a dozen mannequins, as we called them, would come along and display the various dresses, hats, etc. It was a very popular programme.

Once, because of the neglect of Tilly, more popular than was intended. Mitchell:

> All the girls came up in swim costumes and they were in very light materials and when we got them under the lights the costumes turned flesh colour and the resulting transformation, as you can imagine, was fantastic. In fact the engineers stopped work, I believe, for several minutes.

From all these years of excited activity, hardly any visual record survives. Bower:

> There was an enormous sense of frustration because you were engaged in a most intense way over a period of weeks and you then simply blew the thing into the air. It was gone. It was over. If you write a novel at least you've got the thing in your hand but, for us, with no method of recording available, it was just like blowing bubbles – put the pipe in your mouth, the bubble goes up and bursts.

Apart from still photographs, the only record that remains is the Demonstration Film. Its purpose was to serve as a test card for retailers who wanted to adjust newly installed sets and advertise the new medium in their shop windows and it was transmitted by telecine every morning at the same time. It originally consisted of a selection of items from the first four months of EMI transmissions but was constantly updated – many of the items from the *End of Year Programme*, itself a 'résumé of what we'd done during the year', being added or substituted: items which, of course, were originally transmitted live were not filmed for posterity in the studio during transmission. A film camera would get in the way of the television cameras, shoot from a different angle and so not provide an accurate record of what had actually been transmitted on the television screen. Instead, items were reconstructed as accurately as possible by Dallas Bower who produced and directed on a film set at the Stoll Studios in Cricklewood or even on stage at Sadler's Wells. As a result, the Demonstration Film, scratched and faded, still gives today a fairly accurate cross-section of television broadcasting between 1936 and 1939. Here are Margot Fonteyn and Frederick Ashton dancing the tarantella from Walton's *Façade* with Constant Lambert at the piano and full-scale orchestra: Adele Dixon singing television's opening song –

> . . . so there's joy in store
> The world is at your door
> Its joys, its tears, its laughter too . . .

Picture Page with Harry Haines, 'a muffin man', Nina Mae McKinney singing jazz; Eric Wilde and his Teatimers in front of that enormous cut-out teapot and Johnny Nit tap-dancing on a drum so big that it had to be broken up to get it out of the studio door; John Piper looking serious and intense and speaking in soft, modulated tones about art; Minette, a fashion model in a telescopic bathing suit and wrap 'of silver silk oil skin', and Dr Charlotte Wolfe interviewed by Jasmine Bligh:

> *Bligh:* I wonder if you could demonstrate your methods on my hands, Dr Wolfe.
> *Wolfe:* Wiz greatest pleasure. But you must remember zat I am a scientist and a proper analysis takes us more zan one hour so I can only give some general indication. I consider your hand by ze zone of instincts. I imagine zat you can find your way in zee dark?
> *Bligh:* Yes, I can.

Singers, dancers, actors, musicians, presenters, demonstrators, specialist talkers, interviewers, interviewees, curiosities and freaks: the only thing missing is drama. There was only one attempt made to film a studio play. Madden:

> We spent a lot of money doing *The Scarlet Pimpernel*. It was a very big production and it lasted three hours. So, as we had no record of anything, we decided to film it off a screen which, as you can imagine, was not perfect quality because, of course, you can see the lines. However, we did it and we wasted a great deal of celluloid doing it. And we'd no sooner finished than the following morning Alexander Korda rang up and said: 'What's all this I hear about my copyright being infringed?' And I said I was sure we had the rights or we wouldn't have done it. He said, 'I have all mechanical rights. I hear you have been filming the production and you have it on film. Do you want to be sued?' I said we didn't and that we wanted to be friends. He said, 'I'll tell you what you will do. You will take every inch of that film, you will take it out into the open and you will burn it in public. And you will film the burning.' So we did. We had to. We had no option.

And up in Wagnerian smoke went the only record of BBC television pre-war drama. The film of the burning was sent, as proof, to Korda.

13

OUTSIDE BROADCASTS

> The healthiest curiosity, we may hazard, is that which will demand to see as much as possible of the real world, not of artificially composed entertainment . . . the Coronation procession will obviously give a great opportunity to satisfy an eager public. How delightful, again, to see as well as hear, the Derby and the Boat Race; to watch Hammond bat and Larwood bowl; Perry play tennis and Padgham play golf; to follow the expressions and gestures as well as the words of an orator, and get to look at some event or ceremony at which it was impossible to be present. Thus will all the news, all the doings of the great world take on new life and interest.
>
> (*The Times*, 3 Nov. 1936)

Baird made the first Outside Broadcast when he televised the Derby in 1931 but it was OBs that Baird, in 1936, couldn't do. They were only possible with the electronic system of Marconi–EMI and the announcement that the Corporation planned to televise the Coronation procession of King George VI and Queen Elizabeth gave EMI and the BBC engineers just six months to prepare themselves. Birkinshaw:

> The OB evolved in the most natural way with no pressure whatsoever. After a few weeks concentrating on the studio and its works somebody suggested we get one of these EMI cameras and put it on the balcony outside the studio and shine it across Wood Green and the sewage farm and gasworks towards Dagenham and see what we could see. And we did that and, of course, the daylight was ample and we got a jolly good picture. Somewhat lacking in programme interest but technically it worked.

The balcony shot across Alexandra Park was used to cover intervals between programmes. If the interval coincided with the *Flying Scotsman* or some other train steaming along the LNER tracks then that was a visual bonus. Birkinshaw:

> Then the active programme mind began to work and it was realised that adjacent to the BBC area of the Palace was the exhibition hall and it was not long before we staged a boxing match there and we took the cameras out on the longest length of cable that we could run, 1000 feet, rigged some portable lighting by the excellent Campbell and that was one of the earliest OBs. An outside broadcast in the sense that it was not in the studio.

The active programme mind continued to work and the camera on the Palace balcony was taken off its tripod and re-erected on the grass of Alexandra Park. The park became a studio extension and park performances, overseen by Cecil Lewis and Moultrie Kelsall, became regular features. The *Daily Telegraph* (11 Nov. 1936):

> Performing Alsatian dogs were televised yesterday afternoon . . . one of them, Satan, caused a diversion by taking a dislike to the television cameras and bolting into Alexandra Park. In the main, however, the dogs were well behaved and made spectacular leaps over obstacles up to more than seven feet. Two of them, carrying a stick between their jaws on which perched a parrot, jumped together over a number of low hurdles without disturbing their passengers . . . Reception in the *Daily Telegraph* office was extremely good.

Dog shows became routine 'mainly to explain to the viewers the barking that always penetrated the studios'. In addition there were riding lessons with Major Faudel Phillips; demonstrations by Gene Autry and 'Champion'; shots of model yachts on the nearby lake which developed into a full-scale reconstruction of the famous Zeebrugge Raid of World War I; and a new Golden Eagle class locomotive was demonstrated by Leslie Mitchell from the Palace railway station. One of the most regular and popular of these OBs was given by C. H. Middleton who presided over a small patch of converted park and 'told viewers how to grow marrows'. On the part of the producers there was a constant desire to improve, to go one better, to use all the facilities to the fullest extent. *Café Continental* was produced from the garden of the park's refreshment bar until engineers discovered that electrical interference from the London Transport tramway would obliterate the picture and, in 1937, D. H. Munro produced the first OB at night. Munro:

> I think it was August Bank Holiday, 1937, and was done because of a request from the War Office. It was obvious things were going to happen and the suggestion was that TV might do some recruiting for the Territorial Army. An anti-aircraft gun was brought up to AP, all paraded outside in the afternoon. Leslie Mitchell and the officers in charge did a running commentary of how the various things worked and, in the evening, there was to be a mock-attack so the searchlights could be used after dark. Everything went quite well in the afternoon – a very interesting programme, and after the transmission I had a chat with the officer in charge and he said: 'We're up against a bit of a problem. We've run short of blanks. But I've sent a dispatch rider to Woolwich to get enough for the evening.' The dispatch rider came back – Woolwich Arsenal was closed for the weekend, no blanks available. So dear old Percy Cornish and the property men had to improvise bangs of a kind, going off in the studio. And another trouble after that was that the RAF, who had promised to co-operate with an aeroplane to dive-bomb AP, said it was too risky and wouldn't do it. So we had to get on to Elstree Airport to get a private plane to appear in the searchlight beams. And we had to synchronise the bangs of the big drum, with no gun being fired at all but merely the man appearing to fire it. That was two years before war broke out and we had one anti-aircraft gun defending London.

These programmes were more broadcasts from the outside than Outside Broadcasts. As the camera was still attached by an umbilical cable to the parent studio, broadcasts from Alexandra Park were, technically, no preparation for the broadcast of the Coronation. For that, the BBC would need a mobile control room, mobile transmitter, mobile generator, new cameras and men specially trained to operate them.

The site was chosen for the proposed Coronation transmission months before any of the equipment was made. As cameras were not to be allowed inside Westminster Abbey, much to the annoyance of the press and the BBC, the best view of the procession was to be had from Apsley Gate, Hyde Park Corner. Engineer-in-charge was Tony Bridgewater:

> I wasn't so much concerned with the technical operation of the equipment because we knew EMI's were going to be there in force if only because they were delivering the equipment so shortly before the event that we couldn't possibly take it over from them. But we did have to provide the cameramen and the sound people and the vision control and for some weeks I had the rather interesting job of going down to Hyde Park Corner and working out all the details especially how we were going to get the signals over to Alexandra Palace – by radio or cable. On the one hand we would have an aerial – a 'bedstead' aerial 15 by 10 feet supplied by Marconi, and we could send the signals by wireless and, on the other, the cable. This would have to be specially designed and threaded through the ducts of London by the Post Office from Apsley Gate to Broadcasting House to Alexandra Palace. But nobody had ever been able to send a television signal over a cable more than 1000 feet long and we were planning to send it eight miles.

The cable and its supporting equipment was designed and made by EMI; the entire eight miles coiled onto huge drums in the main auditorium at their Hayes factory and tested. The trial television picture was monitored before it entered the cable and when it came out again. There was no difference. It was a technical tour de force. The Post Office laid the cable in a circle round central London with various outlets so that, after the Coronation, it could be used again for other major events.

The idea of a studio on wheels was taken over from sound broadcasting but the MCR (the television mobile control room) was much bigger and more complex than anything comparable used in radio. It was the size of a Green Line bus, had a Bedford chassis and a body with sides which opened – half folding down to form a platform for engineers to stand on and half folding upwards so that the engineers could service the equipment. The inside contained an exact copy of the equipment in the control room of Studio A at Alexandra Palace but in a much more confined space. Racks lined both sides – racks for power equipment, switching gear, pulse generators, amplifiers, channels for four cameras and two picture monitors so that men working inside could see the picture being shot outside. All the wiring was lead-covered tube and, altogether, the van weighed over 10 tons. It was another triumph of engineering for the EMI men who designed and built it – C. O. Browne and his team, John Hardwick, Frank Blythen and Bernard Greenhead:

> We worked night after night after night to get it ready and after we'd got it installed it was so heavy it was surprising it moved at all. The springs had to be stiffened and the equipment placed on rubber blocks. And to test the van we drove it round and round at considerable speed over a road which was full of potholes. And we stood inside. As I watched the racks swaying I felt as if they would fall over and crush me. Frightened the life out of me. But it all seemed to work and nothing fell off.

All the equipment generated great heat and the engineers and programme staff were to learn how to work for hours on end in temperatures of about 100 degrees. In addition to the MCR there was another van of the same size which contained the radio transmitting equipment and a third van which contained an emergency power generator for use where no public supply was available. The units were delivered by EMI to the BBC only two days before the transmission. Bridgewater:

> We planned the transmission meticulously or as meticulously as we could, because we had to be neat and tidy and everything out of the way of the public who were expected to be swarming round. So our cables had to be properly installed and we brought out ladders and got the cables over the top of the arch and then dropped them down to each camera position. There were three. One on the pavement to provide close-ups and two on the arch itself, one facing towards Marble Arch and the other towards the Wellington Arch. Today there would be teams of riggers to do the heavy work but we all mucked in in those days and did everything ourselves.

The mobile units were driven to Apsley Gate, parked, the heavy cables joined, two portable masts erected, an aerial slung between them and the cameras tested. Everything worked. Bridgewater:

> Of course, we were very apprehensive about the whole thing. It would have been so easy to have had a breakdown so we had to double bank and put in spare cables because cables were always failing; they were one of our many weak points.

The picture signals were sent to Alexandra Palace by both radio and underground cable, though, on the day, it was the picture from cable that was transmitted. On the day before transmission, Noel Ashbridge, Gerald Cock and other BBC mandarins made their appearance on site and made the correct noises to their friend the Chief Police Commissioner and Cock 'dished out a few fivers to lesser people, some of the bobbies I think, to make sure they held the crowds out of the way of our cameras.'

The BBC Press Office issued a statement:

> If this first attempt to transmit a real 'outside broadcast' in the television service is a success, not only will it add interest to a great occasion but it will mark an important step forward in the progress of television by extending the scope of programmes beyond the confines of the studios and their immediate vicinity at Alexandra Palace. It will consolidate the lead already won by Great Britain in the world development of television.

On the night before transmission, the BBC demonstrated from the Alexandra Palace Studio 'some of the equipment that has been specially made for the BBC.' On radio, Gracie Fields sang 'The Coronation Waltz':

> Let us sway on our way to romance.
> This is the Coronation Waltz.
> We can dream to extreme while we dance.

And in Scotts Hotel, Langham Street, at the rear of Broadcasting House, the entire television OB team were quartered in dormitories. Bridgewater:

> We were all expecting impossible crowds to throng Oxford Street and we were warned that unless we got on site about two in the morning we probably wouldn't get through – especially as there was a bus strike as well. And the thought of not being on the spot to do our job that we'd prepared for all this time, alarmed us a lot.

After three hours' sleep, the team walked from Broadcasting House to Hyde Park Corner and switched on the van. They got the first test pictures at 6.00 a.m., switched the van off again and sat down for the seven-hour wait – fed from large food hampers supplied by the Corporation: cold chicken, game pie, hams, fruits, cheeses, wine and beers. 'We were treated like lords and we felt like lords and there was nothing we would rather have been on that day than a member of the BBC's television crew.' (John Bliss – cameraman.)

There was no on-site producer. Bridgewater:

> That was strange. I don't know whether they forgot to appoint one or whether it never occurred to them it was necessary. I regarded myself as the producer. I mean, after all, you only had to choose one camera or the other and most of the time it was only too obvious which one should be used. And that was done by our vision mixing chap usually with me standing at the van door looking out to where I could actually see the procession and I'd say, 'Well, I think old chap, I'd try camera 3 now,' and, 'All right, now let's have 2.'

At 2.00 p.m., with cameras warmed up, cameramen checked in their positions, everybody waiting anxiously, the transmission began. The commentator was Freddie Grisewood:

> 'Here we are at Apsley Gate. The route here is lined by RAF troops. They've just had their rations issued to them. They must be quite ready for them poor chaps, they've been here since crack of dawn but then so have we. Now we've got three cameras working today and they're linked up to our new television vans to transmit to the main transmitter at Alexandra Palace. We've got two of our cameras high up on the gate itself, one looking up the East Carriage drive – this will catch the procession as it comes into view and the other that will take the tail of the procession after it's passed by us. The third one on the pavement is within some three or more feet of the royal coach as it comes by. . . .'

The camera team, assembled from the television studios: Harry Tonge and Roland Price were on the arch and, on the ground, John Bliss:

> I had a wonderful view of everything (except, of course, it was upside down in my viewfinder). And, at one stage, an assistant police commissioner thought I was too near and that the camera would frighten the horses. But I reassured him.

Grisewood delivered his commentary from a position on the gate itself:

> '. . . A last look round on the pavement to see that everything's all right. And now, I'm sorry to say, that conditions are against us. It's started to rain and the light is none too good but we'll stick to it and hope for the best. Very bad luck as had it been an hour ago everything would have been perfect. But now here's the

head of the procession. Colonel Grant with four troopers of the Household Cavalry. Band of the First Warwicks leading armed detachments of the Territorials. . . .'

Bernard Greenhead, the EMI engineer in charge, was inside the control van:

Just as we heard that the procession had entered the Marble Arch – we lost the picture. The pictures from all the cameras suddenly disappeared. We had standby generators and transmission channels but switching to them did absolutely no good at all. We could even hear the sound of horses' hooves getting closer and closer and still nothing. I asked a colleague of mine to open up the side of the van and look into the back of the pulse generator changeover to see if he could find out whether any wires had fallen off. Meanwhile, I'd asked somebody else to go round and open the other side of the van behind the changeovers to the standby and transmission panel to see if that had made any difference. They reported nothing. Everybody was getting a bit agitated. In sheer desperation I gave the panel housing the changeover positions a bang with my fist. It worked. The picture came on and I said, 'For God's sake. Nobody move.'

Grisewood kept talking; the audience were quite oblivious of the behind-the-scenes panic.

'. . . and now the troopers give place to the Royal procession of state coaches . . . Queen Mary in *her* state coach . . .'

Bridgewater:

It was obviously a loose joint that Bernard jogged back into position but, of course, it wasn't very comfortable for the rest of the hour expecting at any moment that it might just as easily happen again.

Grisewood:

'. . . and these eight magnificent greys drawing on that almost unbelievable state coach with Their Majesties the King and Queen . . .'

As the weather got worse and the light bad, the film newsreel cameras had to stop turning but the television cameras, despite their comparative lack of sensitivity, were able to continue and, as each horse approached the camera on the pavement, despite John Bliss's assurance, 'every bloody horse shied.' But King George, who had previously agreed to look at the camera, smiled and 'that thrilled us quite a bit.' *Daily Mail*:

When the state coach with the King and Queen appeared the picture was so vivid that one felt that this magical television is going to be one of the greatest of all modern inventions.

Daily Express:

From the moment the great procession was triumphantly shown on several thousand small screens to a vast audience, television had arrived.

L. Marsland Gander, forty-five years later:

I remember well the story I wrote for the *Telegraph*: 'Horse and Foot, the Coronation procession marched into English homes yesterday.' It was just a wonder and I was wide-eyed wondering at this marvel.

Following Madden's dictum that television should start big, the first real OB couldn't have been bigger than the Coronation. Seen by an estimated 50,000 people and received over 63 miles away it was the climax of the first nine months of television, and the more remarkable because it had been achieved not as the result of a gentle run-up but from a standing start. Its technical smooth-running immediately put all sport and national events within television's scope – if not its range. Trooping the Colour, the Lord Mayor's Show, the Chelsea Flower Show and State visits like that of King Carol of Rumania became regular features of BBC Television outside broadcasting. The Remembrance Day Service at the Cenotaph in Whitehall was first televised on 11 November 1937. Philip Dorté, who had been appointed the first OB producer, was in overall charge and the assistant producer, officially described as assistant OB manager, was Ian Orr-Ewing:

> The Cenotaph broadcast was very easily done because we put the cameras just by the Cenotaph and it was very much a set piece. The only problem was some leaves on the trees which existed between my camera position and where His Majesty would stand. So we got a number of us to shake the tree with absolute fury to bring the leaves down so that we could at least see through and get a good picture.

The OB teams were more tested when the broadcast was not of a set piece event but of an occasion that was unexpected, like the return of Neville Chamberlain from Munich. Orr-Ewing:

> It was on 13 Sept. 1938 and he was due to come in the afternoon, and we rang up Tony Rendle, Gerald Cock's deputy, and said, 'Don't you think we could get down to Heston to welcome the Prime Minister when he comes back?' He said, 'Yes. I don't see any reason why you shouldn't.' So I rang up the engineers and we got the vans on the road and down to Heston.

Alan Bray was rack operator and maintenance engineer:

> My job was to find out from the producer where the van had to go. And we were expecting the plane any minute. Then we had to find out whether we were going to have mains supply or whether we'd have to use the old power van which had followed us down. Then, where did he want the cameras? Get the cable out – we had to run our cables where we could across the ground – sound *and* vision – cameras up in position, the cameramen had to do that job. And my responsibility was to find out where everything had to go and then organising to get it there and, in this particular case, as fast as was humanly possible.

Orr-Ewing:

> We were on the roof with one camera for a mid-shot and another camera down to interview him when he got off the plane. The camera was either on a tripod or a small dolly close to the foot of the aircraft steps.

195

Alan Bray:

The 'dolly' was no more than a wooden triangle on wheels designed to carry the tripod. And pushing that triangle was no fun because you could push the camera over so easily, it was so top heavy and if you did move it you had to have a whole row of riggers hanging on to the cable at the back to go with you.

Orr-Ewing:

Alec Hayes and I tossed up to see who should be in the van and who should be on the tarmac and Alec won to be in the van.

Alan Bray:

When we'd got the cameras arranged the senior engineer in charge would get on the phone to AP saying, 'We're all ready. Do you want a signal?' We had a test signal – a cross pattern known as 'bars'. As the producer was rehearsing his shots, AP would want sound tests and then, when the producer was ready to go on air, AP would say, 'We're coming over to you now.' The producer would take over, start talking to the cameramen through our crude, one-way talk-back system. The producer could talk to the cameraman over the headphones but the only way the cameraman could talk-back was by putting a written notice in front of his camera.

The Listener, reviewing the week's television, described what happened:

The triumphant return of the Premier to Heston Aerodrome was seen by tens of thousands of viewers in all parts of London. Despite lowering clouds and rain the pictures were good and clear. We saw, and heard, the machine circle in the air, land and taxi up to the waiting group of cabinet Ministers. We saw Mr Chamberlain step out smiling and erect. We saw traces of writing on that historic memorandum signed by himself and Herr Hitler which he held out and then waved happily in the air before reading it. Then came the surge of the cheering crowd round the waiting car.

Bray:

As a broadcast I was overjoyed – we'd got it working you see. We showed our flexibility. This was a real pat on the back.

Now, in an age of immediate coverage of events worldwide, it is difficult to understand the significance and impact of the Chamberlain OB. But it had, said *The Times*, 'a quality of history in the making which no other outside broadcast has equalled.'

Before the summer of 1937, sport on television appeared only as part of a newsreel. Sports managements welcomed the exposure but, with the advent of OBs wanting to see it 'while it was happening', managements felt suddenly threatened. Like the film producers before them, they became uncooperative. They formed an Association for the Protection of Copyright in Sport and, for a time, it looked as though sports OBs would have no sport to cover. Orr-Ewing:

I used to go and see Jack Solomons, the boxing promoter, and try and persuade him that we ought to televise. I was only allowed to offer him a maximum £300 and that wasn't a fee – that was for facilities like the amount of room or seats we took up – and he quite understandably pointed out that he could sell every ringside seat for £20 and surely it was worth more than £300 to televise to an audience of 10,000.

The Football Association, under Stanley Rous, permitted television coverage of matches like the Cup Final but the Football League forbade any coverage of league matches at all. Orr-Ewing:

> Though the actual risk of attracting audiences away wasn't very great. There were few sets, the image was black and white and imperfectly reproduced. It was more a danger of the future but these people felt that if they once let the doors open, their attractions would be undermined, and attendance affected. . . . The only people who never thought they had anything to fear from televising sport was the All England Lawn Tennis Club but, as tickets there are six times over-applied for, they had perhaps less to risk.

Wimbledon was first relayed in the summer of 1937; the Boat Race, the Derby and the Test Match in which Hutton scored his record-breaking 364 not out, in 1938. Gradually opposition was broken down sufficiently for Outside Broadcasts of sport to become a regular part of the television schedule – golf, motor racing, swimming, polo, rugby and cricket. It culminated in the Boon–Danahar fight on 23 February 1939. The press built up the publicity – anticipating the fight of the century. Cinema interests in a three-way deal between them, the boxing promoters and the BBC operated a big-screen television system to the Tatler and the Marble Arch Pavilion in central London – top price one guinea. 'But,' said the BBC referring to television on the big screen, 'this is an exception, not a precedent. The BBC is not contemplating giving general permission for its television programmes to be shown in places of public entertainment, either cinemas or anywhere else.' Harringay Arena was packed and the fight itself lived up to its pre-publicity: a lightweight contest in which both men floored each other several times only to get to their feet again and slog on. It was a quick action bout and the outcome uncertain until 'the Chatteris boy pounded Danahar to defeat in the fourteenth round.' That OBs were present to televise the action gave as big a boost to television interest and sales as the Coronation itself.

These OB transmissions had to be planned as carefully as any show in the studio. Orr-Ewing:

> I remember having a script board with twenty-six things you had to get done: you had to order the transmission lines you wanted, the lighting, the cameras, the lenses, the make-up girl, everything.

Altogether, the team consisted of about sixteen people. In addition to the Assistant OB manager as producer/director (two OB managers if the cameras were widely separated), the producer's secretary, 'who used to yell out what the producer had to do and hated OBs because there was no room for her in the van,' and the three cameramen, there was a sound engineer, a senior television engineer, two rack operators and the team of slaves. Bray:

'Slaves' was just a term of endearment. The slaves drove the vans and were also the riggers. If we had scaffolding anywhere they'd put that up and helped us put up the cameras because the cameras were heavy. There would be three or four of them but at Wimbledon, for example, we might have as many as six because the rig was so complex – all off the ground, and could take up to a week.

The problems of the OB teams were the same as for their colleagues in the studio – constant breakdowns in cable and camera, 'tilt and bend' and the restrictions of the system itself with the additional problems of having to work at speed, out of doors and in all weathers. Bray:

If you could get the cables for three cameras working, you'd really done a day's work because as fast as you put the cables out they broke down. They were dreadful things. They really weren't up to their job. They broke where they entered the camera and they broke along their length. And with all the cables frequently off the ground, as at Wimbledon, finding the break that had caused the camera to go down was not easy. You had to work all the way down the cable by isolating the furthest section of cable, putting the camera on there, if it didn't work, coming to the next section of cable and so on right back to the van. It took hours but it was the only way we had, just going along, looking.

The three cameras used on an OB were exactly the same Emitrons as used in the studio. For the job outdoors they had the minor disadvantage that the tube was easily burnt out if the camera panned across the sun and the major disadvantage that they could only operate satisfactorily in bright light. From late 1937 the Emitron was gradually supplemented by the Super-Emitron, a camera developed at EMI by Lubszynski and Rodda. It was heavier than the Emitron and, initially, because of the lack of correction, a straight line of troops Trooping the Colour appeared slightly wavy. But, because of increased sensitivity, OBs could work in very low light – even in winter. Orr-Ewing:

Super-Emitrons also allowed you to use telephoto lenses. These were absolutely essential for sports transmissions for the Emitron had a very wide-angle lens and although all right in the studio was quite hopeless at a long distance.

Disadvantages of the Super-Emitron included the difficulty of putting in the tube, the difficulty of changing the lens and the difficulty of focusing. Bray:

The Super-Emitron tube was a dreadful device to get in position. The camera casing was a haywire device and tubes kept getting broken. They cost a lot of money and, as the tubes were hired from EMI, if you broke the tube and EMI said there was another 400 hours of life in it, the BBC had to pay for that 400 hours.

To change the lens meant changing both the viewfinder lens and the taking lens. Bray:

This could take you up to two or three minutes and when we started to get the telephoto it became a bit more difficult as the telephoto stuck right out in front of the camera and made it extremely heavy to hold.

And refocusing took time, too. Bray:

The producer would say to the cameraman, over talk-back, 'Find so-and-so' and the cameraman would have to take his eye out of the viewfinder, locate the person optically, refocus, and then put his eye back to the viewfinder and find the person again.

In the excitement of a football match, speed of operation was essential, often crucial. Orr Ewing:

In the Cup Final of 1938 – Huddersfield versus Preston Northend – there was a penalty in the last minute of extra time that would decide the outcome of the match. And we had one camera not working and the only camera I could take the penalty on had no lens in it because we were busy fitting the 20-inch telephoto so I could fill the whole screen with the net and the man running up to strike the ball. I had about fifteen seconds and we got back on air just in time to see the goal. But the uncertainty of it all was hair-raising.

One of the unexpected advantages of the Super-Emitron was that, occasionally, a tube would be extremely red-sensitive. Bray:

This particular tube made all the red buses peak white but it also penetrated fog. For example, we were doing an ice rink show from the old Empress Hall and it was a foggy winter's day. The fog inside was so thick you couldn't see to the far end of the building with your eyes but the jolly old camera with its red-sensitive tube looked right through the fog and we could see the whole show. And when we found a really red-sensitive tube we'd nurse it because it would prove so useful on a bad day.

Positioning the cameras in the right place was as important as using the right lens. 'Grouping' was the brain-child of Philip Dorté. Orr-Ewing:

I made the mistake early on when we did the Oxford and Cambridge athletics from the White City, in scattering my cameras about. But I soon learned, particularly in football, that you really had to congregate your main cameras otherwise you'd fade from one camera, say, in a rugger match on the 22-yard line, to another one on the other 22-yard line and you lost geography. You couldn't relate who was the man running with the ball and who was the man trying to cut him off. So we then went to grouping our cameras and changing perhaps from a wide-angle lens to a mid-shot to a close-up. But always from the same angle so that the viewer could quickly relocate himself and not lose geography.

Positioning of cameras was the producer's responsibility and the OB producer was always trying to push the system, and the engineers, to the limit. Bray:

We did a show at a lock on a canal and the producer said, 'I want to see the gates open and the boat come through and I want the camera suspended in mid-air over it.' But, of course, he didn't get that and we laughed that producer to scorn. We simply didn't have the facilities. But there was nothing inherently impossible in what he was asking.

The sudden change in the intensity of light that caused problems of 'tilt and bend' for the racks engineers in the studio was, if anything, an even greater problem to the racks engineers on OBs. Bray:

In the MCR, one of the racks operators had his hands permanently on the 'tilt and bend' control. This was then a four-knob business and it needed a lot of experience to do it – especially in a place like Twickenham. If it was a bright day the shadow from the stand was right across the field and if the ball went from the sunlight into the shade, the picture would tilt, electronically – bits of it would go white, other bits would go dark. You had to correct this all the time. It was a 100% pain in the neck.

Wimbledon produced a similar problem. The camera placed nearest the ground for action close-ups was not entirely free from spectator interference. Bray:

If anybody stood up in front of the camera, it put an artificial black into the picture and the whole of the picture would 'sit up'. That is, the main subject would shoot up to white. So, every time someone moved we got this awful effect and there was no means of controlling this from the van end.

The racks engineers became experts at their job. They were visited by Zworykin. Bray:

We all stood to attention because he was such a great man and he went up to the picture in the van and said, 'I don't believe it! How do you get pictures like this?' We'd become so skilled in turning our knobs that we'd got a jolly good picture and he said he'd never seen anything like it.

Every OB had its particular problem. At Wimbledon it was always difficult for the viewer to locate the ball – partly because the ball was small and moved fast; partly because the comparative insensitivity of the cameras made it difficult to distinguish grass-stained ball from grass itself; and partly because of the visual 'noise' on the screen. The link between Wimbledon and Alexandra Palace was difficult because of hilly terrain and was provided by radio signal transmitted from, at first, the flying bedstead aerial and, later, from an aerial on top of the 100-foot turntable ladder of a London fire engine. But there was always 'noise' – white dots all over the screen 'like rice pudding' which made it difficult for the human eye to distinguish pudding from ball. Add to this the difficulty of tilt and bend, the fact that even the camera mounted in the highest position, clamped to one of the stand roof supports, couldn't see the entire court but cut off the corners, and the fact that if the fade between cameras was too frequent or the shot too distant the viewer might not catch sight of the ball at all: OB coverage of Wimbledon was distinctly problematical.

But, with tennis and boxing, the actual action was fairly easy to cover because it was contained in a small, well-defined area. With golf or the Boat Race, it wasn't. Because of the size of the ball and the great distances involved, the coverage of Bobby Locke and Archie Compston in the first golf transmission from Combe Hill was limited to seeing the player tee off and the ball arrive on the green. There was no question of cameras with long lenses or scaffolding towers on which to position them. Similarly, the Boat Race was only covered at the start and the finish. There was no camera on the commentary boat and so the bulk of the action was covered from the studio where two small boats were moved along a diagram of the course to the sound of John Snagge's radio commentary. A small irritant for the cameraman was, when there was a flood, having to stand up to his knees in water and, for the rest of the team, the 'shock' they got from the mobile control room. Bray:

> We put the MCR in a little yard just above the flood water line and it was very difficult to earth. It always got charged up and every time you touched it you'd get a little shock from the static. We didn't worry about it but the producers hated it.

Sound, for national and news events, was covered by hand microphones or boom mikes. Orr-Ewing:

> They were bamboo poles with a mike harness on the end so you could orientate it in the direction you wanted. But they were very rustic and we got ourselves into awful trouble at public events as at Heston with Chamberlain where we put our boom mike right across Movietone News camera coverage.

There were no lip mikes, chest mikes or highly directional mikes. In the case of sport this didn't matter as the microphones were fixed in a position where commentators could see the whole field. But seeing the whole field, for a television commentator, was no advantage. His comments had to be restricted to the picture that was being shown to the viewer at home and, in the beginning, the commentator had no picture monitor. Bray:

> It was essential for the commentators to have monitors so that they were quite certain what the producer, and the viewer, was looking at.

The introduction of commentator monitors was another innovation by Philip Dorté. Bray:

> They were small Pye receivers – reasonable in their own way, but used as monitors, they weren't bright enough for use in the open. The difficulty wasn't great on dull days but, with a cricket match and brilliant sunshine, and despite the use of hoods, the picture was so dim that half the time the commentators really couldn't see what was going on. Though we never admitted that.

'Inside' outside broadcasts became a regular feature from late 1938 when Orr-Ewing was the first person to televise the last night of the Proms. He had to learn everything by heart from gramophone records so that he could make sure to fade to the right instruments just at the right moment and 'what a musician would have done by nature, I had to do by sweat.' There followed, in November 1938, the first live transmission from a London theatre – Priestley's *When We Are Married* from the St Martin's.

Indoor OBs presented a different set of problems. Parking the huge vans in narrow streets was always difficult and police permission had to be sought. Cables had to be laid out of the way of the public and rigged extremely carefully as the plugs and sockets were incredibly heavy – 20–30 lbs of metal which, if they'd fallen, could have done serious if not lethal damage. Sound from the actors on stage was difficult to pick up and cameras could only be positioned front on but the biggest problem was the need for additional light. Orr-Ewing:

> We had to rig a tremendous amount of light, a terrific load, in order to get the
> depth of focus – though I always had the slight feeling that engineers liked the
> maximum amount of light because there was then less chance of their bottoms
> being kicked if the pictures were rather indifferent.

The lights were $2\frac{1}{2}$, 5 and occasionally 10 thousand watts, very big and heavy
and difficult to support in a theatre, and bulbs had to be covered against the
possibility of their bursting – in the very first boxing OB at Alexandra Palace,
two light bulbs fell into the centre of the ring and exploded like bombs only
seconds before the fight started. But the broadcasts were extremely effective
and, after televising *Me and My Girl* at the Victoria Palace and giving the show
another six months of life, managements began to invite television to broadcast
instead of television having to beg permission.

OBs covered concerts, the circus, the zoo, and visited Denham and
Pinewood for interviews with film stars on the set. This was the nearest that the
BBC got to winning over the film producers – and Leslie Mitchell was able to
chat to Margaret Lockwood whilst Desmond Campbell was able to pick up
lighting tips from the film studio lighting cameramen like Harold Rossen and
Georges Perinal. Bray:

> We went to Pinewood several times. There was the famous time when our aerial
> fell through the roof but, apart from that, it was a static sort of OB. We could do
> what we liked. They were so keen to get on the air that it didn't matter where we
> put the cables. So there was no real difficulty about it.

The OB teams worked every Saturday and most Sundays as well and, on
Monday, had a post-mortem. Every producer had to write an account of his
transmissions so that if, in a year, the broadcast was to be made again, lessons
could be learnt and difficulties avoided. And verbal comments were passed on –
the shooting was too frenetic, the cameras wrongly positioned, the commentator thought he was still on the wireless and talked too much and didn't let the
pictures do the work. This way techniques were developed and precedents set.
That there were not even more OBs was the result of a curious ruling from
Broadcasting House. Orr-Ewing:

> BH were always less than enthusiastic about allowing this youngster television to
> exist let alone expand. And they laid down that we had to send our wonderful
> vans to be regularly washed and greased so that two days a week we couldn't do
> any OB at all. At the end of a year, the total mileage they'd done was a thousand
> and I did query whether that was the right use of capital investment – whether
> we wouldn't be better doing with rather less washing and greasing and rather
> more programmes.

BH's directive was probably aimed more at cutting costs than properly
servicing equipment. As there was still no separate licence fee and television
was still directly funded by radio, washing was cheaper than doing an OB –
though OBs were much cheaper to do than studio shows. But OBs, like the rest
of the television service, were determined to establish the medium, expand it,
experiment with it. Jasmine Bligh became the Pearl White of television:

202

I played tennis at Roehampton dressed as in the 1900s with a boater, a long skirt and a funny shaped racquet. I rode on a motor bike with the Royal Corps of Signals at the Royal Tournament and had to take a wheel off while we were going along. And someone had the bright idea of getting me rescued from a burning building.

D. H. Munro:

I faked Jasmine Bligh falling asleep in the studio and the cigarette falling into a wastebasket that started smoking etc. Film was used to show the fire brigade dashing through the streets of Wood Green and eventually arriving at AP and putting the fire out.

Jasmine Bligh:

So I stood outside on a ledge at AP, a hundred feet up, nothing to hold on to and smoke bombs let out around my feet. And, by the time the ladder came up the building, I really needed rescuing. And he was the most marvellous-looking young man with fair curly hair and I remember saying to him, 'There's only one thing you have to remember, keep my skirts down.'

D. H. Munro:

Leslie got his trousers stuck in the telescopic ladder and couldn't move but Jasmine was rescued. She required a very special dress for that, which had to be approved by Leonard Schuster, because he was afraid she might show too much leg.

There was a constant search for visual novelty; always an attempt to push technology to its limits. The transmission in February 1939, from Hanworth air park, was typical of the mood and the achievement as Jasmine Bligh climbed to 100 feet in a helicopter in full view of the television audience and 'Miss Bligh broadcast from the air on a portable wireless transmitter.'

The events broadcast between 1937 and 1939 became the mainstay of BBC Television OBs. Their coverage was established at a time when anyone could try anything – and usually did. But it was an age of innocence when overenthusiasm could sometimes be a disadvantage. Orr-Ewing:

We were so keen to show off and make friends and we were so proud of our vans and abilities and, when we were at Epsom, this chap came into the van and said, 'You know, you're very clever people. Are you going to be able to show us the whole of the Derby including the start, nearly half a mile away?' And I said, 'Oh yes. We've got this 20-inch lens on and we shall show from that tree on the left to just behind the starting gate on the right.' And he said, 'Brilliantly clever. I shall watch tomorrow.' And when I turned up the next morning, there was a huge advertisement starting from the tree on the left, saying 'Seager's Gin', and there was nothing I could do about it.

It was probably the first advert ever seen on television.

14

THE PALACE OF MAGIC

New Year 1939 opened at Alexandra Palace with 'two fully-equipped' studios and all ancillary services thoroughly established and in full working order. The two studios were linked by a central control room, newly built and with apparatus that could fade sound and vision from one programme source to another. For the first time, items in one programme could come from a variety of sources – Studio A, Studio B, telecine or from one of two outside broadcast sources, without loss of programme continuity. T. C. MacNamara, who was largely responsible for the control room construction, wrote in *World Radio*:

> Every attempt has been made in the design and conception of the Central Control Room, to achieve the greatest possible simplicity of working without which the maintenance of 'slick' programme presentation becomes increasingly difficult. At the same time, due allowance has been made for possible future extension.

This included a plan to convert the old Alexandra Palace theatre into one huge studio with twelve picture channels. The studio picture itself had been greatly improved since the introduction of the long-gun Emitron in 1937 and the only area where picture quality remained inadequate was in telecine where, according to a Television Advisory Committee report in October 1938:

> . . . when bad film is scanned, 'tilt and bend' problems arise which result in a non-uniformity of illumination . . . which reduces the convincing nature of the picture.

It remained unconvincing until after the war but, for the press, Alexandra Palace was still a 'Walt Disney Chateau', a 'Palace of Magic'. Television correspondents queued up to be interviewed in vision and write about the experience for their readers:

> . . . the tangle of cables, the focus of a dozen blinding lights, the ranks of white overalled engineers, the terrific heat, the microphones swinging overhead as the camera pushed stealthily towards you and your hands are clammy and a million thoughts race through your head . . .
>
> (Jonah Barrington, *Daily Express*, May 1939)

But for the occupants of the magic palace the excitement of innovation settled down into a more predictable and professional routine. Mitchell:

> I've never been in a happier situation; it was very exciting, very stimulating, but it was not, financially, very rewarding and it was very hard work. Normal days started about nine in the morning and would continue, as far as I was concerned, until approximately ten or eleven at night. That was every day except Sunday.

We did get very good holidays – paid holidays I was astounded to find out, about three weeks, but as we were about to have nervous breakdowns in the first year it was rather essential.

But the magic was always there. Lured to the Palace in ever increasing numbers were the stars of stage, screen and radio to twinkle for a night under the care and cosseting of Elizabeth Cowell or Jasmine Bligh:

I had to look after Vera Lynn. She was very cool. About eighteen. Rather plain with projecting teeth and looked like a schoolteacher. But quite enchanting with this lovely voice. Petula Clark aged twelve, chaperoned by her father and sang like a bird. Gracie Fields appeared for an interview in a fabulous mink coat with at least six inches of petticoat hanging down. Quite unaware of the whole thing. And Frances Day. A big star: blonde and beautiful, gave me a terrible inferiority complex and I hated her. She was very temperamental. Wanted a lot of special attention and many of them were over-fussy about their make-up or what they were going to wear. It was nerves really. They were frightened of the medium because it was unknown and once an actress fainted. She was having a sword battle with someone in a costume play and she was so het up about it that she passed out cold. Didn't matter because everyone thought she'd been run through by a sword.

And studio routine could still produce the unexpected:

There was one time when Leslie was interviewing the Premier of Canada and one of the big lamps exploded and, within seconds, people were on the phone asking 'Has he been shot?'

Munro:

One of the incredible acts that Madden got was an animal act called 'Koringa'. She'd alligators, snakes and God knows what. I happened to be the director of this. The great final act was she would open this alligator's mouth and put her head in it. We'd rehearsed it perfectly. Ted Langley was on Camera 1, a dolly camera, and the idea was the dolly should track in for a close-up. We did the long shot. Everything was going beautifully. I said: 'Now, Ted. Start your track.' I was watching the monitor screen – nothing happened. 'Come on Langley, forward track in.' Koringa was just prising open the alligator's jaws. Nothing happened. I looked out of the studio window and the man who pushed the dolly had disappeared. Langley was left perched alone on the camera. I said: 'Come on Langley, get cracking!' Then I looked round and there was this whacking snake wound round the legs of the dolly. With the cameraman completely unaware that he couldn't move because of a snake at the bottom and the dolly man having done a bunk. We never did get our close-up. Just a quick fade-out.

The unexpected could come even from routine equipment maintenance. Davis, Marconi engineer:

I came up to the Palace to test the sound transmitter and you can't completely screen these transmitters and they have quite a lot of power. And in the studio rehearsing was a celebrated conductor. He had a metal music stand about a quarter of a wave length on 6.8 metres – just the right height – and so you had quite a lot of potential on top of this thing and when he hit it with his baton a great flare of sparks fell out. He was terrified.

And even when, on the odd occasion, there was a breakdown, there was always Leslie. Lawson:

> He was always unflappable. If the picture had gone up the creek, you could put Leslie on and he would keep the ball rolling, just ad-lib until ready. He was the first natural performer for television, he really was.

The staff at Alexandra Palace grew from a mere handful in 1936 to 220 in 1938 and 500 in 1939. The six original producers became seventeen. To get into the BBC in any senior capacity it helped if you were well-connected – 'I was interviewed by one of those rather odd people inclined to ask if you hunted'; if you were non-Catholic – 'Reith was interested in one thing: whether I was a Roman Catholic or not'; and if you were rich but, once there, you were a member of an exclusive, predominantly male, club. Bower:

> It was rather like becoming a senior member of Trinity House. One really was treated with great aplomb.

And there was a togetherness at Alexandra Palace that was missing from Broadcasting House. There was not the great divide between production staff and engineers that existed in radio. Birkinshaw:

> The engineers in radio were regarded as a sort of subspecies who grovelled around with sweat rags doing mysterious things and to be bawled out if things went wrong and I thought if I ever had a position of influence in television I would see there was none of that. And I *did* see there was none of that and there never *was* any of that.

Although Outside Broadcasts were generally regarded as the philistines of the service, there was no great divide between one production department and another. However, 'to know your place' was important. One female member of staff, temporarily promoted to act as deputy head of a small department, was told that, during her 'acting' period, she would not eat in the canteen with her friends who were secretaries. Relations were, at all times, formal. Winthrope:

> The BBC was very starchy then. Everybody was Mr or Miss in those days. There was no question of calling people by their first names.

Male chauvinism reigned supreme at that time, especially for the lady announcers. Bligh:

> You weren't allowed to get married; you weren't allowed to advertise; you weren't supposed to go abroad. Women to the BBC were anathema. And Elizabeth and I were only selected as they thought it would be better to have two pretty girls than to use two good-looking men.

It was BBC policy not to promote married women. Winthrope:

> We women were kept in our places and our decorum was severely looked after. One girl from Broadcasting House walked down Regent Street without stockings

one evening after work because she had a ladder. It was quite 'done' to go without stockings in those days but not for BBC girls. She was called in the next day by Reith's secretary and told she must never go without stockings again. So, presumably they preferred ladders.

Star, 10 June 1937: 'Bare Legs Ban by BBC.' Winthrope:

> And at Alexandra Palace, Gerald Cock's secretary, dear Miss Vickery, who was a nice soul, had jolly well to see that we behaved.

Leslie Mitchell was certain he had lost his job when Reith walked into the announcers' room to find Jasmine Bligh perched on his knee. Mitchell:

> Jasmine was always liable to be late and I'd written out an announcement for her, knowing that she was probably having cocktails or out at a party or something. And she came in and said, 'I'm certainly not going to do a commentary that hasn't been typed.' And I'd been going ever since that morning, was supposed to be in charge, and said, 'You bloody are dear.' And she said, 'I tell you I'm not.' So I said, 'You can go home. I'll do it.' And that was the end of a pleasant relationship for quite a time but, weeks later, I was in the make-up room and Jasmine came in and said, 'Oh Leslie darling, you're not still going on about that nonsense the other night are you?' And sat herself on my knee. At which moment the eminent violinist who was to appear in the studio came in with Lord Reith. Stared in some dismay as I extricated myself. And when they'd gone, I said: 'Now dear, may I thank you for losing me my job. You stupid little nit.' But nothing happened at all.

The Reithian ethos was not, perhaps, as all pervading at Alexandra Palace as it was at Broadcasting House, but it was strong. There were rules – no dogs; no 'drag'; no drink. The 'no dogs' ban applied to staff after Jasmine Bligh had brought her little Aberdeen terrier to work – a present from a friendly boom mike operator – and everyone else wanted to follow suit. 'No drag' applied to actors. Cyril Fletcher:

> In those days you were not allowed to dress up as a woman on television. That was one of the rules just as you weren't allowed to say 'Chink' instead of Chinese or 'Jap' instead of Japanese. But Douggie Byng used to get by. He was the first of the 'drag' comedians to be used on television and in his act he always wore a dinner jacket and then, above the jacket, he used to use furs and things and funny wigs so that he looked like a mermaid – the top part a woman and the bottom part a man. He was allowed to do that – as long as he was half and half and not *all* woman.

'No drink' applied to everybody – to the nervous actress who smuggled a bottle of gin into her dressing room as well as to staff in need of fortification. Bligh:

> Ray Milland was over here and he'd been a sort of chum of mine and when he arrived at Alexandra Palace we went straight to the nearest pub where we had two or three whatever it was and back to the studio under hot lights. It was a very merry interview indeed . . . and the next morning I was sent for by Gerald Cock and told never to have a drink again. So the 'no drinks' rule was more practical than puritanical.

On the premises itself, the only drink was half a bottle of brandy in the matron's cupboard and that was 'only available if someone was dying'.

As well as Reithian puritanism, the infant television took over from radio the Reithian standards of broadcasting – the highest technical standards, the highest production standards and the highest moral standards based on independence from outside interference and a concern for objective truth. Isabel Winthrope, deputising for Head of Wardrobe and Make-up, Mary Allen, sat in on the weekly production meetings:

> The previous year at the Cenotaph there had been a touching scene that had happened completely out of the blue. Somebody had taken a little bunch of flowers and placed them on the Cenotaph. Whoever was in charge of the current year's production of the Remembrance Service suggested that it should be repeated. But, of course, it would be staged and would be phony. Gerald Cock was very angry about that. He would not allow it.

An incident at that 1938 Remembrance Day Service illustrates the difference between television then and now. During the television transmission a man in the crowd drew a pistol and 'alarmed His Majesty.' Philip Dorté, the producer, instead of focusing his cameras on the action, quickly turned them away. The BBC was, then, impeccably correct and impeccably tasteful.

The togetherness, the happiness, the humour and the fun belied the fact that television was a serious business that was highly, sometimes ruthlessly, professional. Bligh:

> We got smug. We thought we knew it all and, at the end of six months we'd got so cocky and so bad that both Elizabeth and I were sent for by Gerald Cock and told if we didn't pull our socks up we'd be replaced. So we pulled our socks up.

Above all, no one was allowed to forget that television was not a plaything for his or her private amusement but was there to provide a service for the viewer – a service as good as that already provided by radio and which, like radio, fulfilled the requirements of the BBC Charter, 'to inform, to educate and to entertain.'

Reception of television programmes was expected to cover a radius of twenty-five miles from the Alexandra Palace transmitter, but reception was often good up to thirty miles and in range of one quarter of the UK population. If a viewer could get his aerial high enough – minimum 30 feet – and conditions were good, regular reception could be had in places well outside the official service area. Places like Norwich, Northampton, Oxford, Brighton, Malvern and Bournemouth had excellent reception. Viewers wrote appreciative letters from Manchester and, under freak conditions, reception of both sound and vision was possible on the Continent.

There was, however, the constant problem of interference, which neither the BBC nor the viewer could do anything about. Television signals were reflected off high buildings and caused a double image on screen. This was to be more of a problem in New York but the gasometer in Southall created considerable havoc. So, too, and more regularly, did cars. A passing car could cause a domestic television picture to disappear in an electrical snow storm: by 1939, 85% of viewers were still complaining that cars upset reception and the problem wasn't overcome until the car manufacturers fitted suppressors to spark plugs as a matter of routine.

When the service began in 1936, HMV (EMI) and Baird both had sets on the market. They were soon followed by other manufacturers like GEC. Initially, the sets had to have a mechanism on them that would allow the viewer to switch from one system (Baird) to the other (Marconi–EMI) but, after February 1937, the sets were simplified. Even so, the *Daily Telegraph* (3 Nov. 1936) had to reassure its readers that sets were not, in fact, difficult to operate:

> A television set has more knobs than an ordinary sound receiver but their uses are soon mastered. When once the picture is obtained satisfactorily, it remains firmly fixed on the screen and there is no need for further fiddling with the controls during the performance.

In the first models marketed by HMV, the screen, the fat end of the cathode-ray tube, was placed in the top of the set facing the ceiling. This was necessary because the CRT was so long that it had to be placed vertically in the wooden cabinet. It was also an advantage for less publicised reasons. Lawson:

> Because you used to get implosion on these things. They were mounted shooting up into the air . . . so the gun, in fact, if it went, it went up and not out into the living room.

The picture was viewed with the help of a front-silvered mirror placed at an angle on the top of the set to reflect the picture back outwards so that it could be seen in the normal way. The quality of the picture, slightly blurred by present-day standards, was still a great improvement on what had gone before.

By May 1937, the television manufacturers had sold about 2000 sets. That they hadn't sold more was partly because the screen was so small – people couldn't adjust to the tiny images compared to the elephantine ones they were used to seeing on the cinema screen – and partly because they weren't convinced, having seen so many changes in the preceding years, that there weren't yet more to come that would again make sets obsolete. But the major reason was the cost of the sets. The HMV set could be had in two versions, the cheaper one, without radio, costing £90. Sales were so slow that it was reduced to £60 and people who had bought at the higher price were given a refund. But, even at that price and with the boost from the broadcast of the Coronation, sales didn't increase as much as expected. Television sets were beyond most people's pockets. Super versions, at £120 incorporating radio and gramophone, were equivalent to the price of a small car or quarter the price of a fair-sized house. Even the weekly hire charge of £1 was prohibitive for most people and television became, in the words of one producer, 'a rich man's toy'. In consequence, the BBC estimated that, for a major outside broadcast, five times as many people would watch as had sets.

By August 1938, the price of cheaper sets had fallen to as comparatively little as £22 and the deputy Director-General of the BBC, Mr C. G. Graves, gave a headmasterly pep talk to the viewing nation or, rather, the un-viewing nation:

> In Television, Great Britain, with its established home service, has a two-year lead on any other country. American and other foreign friends of ours are impressed by what's been done here. We are creating a great national industry. It's true to say that television offers you the enjoyment of a unique service of interest and entertainment, while *you* are helping to build up this new industry. The wireless trade are doing their share with courage and energy by providing thoroughly reliable sets at very reasonable prices. We want *you* to wake up to the fact that the so-called fairy story of television has come true.

By 1939, the number of sets had increased to 20,000 and the viewing public to 100,000 – tiny in comparison with today's millions but, nonetheless, a tenfold increase over two and a half years. The Radio Manufacturers Association suggested the audience might be even bigger with more 'lowbrow' entertainment in place of 'morbid, sordid and horrific' plays.

Television in the late thirties was largely a 'high-' to 'middle-brow' occupation. The television owner and the television producer shared a common socioeconomic background. Programmes reflected their joint taste. Middle-class entertainment *by* middle-class people *for* middle-class people. Birkinshaw:

> Undoubtedly the initial audience was more middle-class than anything else and they would have dinner and about twenty minutes before the programme would start, they would gather in the sitting room, switch on, let the set warm up and there would be a pleasant atmosphere of expectancy. Cigarettes, coffee, would be handed round. It was like going to the theatre and then, finally, they would turn the lights out and on would come the programme at nine o'clock. Utterly, utterly different from nowadays when 'the box' – a hateful term – is often allowed to play to itself in the corner with nobody taking much notice.

The only direct contact the programme makers had with their audience was through the 'appreciative letters' that arrived at Alexandra Palace and the telephone calls. Cyril Fletcher:

> After a programme people would ring up. There were so few of them that you would get to know them. The phones were in the corridor outside the studios and on one occasion this old girl rang up and said: 'Oh, it's marvellous tonight, Mr Fletcher, I have enjoyed it. It's all in colour.' And so I said: 'What sort of colour?' She said: 'It's all in marvellous red shades.' And I said quickly: 'Switch off. Your set's on fire!' As, indeed, it was.

In January 1937, the BBC introduced Viewer Research. Its aim was to find out how many sets were in operation; the conditions under which programmes were being viewed – at home, at a neighbour's; where sets were installed for demonstrating programmes to the general public and, most important for the broadcasters, to find out viewers' opinions of the programmes. The sample who filled in the original questionnaires was small – just seventy-four people – twenty-one of whom viewed on a Baird receiver, seventeen on HMV, fourteen on Cossor, twelve on Marconi, four on GEC and six on other makes, or their own make. A quarter of the sample still found difficulty in adjusting their sets for vision reception.

As viewers were not asked to comment on specific programmes but on programmes in general, their answers tended to be vague. However, certain facts emerged: light entertainment was enjoyed by 75% of the sample though some people felt that the technical level of television was inadequate for perfect enjoyment of swift-moving acts like acrobats and jugglers; 80% approved of *Picture Page*; 90% approved of OBs – from the grounds of Alexandra Palace prior to the Coronation – and made suggestions for future transmissions, especially sport, 'when technical conditions make them possible'; 90% liked the drama – 'which rather surprised us, that a full-length play would hold the attention,' but ballet and music were approved by only 50%. Films, such as they were, were approved though viewers objected to 'frequent repetition' of news film and asked for the inclusion of travel films. 'A substantial body of viewers ask for more and longer films and there were several requests for cartoon films.' The only programme area to get an unfavourable reception were studio demonstrations and talks where two-thirds of the sample complained. 'Disapproval concentrated largely upon demonstrations of cooking, washing, ironing etc. which were condemned as of little interest to those who could *afford* television sets.'

The BBC took note of the audience's demands. Demonstrations in the studio became rare after the spring of 1937; cartoons increased; so, of course, did OBs but, because of the ban by film producers, the demand for more films remained largely unsatisfied. Audience approval continued into 1938 and grew: 'the unanimity of general appreciation was striking. In a batch of 150 letters only one was unfavourable.' (In 1980, 60% of viewers who wrote or telephoned the BBC did so to complain.) Audience satisfaction was reflected by the press. *The Observer* (26 Sept. 1937) thought programmes were 'full of interest – never a dull moment.' And:

> Once you get used to the smallness of the screen compared to a cinema, the entertainment value of this latest modern miracle is something that you cannot imagine until you have seen it with your own eyes.

The *Daily Mail* began to notice a difference in attitude between the output of BBC Radio and BBC Television. Referring to variety shows, it commented:

> With television cabaret one had the feeling that it was put on for the pleasure of the public. With the radio cabaret one got the impression that it was put on to amuse officials of the BBC.
>
> (3 Feb. 1937)

Despite its almost exclusively middle-class clientele, television was already becoming more populist than its longer established rival and the comments of the *Mail* and other papers did not help to improve the poor relations that existed with Broadcasting House, who were financing television out of the radio licence fee only to find that it was the 'glamour boys' at Alexandra Palace who were catching all the approving headlines. The only constant complaint directed at television was about the number of repeats – programmes transmitted in the afternoon repeated in the evening – but it was generally acknowledged that, whilst television was being financed from BH, it certainly was not being financed enough.

Compared with the daily television diet of half a century later, the only programme areas missing from the output between 1936 and 1939 were hard-edged, current affairs journalism, filmed documentaries, children's programmes and, of course, movies. However, in the spring of 1939, from almost 5000 viewers replying to a BBC questionnaire, 60% thought the programmes were satisfactory and only 6% didn't. Almost 80% thought the standard of programmes was improving and only 4% didn't.

On 1 September 1939, the BBC Television Service closed for the war. Its last programme was a Disney cartoon and Mickey Mouse's final words were: 'I tink I go home.' Munro:

> We were at Olympia, really preparing to launch television to the public. The manufacturers had hundreds of sets ready and everything was coming down to a reasonable price. Down at Olympia, Elizabeth Cowell was doing 'Come and Be Televised', with members of the public. Supervising was Pat Hilliard. I was at central control at AP with the engineers. John Bliss was senior engineer at that time and we knew that something dreadful was going to happen but we'd carry on as long as we could. We always had a couple of stand-by cartoon films in the event of a breakdown so, instead of closing down at Olympia at noon, I got on to Pat and said: 'Look, we've had the bad news. We're finished. Tell Elizabeth to give a summary of the afternoon's programmes and what we're going to do tonight. While she's preparing it with you, I'll run a Mickey Mouse film up here.' And the last thing that went out on sound and vision was Elizabeth Cowell announcing Mantovani and his orchestra for the afternoon programme and the Galsworthy play. Neither went out. We knew they wouldn't. But, officially, we never closed.

It has been suggested to Lord Orr-Ewing by Lord Swinton, Secretary of State for Air (1935–8), that the government only gave the go-ahead for the service in the first place 'to make sure that there was the manufacturing capacity for cathode-ray tubes in this country which was essential to our radar defence.' Whatever the truth of that statement, most of the BBC Television personnel who went into the services were drafted into intelligence or radar. When they regrouped in 1946 and the service was reopened by Jasmine Bligh with the words 'Hello, remember me?' the excitement, the impetus and certainly the advantage that Britain had over other countries in the television field was gone. The United States had caught up. The proposal put forward by Lord Hankey for a system of 3D colour television with 1000 lines, which could have given Britain the lead again, was turned down.

But the achievement of pre-war television remains. In three short years the production teams and teams of engineers who worked at Alexandra Palace, and the teams who serviced them, established a new medium. In engineering terms they established the BBC as the father of black and white, high-definition television: in production terms, they learnt and established the techniques of television broadcasting and established the kind of programmes that are in use throughout the world today. Their achievement was internationally recognised as early as 1937 when Dr Beal, director of research at the Radio Corporation of America, watched television at the home of his EMI opposite number, Isaac Shoenberg. At the end of the short BBC transmission, Beal turned to Shoenberg and said, 'Well, Mr Shoenberg, I congratulate you. That is the kind of television broadcast that I have dreamed about but have only this evening seen for the first time.'

Sir Isaac Shoenberg made two prophetic statements about television. After seeing a successful demonstration of the first Emitron he turned to his team and said: 'Well, gentlemen, you have now invented the biggest time waster of all time. Use it well.' He also said, paraphrasing Bishop Latimer before his death at the stake, 'We are lighting a candle, gentlemen, which will not be put out.'

13g The Lord Mayor's Show, 9 November 1937. The cameraman's view from the top of the control van

13h Wimbledon, 30 June 1938. 'Fire Escape' aerial and OB vans in the car park

13i Memorial service at the Cenotaph, 11 November 1938. Super-Emitron camera (left) and offending tree. The other cameras are for film newsreels

13j Farming. Regular transmissions were made from Bulls Farm, Enfield, Middlesex. Note 'Long Gun' Emitron and boom microphone. A.G. Street discusses a Clydesdale mare in foal

13k The arrival of the Prime Minister, Mr Neville Chamberlain, at Heston Airport on his return from visiting Hitler, 13 September 1938

215

13l Anti-Aircraft defence demonstration at Alexandra Palace, 12 December 1936. The first night-time OB and a sign of the approaching war. Television camera and lights in foreground

13m Amateur Boxing, Alexandra Palace, 1 December 1938. Note the camera platform suspended on the scaffolding and the special overhead light

13n Cricket Test Match, England v. West Indies at Lord's, 24 June 1939. Commentators, T. Woodroffe and T.L. Rich

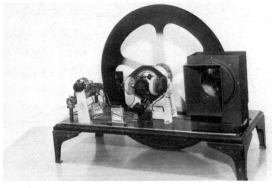

14a *(Right)* Baird 30-line televisor
c. 1928. The case has been removed to
show the disc. The picture was viewed
through the magnifying glass on the
right

14b *(Below)* This Marconi set was
advertised in *Radio Times* in February
1937. The picture on the set on the left
was viewed as a reflection in a mirror

TELEVISION
for
A WEEKLY PAYMENT OF
20/-
This important
MARCONI
ANNOUNCEMENT

. . . is News!—Really Great News! Now that the B.B.C.,
following the period of experiment, will be televising pictures on
one system only, Marconiphone are able to increase greatly their
plans for the production of Television sets for the home. The
Marconiphone Company Limited have, therefore, pleasure in
announcing the following home Television Receivers now available for immediate delivery, on Hire Purchase terms for a small
deposit and payments at the rate of £1 per week!

Model 701. *Television Sight and Sound, and Long, Medium
and Short-wave Radio. Cash Price* **80 guineas.**
Model 702. *Television Sight and Sound Receiver. Cash Price*
60 guineas.

These sets are installed free of charge including provision of a
Television aerial, within the service area of the London Television
station, and are covered by a guarantee of a year's free
maintenance.

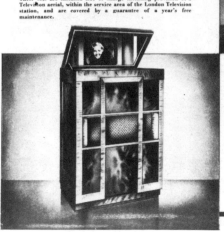

WHY NOT ENJOY A DEMONSTRATION?

*Marconiphone Television Receivers are available from dealers
throughout the London Television area. Demonstrations can be
arranged without any obligation to purchase. Just send your
name and address on this slip to The Marconiphone Company
Limited, Radio House, Tottenham Court Road, London, W.1.*

NAME ....

ADDRESS ....

R.T.19/2/37

....

MARCONI—   THE REAL THING

217

BIBLIOGRAPHY

Most of the information in this book has come from the BBC Written Archives Centre, the archives of the Royal Television Society, the records of GEC-Marconi Electronics Ltd and, in particular, from the testimony of more than fifty interviewees. I have also consulted the following books and articles:

Baird, Margaret, *Television Baird*, Haum, Capetown, 1973.

Benzinnra, B. J., 'A. D. Blumlein – an Electronics Genius', *Electronics and Power*, 1967.

Bridgewater, T. H., *A. A. Campbell Swinton*, Royal Television Society, 1982.

Briggs, Asa, *History of Broadcasting in the U.K.* (Vol. 2. *The Golden Age of Wireless*), OUP, 1965.

Burns, R. W., 'J. L. Baird: Success and Failure', *Proceedings of the Institution of Electrical Engineers*, Vol. 126, No. 9, 1979.

Davis, Janet, 'Ballet on British Television', *Dance Chronicle*, Vol. 5, No. 3, 1982–3.

Fox, W. C., unpublished written records of Baird Television Ltd (1929–31).

Gander, L. Marsland, *Television for All*, Alba Books Ltd.

Garrett, G. R. M. and Mumford, A. H., *The History of Television*, *Proceedings of the Institution of Electrical Engineers*, Vol. 99, No. 17, 1952.

McGee, J. D., 'The Early Development of the Television Camera', unpublished MSS, 1971.

McGee, J. D., 'The Life and Work of Sir Isaac Shoenberg' (Shoenberg Memorial Lecture), 1971.

Moseley, Sydney, *John Baird*, Odhams Press, 1952.

Pawley, Edward, *BBC Engineering (1922–72)*, BBC, 1972.

Percy, J. D., *The Founder of British Television*, Royal Television Society, 1952.

Salter, Lionel, 'The Birth of Television Opera', *Opera*, March 1971.

Shiers, George, 'Television Fifty Years Ago', *Journal of Broadcasting*, 1975.

Swift, John, *Adventure in Vision*, Lehmann, 1950.

Tiltman, R. F., *Baird of Television*, Seeley Service and Co., 1933.

Udelson, J. H., *The Birth of Television in America*, University of Alabama Press, 1982.

Waddell, Peter, 'Seeing by Wireless', *New Scientist*, Nov. 1976.

Other articles in *Nature*, *Electronics and Power* and other magazines and newspapers are listed in the text.

INDEX

Page numbers in *italic* refer to illustrations

INDEX

Douglas, Fred, *81*
drama, 61–2, 157–9, 183, 185

Eckersley, P.P., 55, 58, 70, 141
Edwards, Percy, 67,
Edwards, Tom, 184
electronic television, 93–109
Ellington, Duke, 13, 16
EMI, 98–104, 105, 191
Emitron cameras, 19, 94, 98–100, 103–4, 107, 134–8, 198, 204; *113*

fading, 19–20, 62, 136, 168
Farnsworth, P.T., 107, 128
Farnsworth camera, 128, 129, 133
Fernseh A.G., 57, 73
Fields, Gracie, 61, 92, 118, 153, 192, 205
films, 14, 64–5, 98, 100, 128, 133–4, 149, 169
finance, 13, 108, 152, 180
Flamm, Donald, 71–2
Fleming, Sir Ambrose, 46, 50, 59, 60
Fletcher, Cyril, 153–4, 207, 210
flicker, 15, 17, 42
flying spot system, 55–7, 84–5, 119, 129, 132–3, 142
Fonteyn, Margot, 167, 168, 188; *173*
405-line system, 17, 107–8
Fox, Bill, 31–2, 36–7, 42–3, 51, 57; *76*
Fugue for Four Cameras, 168

Gance, Abel, 72
Gander, L. Marsland, 23, 88, 91, 92, 128, 150, 194–5
Gardner, John, 146
Garson, Greer, 144, 157, 159, *173*
Genée, Adeline, 84, 166, *111*
General Electric, 41, 57, 66, 96
Gingold, Hermione, 91
Glage, G., 95
Goossens, Sidonie, 163, 167–8
Grant, Rita, 21–2
Graves, Cecil, 122, 209–10
Greenbaum, Hyam, 16, 18–19, 122, 163–4
Greenhead, Bernard, 19, 102, 137, 138, 169, 191, 194; *113*
Grey, Earle, 61, 62–3; *79*
Grierson, John, 143
Grisewood, Freddie, 193–4

Hadamovsky, Eugen, 128
Haines, Harry, 188
Hall, Henry, 86, 142, 164
Hankey, Lord, 212
Hardwick, John, 191
Harlow, Jean, 71
Harris, Georgie, 88–9, 90–1
Harris, Mrs, 88
Harvey, Rupert, 67
Haskell, Arnold, 84, 160
Helpmann, Sir Robert, *173*
Henry, Leonard, 22–3
Here's Looking at You, 14–20, 125–6, 136, 151, 166, 181, 184; *74*
Hertz, Heinrich, 95
Hildegarde, 162
Hill, Ronnie, 14
Hilton, John, 156
HMV, 97, 98
Hoover, Herbert, 47, 72
How He Lied To Her Husband, 157; *173*
Howard, Leslie, 150
Howard, Sydney, 60
Howard, Trevor, 158
Hughes, Spike, 162
Hutchinson, Oliver George, 40, 41, 43, 45, 47, 49, 61, 68
Hutchison, William, *174*
Hylton, Jack, 21, 143
Hyslop, Charles, 159

iconoscope, 96–7, 100–1, 105
infrared light, 45–6
Innes, George, 61, 79
interference, 208–9
Intermediate Film Technique, 14–15, 106–7, 108, 121, 125–6, 128–32, 133, 134, 138; *113, 115*
International Cabaret, 152, 169
intervals, 126, 189
interviewing, 21–2, 146–8

Jackson, Dora, 140
Jackson, Jack, 153
Jacomb, W.W., 50, 51, 55, 105
Jenkins, C.F., 30, 39–40, 57, 97
Joyce, Eileen, 146–7

Kaye, Danny, 154; *172*
Kelsall, Moultrie, 189